THE BLACK HAND OF REPUBLICANISM

THE BLACK HAND OF REPUBLICANISM

Fenianism in Modern Ireland

EDITED BY
FEARGHAL McGARRY
and JAMES McCONNEL

IRISH ACADEMIC PRESS
DUBLIN • PORTLAND, OR

First published in 2009 by Irish Academic Press

2 Brookside,	920 NE 58th Avenue, Suite 300
Dundrum Road,	Portland, Oregon,
Dublin 14,	97213-3786
Ireland	USA

www.iap.ie

British Library Cataloguing-in-Publication Data
An entry can be found on request

ISBN 978 0 7165 2999 6 (cloth)
ISBN 978 0 7165 3000 8 (paper)

Library of Congress Cataloging-in-Publication Data
An entry can be found on request

Printed by the MPG Books Group, Bodmin and King's Lynn

Contents

III THE FENIAN DIASPORA

IV PRINT CULTURE

V CONTEXTS AND CONCEPTS

Acknowledgements

This book resulted from an international conference on Fenianism hosted in Belfast in June 2008 by the School of History and Anthropology at Queen's University Belfast and the School of History and International Affairs at the University of Ulster. We would like to thank all of those who contributed to the conference in different ways, particularly Shaun McDaid, Caoimhe Nic Dháibhéid, Olwen Purdue and Colin Reid. We are grateful also to the Academy for Irish Cultural Heritages, University of Ulster; the Humanities Research Institute, University of Ulster; Tommy Graham and *History Ireland*; and Lisa Hyde, Aonghus Meaney and the team at Irish Academic Press.

Notes on Editors and Contributors

Richard Vincent Comerford has been head of History at NUI Maynooth since 1989. He is currently directing a project on associational culture in Ireland, funded by the IRCHSS.

Richard Davis, originally a Trinity College Dublin graduate, is an emeritus professor of history at the University of Tasmania. He has published several works on Young Ireland, including *Revolutionary Imperialist: William Smith O'Brien, 1803–1864* (Dublin, 1998).

Peter Hart is Canada Research Chair in Irish Studies at Memorial University, Newfoundland. He is the author of *The IRA and its Enemies* (Oxford, 1998), which won three awards, including the Christopher Ewart-Biggs Memorial Prize; *British Intelligence in Ireland 1920–21: The Final Reports* (Cork, 2002) and *Guerrilla Days in the UK: Revolution in Ireland and Britain* (forthcoming).

Matthew Kelly teaches history at the University of Southampton. His first book, *The Fenian Ideal and Irish Nationalism, 1882–1916*, was published in 2006. He is currently finishing *Finding Poland: From Tavistock to Vilnius and Back Again*.

Fergal McCluskey received his Ph.D. from Queen's University Belfast in 2007 and currently holds an Irish Research Council for the Humanities and Social Sciences (IRCHSS) Fellowship at the National University of Ireland, Galway. He is the author of a forthcoming *Irish Historical Studies* article, 'Fenians, Ribbonmen and popular ideology's role in nationalist politics: East Tyrone 1906–1909'.

James McConnel teaches history at Northumbria University. His publications include articles in *Irish Historical Studies*, *Historical Journal* and *Past and Present*.

Fearghal McGarry teaches history at Queen's University Belfast. His publications include *Irish Politics and the Spanish Civil War* (Cork, 1999) and *Eoin O'Duffy* (Oxford, 2005). His latest book, *The Rising: Easter 1916*, will be published in 2010.

William Murphy is a lecturer in Irish Studies at Mater Dei Institute of Education, Dublin City University. He has published on various aspects of Irish politics and culture, including political imprisonment. His *Political Imprisonment and the Irish, 1910–1921* will appear in 2010.

Margaret O'Callaghan lectures in Irish history and politics at Queen's University Belfast. Her publications include *British High Politics and a Nationalist Ireland: Criminality, Land and the Law under Forster and Balfour* (Cork, 1994). She is currently editing the Irish political and cultural writings of Roger Casement for publication by the Irish Manuscripts Commission.

Máirtín Ó Catháin is a lecturer in history at the University of Central Lancashire and author of *Irish Republicanism in Scotland, 1856–1916: Fenians in Exile* (Dublin, 2007).

James Quinn is the Executive Editor of the Royal Irish Academy's *Dictionary of Irish Biography*. He is the author of the biographies *Soul on Fire: A Life of Thomas Russell* (Dublin, 2002) and *John Mitchel* (Dublin, 2008), and has published numerous articles on various aspects of nationalism and republicanism in eighteenth- and nineteenth-century Ireland.

Marta Ramón holds a Ph.D. from the University of Oviedo in Spain. She is a former IRCHSS Postdoctoral Fellow and is the author of *A Provisional Dictator: James Stephens and the Fenian Movement* (Dublin, 2007).

Paul Rouse holds a Ph.D. from University College Dublin. He has written on the sporting and cultural history of Ireland in the nineteenth and twentieth centuries. He is currently a director of the GAA Oral History Project and has written extensively about the history of the GAA. He is an editor, with Mike Cronin and William Murphy, of *The Gaelic Athletic Association 1884–2009* (Dublin, 2009).

Frank Rynne is completing a doctoral thesis on the Fenians and the Land War in West Cork at Trinity College, Dublin. He is a contributor to *History Ireland* and has written articles and broadcasts for, among others, the *Irish Times* and BBC World Service Radio.

Niall Whelehan is completing a Ph.D. in history at the European University Institute, Florence on the subject of the Skirmishing Fund. He was recently a visiting scholar at Glucksman Ireland House, New York University. His research interests include political violence in the nineteenth century; comparative history; Italian and Spanish anarchism; migration; and political exile.

Introduction

Fearghal McGarry and James McConnel

On St Patrick's Day, 1858, a revolutionary society was formed in Dublin to bring about a democratic Irish republic by force. The Irish Republican Brotherhood – or the Fenians as its members would popularly become known – developed into the most important republican movement in modern Irish history.[1] Not only did it direct political and revolutionary struggles in Ireland for over half a century, it infiltrated Ireland's literary and sporting cultures (most famously, the Gaelic Athletic Association and the Gaelic League), constructed political machines in urban America, engaged in military operations across the globe (twice invading Canada) and established an organised presence throughout all six continents. Most importantly, by shaping popular perceptions of the Irish nation and how its struggle for independence from Britain should be conducted, it influenced not only political developments but notions of national and cultural identity. For good or ill, modern Ireland has been profoundly shaped by Fenianism: 'In so far as such things can be dated', Tom Garvin has observed, 'the Irish revolution started with the founding of the IRB in 1858.'[2] It was the IRB that planned the Easter Rising which proclaimed the Irish Republic in 1916, and it was Michael Collins' Fenian élite who guided the Irish Republican Army's campaign during the War of Independence.

This book is published to mark the 150th anniversary of the founding of the Brotherhood. Ironically, the most striking aspect of this anniversary, which has just passed, was how little attention was devoted to an organisation which excelled like no other Irish movement in the organisation of historical commemoration. As the funerals of Terence Bellew MacManus in 1861 and O'Donovan Rossa in 1915 illustrate, it was the Fenians who pioneered the tradition of the political funeral as national spectacle, a tradition which remains part of the political culture, as evidenced by the recent state funerals for Kevin Barry and the other War of Independence Volunteers executed by the British authorities. It was the IRB who transformed the botched rescue of Fenian rebels in England – which resulted in the death of an unarmed policeman and the subsequent execution of the 'Manchester Martyrs' – into an annual demonstration of republican resilience through decades of unpopularity; and it was the same organisation that popularised the annual pilgrimage to Wolfe Tone's grave in Bodenstown, a tradition continued by present-day political parties including Fianna Fáil and Sinn Féin. For a country that takes its commemorations seriously – some would say too

seriously – the absence of public and political commemoration to mark the
150th anniversary of the most influential organisation in the history of republicanism is intriguing.[3] Although Fianna Fáil, Fine Gael and Sinn Féin regularly engage in ownership disputes over the title deeds of the republican tradition – as most recently illustrated by the government's embarrassment at
having to move the official state commemoration of the ninetieth anniversary
of the founding of the Dáil forward by one day due to Sinn Féin's success in
booking the Mansion House on the exact date – there has been little com-
petition for the Fenian legacy.[4]

One explanation for this reticence is Fenianism's identification with violence and terrorism. The bombing of London's Underground and other symbolic targets such as the House of Commons and Scotland Yard is not as
recent a phenomenon as many people would think: the Fenians were doing
it in the 1880s. It was the IRB's activities that prompted the formation of
Special Branch (initially known as the Special Irish Branch) in London, and
it is not surprising that the post-9/11 surge of interest in the historical origins of modern global terrorism has led to a renewed focus on this dimension
of Fenianism.[5] Although – as with other common assumptions about
Fenianism – the historical basis for identifying the IRB with modern global
terrorism is questioned in this book, there remain intriguing parallels
between present-day perceptions of Islamist terrorism and Fenianism, an
earlier enemy within which proved equally capable of periodically haunting
the public imagination in the late nineteenth century, provoking press hysteria and public and political alarm out of all proportion to its competence
and capabilities.

In contrast to the United Irishmen – enthusiastically, and almost plausi-
bly, commemorated as democratic pioneers of non-sectarian republicanism
during the recent bicentenary of the 1798 rebellion – the Fenians have left
behind a more problematic legacy for post-ceasefire Ireland. It is surely no
coincidence that Sinn Féin – the only political party to mark the IRB's 150th
anniversary – is the republican party most comfortable in identifying with its
'physical force' past.[6] Or that the very term retains a resonance in Northern
Ireland – whether embraced by 'unrepentant Fenian bastards' or deployed as
a sectarian term of abuse ('Fenian scum') – which it has long ceased to enjoy
in the Republic of Ireland. Conversely, Fine Gael – the political party with
the best claim to the institutional ownership of the IRB's legacy – has no
interest in it, having long disassociated itself from the militant republican
tradition and its sentimental veneration.

Aside from Fenianism's troubling associations with such problematic features of past Irish political life as insurrection, assassination, bombing campaigns and terrorism, there may be other reasons for ambivalence in its official commemoration by politicians and the state. After all, the Easter Rising,
an act of symbolic violence orchestrated by the IRB, continues to be widely
and enthusiastically commemorated, as does the founding of Dáil Éireann and
the War of Independence, events underpinned by a violent IRA campaign

directed by the IRB. Perhaps equally troubling is the association of Fenianism with conspiratorial methods: whereas the Easter Rising is celebrated as a public declaration of national independence, and the establishment of the Dáil – even less problematically – as a dignified assertion of sovereignty rooted in the democratic mandate provided by the general election of December 1918, the Fenians remain best known as a conspiratorial, oath-bound secret society.

The tensions between conspiratorial physical-force republicanism and democracy – an important and enduring feature of modern Irish political life – were never more evident than in the final years of the movement, which would provide further grounds for the IRB's uncertain posthumous reputation. Although the Brotherhood can claim much of the credit for bringing about the Irish revolution of 1916–21, it shares some of the responsibility for the traumatic way in which that revolution came to an end. Like every other republican organisation, the IRB was split by the Anglo-Irish Treaty of 1921 and the Civil War that followed. But, in contrast to other organisations such as Sinn Féin, the IRB was singled out for blame for contributing to that split. Anti-treaty republicans alleged that the IRB's conspiratorial methods had exacerbated the confusion that led to the split, and that Michael Collins had manipulated the movement in order to secure support for disestablishing the Irish Republic.[7] These claims may have contributed to the IRB's sinister reputation as 'a ruthless mafia' – 'the Black Hand of republicanism stretching from New York to London', in Peter Hart's evocative phrase – but it was also true that Collins sought to use the fraternal bonds of the IRB to prevent rather than precipitate violence between republicans during this divisive period.[8]

The treaty split and violence that followed raised fundamental questions about the methods and objectives of Fenianism. For anti-treaty legitimists, the subversion of the Republic proclaimed by the Easter rebels contradicted the very essence of the Brotherhood. For Fenian pro-treatyites, such as Michael Collins, the goal of the movement had always been to bring about the substance of independence as much as the formal political structures of a republic, an aspiration that reflects the pragmatic formulation adopted by Sinn Féin at its historic October 1917 convention, which succeeded in fashioning a united republican movement out of an inchoate coalition of IRB conspirators, Volunteer gunmen and monarchist, separatist and republican politicians.[9] In 1922, both pro- and anti-treatyites could draw on the writings and actions of past leaders of the Irish Republican Brotherhood in support of their irreconcilable claims.

In the end, the IRB went out with a whimper rather than a bang. Its ultimate demise – in appropriately murky and contentious circumstances – occurred in 1924 when it was wound up after it had been secretly revived by the leadership of the National Army as a means of out-manoeuvring a rival faction within that force.[10] Despite the effectiveness of the IRB in certain periods of Irish history, there could be few clearer illustrations of the prob-

lems that invariably characterised oath-bound secret societies than the circumstances of its prolonged demise between 1921 and 1924.

The ignominious Army Mutiny dispute (involving – like most republican
splits – a potent cocktail of self-interest, patriotism, principle and factional
rivalry) demonstrated another enduring feature of the IRB: how a movement
whose members claimed an unbroken ideological and institutional continuity repeatedly found itself used as a vehicle for competing factions, a problem which must have proved difficult to ignore following the fiasco that characterised the final days of the preparations for the Easter Rising. In his
recent valuable study of the IRB, Owen McGee provocatively suggests that
the Irish revolution marked the eclipse rather than the triumph of republicanism, as the radical democratic ideology of late nineteenth-century
Fenianism was hollowed out by a generation of Catholic, Irish-Ireland nationalists.[11] No less controversially, John Regan has argued that Michael Collins
revived the IRB after the treaty split in order to achieve a military dictatorship during the Civil War.[12]

Whatever the substance of such claims, given the IRB's divisive role in
the treaty split it was hardly surprising that leading politicians such as Éamon
de Valera – who, like other prominent republicans, had conscientiously broken his links with the IRB after the rebellion due to his belief that such an
organisation was no longer necessary or even desirable when republicans
could work openly within the Irish Volunteers and Sinn Féin – may have
experienced some ambivalence about commemoration of that organisation in
independent Ireland.

The most revealing aspect of commemoration – and the reason why so
many historians remain interested in the process – concerns what is remembered and what is forgotten or obscured. Following independence, as McGee
has noted, the Irish state and Fenian memoirs (such as those of John Devoy)
chose to emphasise the militaristic dimension of Fenianism – the rebellions
of 1867 and 1916 – rather than the decades of radical political activism in the
intervening period.[13] Commemoration of Fenianism has generally made much
of the IRB's militancy: it is the image of the Fenian as rebellious, defiant,
uncompromising – unrepentant – that accounts for the movement's appeal
to many present-day republicans. Such contemporary perceptions are partly
justified: the IRB's distinctiveness as a republican movement was that it was
the first such organisation that was dedicated from the outset to achieving a
republic by violent means. And the IRB's rejection of deference to authority
– whether in the form of policeman, landlord or even priest – did form an
important part of its popular social appeal. Charles Townshend is not alone
in arguing that the real importance of Fenianism lay in its attitude rather
than its ideas: 'it embodied an inspirational sense of character-building, a
posture of self-respect, and the repudiation of servility'.[14]

Similarly, there was a fairly clear basis – albeit an often theoretical and
rhetorical one – for distinctions between Fenian militancy and constitutional
nationalist moderation. Constitutional politicians such as Daniel O'Connell

and Charles Stewart Parnell sought self-government within the union by essentially peaceful agitation. Fenians supported the goal of a republic to be achieved, if necessary, by force. And underpinning these differences over means and ends were divergent ideologies and mentalities. Drawing on mid-nineteenth-century European romantic nationalism, Young Ireland and Fenian revolutionaries placed more emphasis on Ireland's distinctive culture as a justification for independence, and greater stress on the importance of non-sectarian and secular ideology. Constitutional nationalist politicians, a more pragmatic and utilitarian breed, were more attuned to the sectarian realities of Irish society, and tended to base arguments for self-government more on principles of democracy and good government than on essentialist criteria such as language, culture or the spirit of the nation (although they were certainly not immune to these). Constitutional nationalists, whose ambitions for self-government were dependent on securing the agreement of allies within the British political system they formed a part of, tended to attribute English opposition to their demands to fear, ignorance or stupidity. Separatist rhetoric, as exemplified at its most extreme by John Mitchel's popularisation of the idea of the Great Famine as an act of English genocide or indeed much of the discourse of Fenianism, was more inclined to depict England as an intrinsically evil entity, motivated by ill-will towards Ireland, and their more moderate nationalist rivals as self-serving and morally corrupt.

But it was also in the interest of Fenians and those who would later commemorate them to retrospectively exaggerate their rejection of parliamentary politics in a way that obscured the significance of their interventions in Irish politics, most notably their support for the Parnellite party during the Land War. Where IRB men propose a crude dichotomy between the spirit of Fenianism (signifying authentic nationalism) and constitutional politics (compromise and betrayal), historians detect a more complex spectrum of shifting loyalties: Irish politics under the union did not allow for clear boundaries between these intertwined political traditions. Daniel O'Connell is believed to have been a United Irishman in his youth; Charles Stewart Parnell, who may well have taken the Fenian oath, achieved political dominance in Ireland on the back of an uneasy alliance with the IRB, and even John Redmond – the most moderate (or, his detractors would allege, imperial) of the great constitutional nationalist leaders reluctantly found himself at the head of Ireland's largest (and largely Fenian-controlled) paramilitary organisation in 1914.[15] On the other side of the fence, many Fenians became prominent parliamentarians in later life, some accepting high office and royal honours elsewhere in the British empire.

Debates about the differences between constitutional nationalism and Fenianism are bound up with complex and problematic issues of popular support and democratic legitimacy. How many people shared Fenian attitudes, admired its objectives, or privately regarded its uncompromising approach to the national question as a legitimate, if unrealistic, one? We don't know. Historians, particularly those identified with the 'revisionist' controversy of

past decades, have often emphasised the lack of electoral support for advocates of separatism throughout the period between the Act of Union and the
Easter Rising. Although physical-force republicans sometimes enjoyed a good
deal of popular sympathy (particularly in retrospect), they consistently failed
to mobilise this support in an effective military or political form. Despite
this, some contemporaries, including Archbishop Croke, believed that 'the
great bulk of our Irish Catholic people are Fenian in heart or sympathy'.[16]
Recent research, which might be described as post-revisionist, has shifted in
this direction.[17] Despite the marginal nature of the IRB throughout much of
its existence, particularly in the decades following the death of Parnell, Matt
Kelly has argued that the Fenian ideal successfully transcended the narrow
organisational confines of its host, commanding far greater sympathy than
the decrepit organisation's tiny membership suggested. Fenianism was 'the
central influence in an Irish nationalist culture that was deeply embedded in
the texture of Irish identity', he argues in his recent study of the IRB:
'although some Irish nationalists dismissed Fenian and separatist ideals as
archaic and foolish, home rule did not achieve the same level of emotional
resonance with the Irish people'.[18]

Perhaps, then, the ultimate triumph of Fenianism has been its ability to
transcend the factional, contested and often inconsistent aspects of the Irish
Republican Brotherhood's institutional history, as evidenced by its success in
portraying itself as the central link in an unbroken chain of resistance
stretching back to the rebellions of 1848, 1798 and the mystical dawn of the
struggle for Irish freedom. Where republicans emphasise a seamless continuity, historians identify a more complex and fascinating history of tensions and
discontinuity. This further reinforces the need – distinct from the revisionist debates of a generation ago – for historians to carry on placing the 'Fenians
in Context'. Indeed, in this respect, the title of this book should be taken
seriously as a statement of one of the things we hope to achieve here. The
point is not that the IRB was linked directly to the Serbian secret society,
Црка рука; rather, it is that both were influenced by a wider European and
transnational grammar of political violence in the forms and methods they
adopted.[19] And we can perhaps go further than this: both also fit into a broader
tradition of radical – though not necessarily congruent – political thought.
The Black Hand encompassed not only pan-Serbian and monarchist strands
but also elements linked to European revolutionaries and to British
Fabianism.[20] Likewise, mid-Victorian Fenians – if not their Edwardian counterparts – showed interest in the European democratic left and in Karl Marx,
while some socialists were, in turn, curious about the IRB.

The pre-Connollyite history of Marxian socialism and Fenianism has
received some scholarly attention over the years, though historians have
tended to agree with John Devoy – himself a member of the International
Working Men's Association (IWMA) and, in Roy Foster's memorable phrase,
'the Lenin of the movement' – when he wrote on Marx's death in 1883 that
'Whatever Irishmen may think of the general policy of Karl Marx, it must

never be forgotten that he was a sincere friend of Ireland.'[21] In fact, even if Irish republicans were never 'reds wrapped in green',[22] figuring out what ordinary Irishmen and women thought – if anything – about Marx, socialism or other European systems of thought must await the kind of pioneering work conducted by David Vincent and Jonathan Rose for nineteenth-century Britain.[23] What can be said is that, as Matthew Kelly argues in this collection, central aspects of the *Irish People*'s journalism were class-based and 'though a schematic Marxism is not to be found in the newspaper, much of their argument chimed with English radicalism'. Moreover, as Peter Hart shows in his chapter, by situating the IRB within broader European revolutionary traditions, we can see Fenianism in terms of new and unfamiliar chronologies and patterns. Finally, as Máirtín Ó Catháin shows, the imaginative space in which Fenianism operated was not uncontested, but profoundly shaped by its enemies. So, while there were probably very few well-thumbed copies of *Das Kapital* (1867) circulating in late nineteenth-century Ireland, this did not stop the Church linking Fenianism to socialism, or hostile British commentators connecting the dots between the IRB and continental socialists, nihilists and anarchists.[24]

One reason, perhaps, why the linkages between Irish republicanism and other contemporaneous radical strands have not been explored fully is the fact that by far the most influential interpretation of mid-Victorian Fenianism – that of Vincent Comerford – argues that ideology *per se*, irrespective of whether it was socialist or republican, had very little to do with the popularity of the IRB in the 1860s. In fact, according to this thesis, Fenianism appealed primarily to 'respectable' lower-middle-class, urban-dwelling artisans and tradesmen because it provided them with social and recreational opportunities otherwise denied them by a society dominated by priests, landlords and peelers.[25] Although Newsinger's critique of Comerford's 'patriotism as a pastime' thesis sought to restore the radical credentials of the IRB,[26] it is only more recently that a serious attempt has been made to reassert the importance of ideas within Fenianism, albeit firmly grounded in domestic thinking and practice. Thus, Owen McGee presents the Fenians as a fraternal organisation dedicated to instilling radical democratic, egalitarian and republican principles in Irish society as an essential precondition to revolution in Ireland,[27] while Fergus Campbell has stressed the ideological dimensions of Fenianism's grassroots, detecting in the revolutionary currents of Victorian and Edwardian Co. Galway a social and economic potential more radical than simple support for land redistribution.[28]

Many of the chapters included in this collection have developed out of this evolving historiography or seek to address core questions thrown up or elided by the literature. What were the formative organisational and intellectual influences on the early IRB? How far was it the product of the mid-Victorian culture it emerged from? How did Irish republican networks communicate with one another, whether in Dublin and Mayo or Dublin and New York? To what extent does the concept of a 'Fenian diaspora' help us to understand the global phenomenon of Irish revolutionary activity?

The politics of continuity have long been central to Irish republican thought and this collection seeks to tackle the issue by revisiting the question of how robust notions of nationalism, with a capital and lower-case 'n', really were in the 1860s. In his chapter, James Quinn questions the perception of the Fenians as the successors to the Young Ireland tradition, demonstrating how the IRB generally failed to win the approval of Young Ireland leaders in its early years. Marta Ramón's chapter also emphasises the tensions between the IRB and more moderate nationalists in the 1860s, including former Young Irelanders, analysing these through the often neglected prism of class. The clash between the National Brotherhood of Saint Patrick and constitutional nationalists provoked by the fight over the bones of Terence Bellew MacManus was a consequence of the tensions between working-class, popular activism and the desire of middle-class élites to retain control of nationalist politics. Kelly's exploration of the *Irish People* also illustrates just how clearly Fenians regarded themselves as representing a break from earlier, unsuccessful models of republicanism, not least Young Ireland, whose 1848 insurrection was 'depicted as a national embarrassment rather than a focus for celebration'. More radically, Vincent Comerford questions the way in which observers (not excluding historians) have too readily conceptualised Fenianism as a consistent ideological tradition, rendered explicable through 'the mythic aura of the Fenian organisation' rather than 'normal nineteenth-century social activity'.

Due in part to the surviving evidence and also to the Fenians' own propaganda, historians have tended to see the IRB in rather monolithic terms. However, the recent renaissance in regional studies of the Irish revolution has spread and is leading to micro-historical examinations of other phases of nationalist agitation. As three chapters in this collection underline, far from being a monolith, both the IRB's durability and its organisational limitations reflect the pronounced localism at its grassroots. This is seen clearly, for instance, in Frank Rynne's chapter on the Land War in Co. Cork. The struggle for the land after 1879 divided the IRB's leadership; yet, as Comerford appreciated over a generation ago, it was a key driver of rank-and-file Fenian activism in small towns and their rural hinterlands, and, as Rynne shows, provided republicans in Ballydehob with an opportunity to seize the political initiative. Still, the IRB's secrecy makes it difficult to determine the extent to which Fenian agitation was directed or co-ordinated by Dublin. However, Paul Rouse's chapter on the IRB and the early history of the GAA suggests that Fenian attempts to hijack that organisation in the 1880s faltered – beyond controlling the association's executive – because local branches jealously guarded their autonomy. This, in turn, raises the possibility that not only were some of these local opponents of the GAA's takeover themselves also grassroots Fenians, but that we need to better understand the Brotherhood's chains of command and the operation of centripetal and centrifugal forces within the organisation. That a grassroots Fenian agenda could exist alongside that of the supreme council appears to be borne out by Fergal

McCluskey's discussion of the Hibernian-Fenian nexus in turn-of-the-century Co. Tyrone. Here, Fenian infiltration of the Ancient Order of Hiberians (AOH) was the product not just of the IRB's classic strategy of entryism but also reflected the need of provincial republicans for an associational outlet which allowed them to publicly articulate their democratic principles in a local setting.

Questions about the organisational circuitry of Fenianism are pertinent not only to the movement in Ireland but also with regard to the linkages between Irish republicans in such far-flung places as Britain, Australia, New Zealand, South Africa, Canada and the USA. Excepting occasional references to a still-born revolutionary directory set up in 1876 to co-ordinate Irish, North American and Australasian operations, studies of diasporic Fenianism have tended to favour discrete, localised studies, thereby losing sight of the transnational dimensions of Fenianism. This is not to substitute one monolithic model of Fenianism for another. Notwithstanding the advent of tramp steamers, international postal services and submarine telegraphic cables, the world apparently was still not yet small enough to sustain a genuinely global secret society. None the less, as the recent work of Ó Catháin on Scotland has contended, Fenianism was in many ways a product of the Irish diaspora and cannot be understood without reference to this wider context.[29] Moreover, Ó Catháin's contribution to this collection demonstrates how the IRB's own enemies were instrumental in shaping British public perceptions of the Fenians as a global threat. This parallels other work – principally that of Brian Jenkins – which has recently re-examined the vectors of both diasporic Fenianism and state responses to it in the light of 9/11.[30] One incident which at first glance seemed to confirm the Fenians' 'global reach' was the attempted assassination in Sydney of Queen Victoria's second son, Prince Alfred, in 1868 by a self-confessed Fenian. In his chapter, Richard Davis echoes contemporary doubts about the assassin's Fenian credentials and, indeed, his sanity, and suggests that the incident's real value is the light it throws on the ethnic and confessional fractures in Australian colonial society. While Orangemen and militant Protestants sought to harness popular hostility towards Fenianism against local Catholic educational demands, Irish Catholics themselves struggled to convincingly deflect accusations that even if there were few sworn Fenians in their midst, there were still many who sympathised with the republican cause. While incidents such as the unsuccessful assassination attempt of 1868 or the killing of the notorious informer James Carey in South Africa in 1882 (by another 'Fenian' assassin with dubious credentials) throw suspicion on the wilder claims of both the Victorian IRB and their enemies in British intelligence, one of the things Niall Whelehan's chapter demonstrates is that American Fenianism certainly conceptualised itself transnationally. Thus, Jeremiah O'Donovan Rossa and his US-based Skirmishing Fund bankrolled a bombing campaign in 1880s Britain which did much to justify British paranoia about the thick green line of Fenianism advancing against the empire. And yet, as Whelehan also demonstrates, the use of 'infernal machines' was rooted less in the politics of revolution and much more in the parochial, even insular, world of the eastern United States, where settling day-to-day grudges and disputes with dynamite was far from unusual.

If we know little of the secret conversations, whether at cricket games in Co. Cork or smoke-filled pubs in Manchester, Chicago or practically anywhere the Irish congregated in large numbers, we do know more and more about how Fenians talked to themselves and one another through their newspapers. Among other things, Anthony McNicholas' recent study of Irish republicans and the English press shows that Fenian journalists like J. J. O'Kelly had spells on nationalist newspapers right across the Irish world, thereby lending them a degree of intellectual cohesion.[31] In his chapter already mentioned, Kelly not only reconstructs the Spartan aesthetic of the *Irish People*'s editors, but also speculates as to how the – sometimes not so – simple act of getting hold of the paper by provincial Fenians may have been an important act of defiance in its own right. The earnestness of Kelly's provincial IRB men, looking forward to holding and reading each new issue of the *People*, contrasts strongly with the venality of one of the hacks at the heart of Dublin's newspaper business: Richard Pigott. Margaret O'Callaghan's fascinating sketch of Pigott's rise and fall traces in detail one example of the personal and commercial opportunism seen elsewhere in connection with the Fenian phenomenon. Pigott apparently saw Irish republicanism as a business opportunity from early on and this helps to explain his later ignominious end. William Murphy's chapter on Irish republican prison memoirs also makes an interesting point in this respect, since Pigott busily encouraged released prisoners to put pen to paper after 1870. And while these works were primarily written for political purposes, they can also be related to the idea of the Fenian hero as celebrity. While some former prisoners may well have baulked at having their lives repackaged to conform to the genre conventions of the prison memoir, others may have been like the fictional character 'Dick Fitzgerald' in J. D. Maginn's 1889 novel *Fitzgerald: The Fenian*, in which the hero impresses his future wife by telling her that his prison memoir is in its third edition and is attracting interest from London publishers. Michael Davitt was surely not the only Fenian who was beguiled by the cult of Victorian celebrity.

Ultimately, as the contributors to this book make clear, it is not simply the nature of Fenianism that remains contested but the concept of Fenianism as a coherent ideological position over time, and even the very use of the name to describe this political tradition. Their research will have little impact on popular perceptions of Fenianism or the assumptions of present-day republicans who see themselves as part of that tradition. More representative of popular and republican sentiment is the approach of *The Fenian Anthology*, the only other publication to mark the 150th anniversary, which bookends its compendium of 'thrilling tales of escape, speeches from the dock, extracts from memoirs, ballads, novels and correspondence' with the Parisian diary entries of Wolfe Tone and Bobby Sands' Long Kesh writings.[32] The sense of legitimacy which derives from such notions of heroic continuity are perhaps nowhere better illustrated than in the Proclamation of the Irish Republic, the foundational text of the independent Irish state. Although the articles in this book outline a more complex Fenianism than that allowed for by popular sentiment or republican politics, the history of Fenianism, for some, will continue to be seen as too important and useful to be left to the inquiring minds of sceptical historians.

NOTES

1. On the use of 'Fenian', see John O'Leary, *Recollections of Fenians and Fenianism* (London: Downer, 1896); Mark F. Ryan, *Fenian Memories* (Dublin: M. H. Gill & Son, 1946, 2nd edn). Also see Pearse's famous graveside oration: 'the fools, the fools! – they have left us our Fenian dead', in Brian MacArthur (ed.), *The Penguin Book of Historic Speeches* (London: Penguin Books, 1996).
2. Tom Garvin, *Nationalist Revolutionaries in Ireland, 1858–1928* (Dublin: Gill & Macmillan, 2005 edn), p. 5.
3. The only formal commemoration occurred at local rather than state level. Prompted by a Sinn Féin resolution, Dublin City Council voted to erect a plaque on 16 Lombard Street where the IRB first met. Sinn Féin's intervention highlighted the survival of a characteristically Fenian reading of history. Questioning Taoiseach Bertie Ahern in the Dáil (on 5 December 2007) on the lack of state commemoration, Sinn Féin TD Caoimhghín Ó Caoláin suggested renaming Dublin's Victoria Quay to Fenian Quay on the grounds that it was currently named after the 'Famine Queen' responsible for 'the genocide of the Irish people at the time'.
4. *Irish Independent*, 13 Jan. 2009.
5. See, for example, Michael Burleigh, *Blood and Rage: A Cultural History of Terrorism* (London: Harper Collins, 2008).
6. *An Phoblacht*, 13 Mar. 2008.
7. The Earl of Longford and Thomas P. O'Neill, *Éamon de Valera* (Dublin: Gill & Macmillan, 1970), pp. 172–6. For the role of the IRB during this period, see John M. Regan, *The Irish Counter-Revolution, 1921–1936* (Dublin: Gill & Macmillan, 1999), pp. 30–3.
8. Peter Hart, *Mick: The Real Michael Collins* (London: Macmillan, 2005), pp. xiii, 378.
9. Michael Laffan, *The Resurrection of Ireland: The Sinn Féin Party 1916–1923* (Cambridge: Cambridge University Press, 1999), pp. 116–21.
10. Regan, *Irish Counter-Revolution*, pp. 189–97.
11. Owen McGee, *The IRB: The Irish Republican Brotherhood from the Land League to Sinn Féin* (Dublin: Four Courts Press, 2005), pp. 355–62.
12. John M. Regan, 'Michael Collins, general commanding-in-chief, as a historiographical problem', *History*, 92/307 (2007), pp. 318–46.
13. McGee, *The IRB*, p. 369.
14. Charles Townshend, *Ireland: The Twentieth Century* (London: Edward Arnold, 1999), pp. 26–7.
15. Patrick Geoghegan, *King Dan: The Rise of Daniel O'Connell, 1775–1829* (Dublin: Gill & Macmillian, 2008); Patrick Maume, 'Parnell and the IRB oath', *Irish Historical Studies*, 29/115 (1995).
16. Townshend, *Ireland*, p. 26.
17. For a discussion of two important studies of the IRB, see Alvin Jackson's review of Kelly and McGee in *Victorian Studies*, 50/2 (2008), pp. 307–10.
18. M. J. Kelly, *The Fenian Ideal and Irish Nationalism 1882–1916* (Woodbridge: Boydell & Brewer, 2006), p. 123.
19. Walter Laqueur, *A History of Terrorism* (Edison, NJ: Transaction Publishers, 2001), p. 113.
20. Frederick Singleton, *A Short History of the Yugoslav Peoples* (Cambridge: Cambridge University Press, 1995), pp. 115–16.
21. R. F. Foster, *Modern Ireland, 1600–1972* (London: Penguin Books, 1988), p. 393; *Irish Nation*, 14 March 1883, quoted in Paul Bew, *Ireland: The Politics of Enmity, 1789–2006* (Oxford: Oxford University Press, 2007), p. 248.
22. Patrick Quinlivan and Paul Rose, *The Fenians in England, 1865–72: A Sense of Insecurity* (London: John Calder, 1962), pp. 165–6. On this relationship see Emile Strauss, *Irish Nationalism and British Democracy* (London: Methuen, 1951); Eric Hobsbawm, *The Age of*

Capital, 1848–1875 (London: Weidenfeld & Nicholson, 1962), pp. 92–3; Desmond Ryan, *Fenian Chief: A Biography of James Stephens* (Dublin: Gill & Macmillan, 1967), p. 235; James Connolly, *Labour in Irish History* (Dublin: New Books Publications, 1967 edn), p. 135; John Newsinger, 'Old Chartists, Fenians and new Socialists', *Éire-Ireland*, 17/2 (1982), pp. 19–45; Peter Beresford Ellis, *A History of the Irish Working Class* (London: Pluto Press, 1985, 2nd edn), p. 124; Roman Szporluk, *Communism and Nationalism: Karl Marx Versus Friedrich List* (New York and Oxford: Oxford University Press, 1991), p. 178; Franz Mehring, *Karl Marx: The Story of his Life* (London: Routledge, 2003, 2nd edn), p. 391; Fintan Lane, *The Origins of Modern Irish Socialism, 1881–1896* (Cork: Cork University Press, 1997), p. 21.

23. David Vincent, *Literacy and Popular Culture, England 1750–1914* (Cambridge: Cambridge University Press, 1993); Jonathan Rose, *The Intellectual Life of the British Working Classes* (New Haven, CT: Yale University Press, 2001).

24. For example, see Alexander Ewald, *The Right Hon. Benjamin Disraeli, Earl of Beaconsfield, KG, and His Times*, 5 vols (London: William Mackenzie, 1882), p. 365; H. B. C. Pollard, *The Secret Societies of Ireland* (London: Philip Allen, 1922), p. 64.

25. R. V. Comerford, *The Fenians in Context: Irish Politics and Society, 1848–82* (Dublin: Wolfhound Press, 1985).

26. John Newsinger, *Fenianism in Mid-Victorian Britain* (London: Pluto Press, 1994).

27. McGee, *The IRB*.

28. Fergus Campbell, *Land and Revolution: Nationalist Politics in the West of Ireland, 1891–1921* (Oxford: Oxford University Press, 2005).

29. Máirtín Ó Catháin, *Irish Republicanism in Scotland, 1858–1916: Fenians in Exile* (Dublin: Irish Academic Press, 2007).

30. Brian Jenkins, *The Fenian Problem: Insurgency and Terrorism in a Liberal State, 1858–1874* (Liverpool: Liverpool University Press, 2008).

31. Anthony McNicholas, *Politics, Religion and the Press: Irish Journalism in Mid-Victorian England* (Oxford: Peter Lang, 2007).

32. Joe Ambrose (ed.), *The Fenian Anthology* (Cork: Mercier Press, 2008).

I
MID-VICTORIAN FENIANISM:
CONTINUITY AND TENSION

1

The IRB and Young Ireland: Varieties of Tension

James Quinn

I

The Young Ireland movement is traditionally seen as the seedbed out of which the IRB emerged.[1] Many Fenian leaders recorded that it was the Young Ireland newspaper, the *Nation*, that first inspired their national enthusiasm, and many future IRB men were involved in the attempted rebellion of 1848. In nationalist historiography, the elder statesmen of Young Ireland were often portrayed as handing on the torch to the younger men of the Fenians, who added an element of ruthlessness to their predecessors' idealism and generally tempered the romantic nationalism of the *Nation* with a harder and more practical edge.[2]

II

The Young Irelanders seceded in 1846 from Daniel O'Connell's Repeal Association because of their refusal to discountenance the use of physical force in all circumstances, and founded the Irish Confederation in January 1847. Many future IRB leaders became members of the local clubs spawned by the Confederation and it is these Confederate clubs, which had a more plebian and democratic tone than the Young Ireland leadership, that can be regarded as the true progenitor of the IRB. Membership of the clubs grew rapidly throughout the early months of 1848, their numbers increased by the overthrow of the monarchy in France in February 1848 and the arrest of leading Young Irelanders on charges of sedition in March. Encouraged by the inflammatory rhetoric of John Mitchel's *United Irishman*, new clubs adopted names such as Wolfe Tone, Robert Emmet and Hugh O'Neill that invoked Ireland's revolutionary past, and many also began to procure arms and drill. Mitchel's conviction for treason felony at the end of May saw a further surge in the number of members and many new clubs named after him were founded.[3] By late July 1848 there were 200 clubs, with about 40,000 members, and their impatience with the passivity and moderation of the

Confederation's leadership helped to catapult those leaders into open rebellion in July 1848. The Young Ireland leaders were, however, reluctant insurrectionists, and their failure to harness adequately the manpower at their disposal in Confederate strongholds such as Dublin and Cork contributed to the speedy collapse of their attempted uprising.[4]

After the imprisonment and exile of the Young Ireland leadership and the disintegration of the Irish Confederation, some of those who had been prominent in the Confederate clubs took the initiative in forming the Irish Democratic Association – a network of loosely linked popular clubs in 1848–9. Many of these urban democrats were also sworn into various secret societies that continued to plan insurrection. This shadowy network attempted to mount an insurrection in September 1849 that resulted only in an unsuccessful attack on the police barracks at Cappoquin, Co. Waterford.[5] It declined thereafter, but pockets of disaffection remained and provided a nucleus for the foundation of IRB cells after 1858.[6]

Seeking to learn from the mistakes of their predecessors, the founders of the IRB maintained that spontaneous revolt was impossible and that secrecy and organisation, enshrined in a disciplined body dedicated to revolution, were the keys to success in the future. Some, such as James Stephens, were also influenced by their experience of political secret societies in France in the late 1840s and early 1850s. Stephens, a member of the Kilkenny Confederate club, had taken part in the attempted insurrection of July 1848 under the leadership of William Smith O'Brien and had been clearly unimpressed by O'Brien's indecision and his chivalrous approach to insurrectionary warfare.[7] Stephens, though, was keenly aware that the political prestige of Young Ireland leaders would help to bolster his organisation and made approaches to a number of them for assistance in 1858. The response he received was poor: both Smith O'Brien and John Blake Dillon were opposed to secret societies and refused to assist him.[8]

Taking his case to America, Stephens called on T. F. Meagher in New York and John Mitchel in east Tennessee. The accession of Mitchel was looked upon as particularly important by the IRB leadership, as he was regarded as far more committed to the insurrectionary tradition than other Young Irelanders. After he had been sentenced to fourteen years' transportation in May 1848, many of the Confederate rank-and-file talked of mounting a rescue attempt, but their leaders ordered that no attempt should be made.[9] Young Dublin Confederates such as John O'Leary and John Savage, who later became prominent Fenians, experienced their first disillusionment with the Young Ireland leadership and were bitterly angry to see their 'foremost man' being transported without a struggle.[10] Transportation, however, meant that none of the blame that was attributed to the other leaders for the debacle of the 1848 insurrection attached itself to Mitchel, and for physical-force nationalists he remained the most inspirational and revered of all the Young Ireland leaders. However, Stephens' approaches to Meagher and Mitchel were not successful – in both cases initial sympathy gave way to deep suspicion. Stephens and Mitchel did not take to each other (neither had a good track record in co-operating with or deferring to others), and soon developed a sharp mutual antipathy.[11] Mitchel dismissed Stephens as 'a humbug', while Stephens scorned Mitchel as 'a disgruntled egoist and a man of the past'.[12] According to John O'Leary, the failure of these approaches permanently soured Stephens' attitude to all those associated with Young Ireland 'and he infused his own feelings largely into the mass of his followers'.[13] Such views were reciprocated and American-based Young Irelanders such as Thomas Francis Meagher, Richard O'Gorman and Thomas D'Arcy McGee looked coolly on the new organisation and refused to become involved. It was their reluctance that forced John O'Mahony, another who had taken part in the events of 1848, into assuming a leadership role in the American organisation. O'Mahony believed that the exiled leaders had let the cause of Irish nationalism down and in late 1858 he wrote to Stephens: 'I am sick of Young Ireland and its theatrical leaders, whose want of steadfastness of purpose and childish pettiness with the people that were disheartened by their own resolution and want of forecast makes me more despair of my country than any fickleness of its populace.'[14]

Early in 1858 Stephens had also sought the assistance of A. M. Sullivan, the influential proprietor of the *Nation*, who, although not an original member of the Young Ireland grouping, identified strongly with their legacy and sought to carry on their tradition in his newspaper. Sullivan was strongly opposed to secret societies and refused to help.[15] Some time later, Sullivan heard accounts that some of those active in founding the proto-Fenian Phoenix Society in west Cork had claimed that Sullivan, John Mitchel and William Smith O'Brien were all leaders of the society. Attempting to counter these claims, Sullivan publicly dissociated himself from the Phoenix Society in an editorial in the *Nation* and decried the fact that young men were becoming involved in secret conspiracies; he also quoted a letter from O'Brien repudiating such groups and denying any connection with them. Sullivan appealed to patriotic young Irishmen 'to avoid the hopeless perils and demoralizing effects of secret societies', which he claimed had only ever brought misery to Ireland and were 'more perilous to society than open tyranny'.[16] Some weeks after this editorial fifteen members of the Phoenix Society were arrested in the south-west. Many members of the IRB, especially Stephens, laid the blame squarely on the shoulders of Sullivan, claiming that his editorial had alerted the authorities to the existence of the society, and denounced him as an informer and a 'felon-setter'. Although Sullivan was sympathetic to the arrested men, and was the chief promoter of a fair trial fund to assist them, these cries were taken up by many of Stephens' lieutenants and Sullivan became a hate figure for physical-force nationalists. Sullivan defended himself in the *Nation* and wrote a lengthy pamphlet setting out his side of the story. He argued that Fenianism was little more than a system of moral subversion and character assassination, distinct from the open and honourable nationalism of Young Ireland and their followers.[17]

The feud between Stephens and Sullivan simmered on through the 1860s. Stephens resented the political influence of those who remained aloof, often referring derisively to prominent Young Irelanders as 'trusted leaders', and dismissed Sullivan as the foremost among the 'patriotic journalists' he despised.[18] For its part, the *Nation* became an increasingly outspoken opponent of any initiatives that originated with Stephens. When the National Brotherhood of St Patrick was founded in March 1861, and was soon seen to be a front for the IRB, Sullivan condemned the secretive moves that led to its foundation as 'a coup ... born of trick, surprise, and subterfuge' and claimed that 'the National Brotherhood was ushered into the world to begin a life of dubious character and fortune'.[19] All the leading Young Irelanders kept their distance from the National Brotherhood, and some such as John Martin openly expressed reservations about its secretive nature and the composition of its leadership.[20]

III

Stephens, however, had no compunction about laying claim to the Young Ireland legacy when it suited him and he became one of the main promoters of the proposal to honour the remains of Terence Bellew McManus, a prominent figure in the 1848 insurrection. McManus had been transported to Tasmania for his part in the insurrection, had escaped after four years, and died in poverty in San Francisco in January 1861. The American Fenian Brotherhood decided that he should be buried in Ireland, and in August they exhumed his body and shipped it across the Atlantic. After several days lying in state at the Mechanics' Institute in Dublin, McManus was reburied in Glasnevin cemetery on 10 November. On a cold, wet day in Dublin, an estimated 150,000 people lined the streets as the massive funeral procession of various nationalist organisations made its way to the cemetery. However, this show of strength masked some deep divisions. Most of those who had shared McManus's years of exile in Tasmania – notably Smith O'Brien, Mitchel and John Martin – were opposed to the idea of using his remains to mount a political demonstration, and believed that his original resting place should have been left undisturbed.[21] However, they could not be seen to obstruct the honouring of a former comrade and, anxious not to be elbowed aside by lesser-known figures, they eventually reconciled themselves to the proceedings.

The Young Ireland priest Fr John Kenyon was originally scheduled to give the funeral oration. Stephens and Thomas Clarke Luby expressed the hope that he would emphasise that the funeral was 'something that ought to rekindle patriotic feeling in Irish breasts and animate our people to renewed efforts to win back their lost independence'. Kenyon, however, was unhappy at this and apparently replied that the furthest he would go would be to state that the funeral was evidence that 'the Irish people still keep alive in their souls the *aspiration* after national independence'.[22] This was unacceptable to the IRB leadership, who feared that the Young Irelanders might take the opportunity to praise McManus and bury Fenianism, and Stephens then wrote a speech himself to be delivered by Captain Michael Smith, one of the American delegation that had accompanied the remains. There was much jockeying for position over procedural arrangements and Kenyon's attempt to have the moderate nationalist, The O'Donoghue, elected as chairman of the funeral committee caused uproar among the IRB. A furious battle also erupted over the question of the funeral oration, with Kenyon leaving the meeting threatening to prevent the funeral by seizing the body, and the IRB taking the precaution of placing a guard around McManus's coffin that night to prevent any attempt to remove it.[23]

In the end Kenyon's threats of disruption came to nothing, and the funeral passed off impressively. However, relations between Young Ireland and the IRB were deeply soured: Thomas Clarke Luby, for example, who had previously been on amicable terms with the Young Irelanders, accused them of trying to sabotage the funeral and became a bitter enemy. For his part, Stephens was elated at his success in achieving a triumph over the nationalist establishment and sought to monopolise credit for the event, writing to John O'Mahony in New York: 'We can allow no share at all to mere outsiders; the work was ours from beginning to end ... the "trusted leaders" and their small tail were thoroughly aware of the work being ours in all its bearings ... Poor purblind and bungling cravens!' He singled out Kenyon and Martin as his main adversaries and claimed that on the night before the funeral 'a great principle – the sovereignty of the people – was for the first time really struggled for and nobly won in Ireland'. In comparison, the Young Irelanders had shown themselves to be cowardly incompetents: 'Never, it may be fairly said, did such little natures chance to lead a people. At no time and in no way can they give proof of anything but littleness.'[24]

The funeral was a great propaganda coup for the IRB, allowing them to represent themselves as the primary heirs of the tradition of armed resistance to British rule. But other nationalists felt estranged and alienated by Stephens' machinations. These feelings were exacerbated by Stephens' subsequent policy of attempting to sabotage nationalist initiatives that did not originate with him. On 5 December 1861 a meeting at the Rotunda in Dublin was convened by A. M. Sullivan and chaired by The O'Donoghue to take advantage of Anglo-American tensions and discuss the founding of a new nationalist organisation. Stephens, however, managed to pack the meeting with IRB men and block the progress of any new organisation. When packing committees did not suffice, Stephens was perfectly pre-pared to disrupt meetings by more direct methods. When A. M. Sullivan held a meeting in Dublin in 1864 to call for a statue to be erected to Henry Grattan, Stephens infiltrated it with a large number of his followers, who shouted down O'Sullivan and prevented him from addressing the meeting. The Fenian paper, the *Irish People*, claimed that 'The people of Dublin gained a glorious moral triumph ... they will never tolerate ... a felon-setter acting the part of a patriot.'[25]

IV

Stephens kept a close watch on all nationalist initiatives outside his control and when John Martin and The O'Donoghue founded the National League in January 1864 the *Irish People* poured scorn on its moderate objectives, reliance on constitutional methods and lack of public support, dismissing it as 'the erection of a great talking shop ... where every idle fool may dis-port himself at fancy'.[26] Contingents of IRB men regularly disrupted National League meetings with demands for 'a war policy' and shouts of 'rifles are what we want'. On one occasion at a League meeting in August 1866, John Martin, a figure admired by most nationalists for his decency and integrity, rebuked those IRB members present for their rowdy behav-iour and in return was showered with eggs.[27] Most moderate nationalists were appalled: William Smith O'Brien called such actions a 'disgrace upon the nationalists of Ireland ... I utterly despair of any advancement of the cause of our country when ... men who call themselves patriots demean themselves like a mob of ruffians'.[28]

The disruption of these meetings widened the breach between the IRB and the Young Irelanders, who regularly denounced Stephens and his followers for their 'ruffianism'. The neo-Young Ireland press also claimed that such boorish behaviour highlighted one of the clearest differences that existed between the two groups, namely that of social class. Most of the Young Ireland leaders were men of some social standing, while such figures were unusual in the Fenians. John O'Leary admitted that Stephens' main influence was on 'the uneducated or half-educated',[29] and opponents of the IRB often denigrated the organisation by comparing its leadership unfavourably with that of the Young Irelanders and intimated that they lacked the background and abilities to aspire to the leadership of Irish nationalism: John Rutherford, for example, noted that 'From beginning to end, Irish Fenianism was singularly wanting in the gentleman-like element. There was no culture – no refinement in it. Neither did it include anything like genius. Not one single individual of its hundreds of thousands of converts could be compared for a moment with "the men of '48", either in mental or social standing.'[30]

Far from being offended at such comparisons, most IRB men were proud of the plebeian composition of their organisation and saw themselves as the true successors to Wolfe Tone's 'men of no property'. They regarded their struggle as a democratic one and often criticised Young Irelanders such as John Martin and John Blake Dillon for their efforts to enlist men of property into their various political organisations.[31] To reinforce their democratic credentials the Fenians took an attitude of deliberate irreverence towards gentrified nationalists and mocked them mercilessly for their social pretensions. William Smith O'Brien's claims to be a lineal descendant of Brian Boru and The O'Donoghue's pride in his ancient Gaelic title were frequent lampooned.[32] The *Irish People* proudly proclaimed that 'The nationalists of today have no slavish hankering after aristocratic leaders', and argued that the landed classes could never be relied upon to lead a popular struggle. It noted that 'The Volunteer movement of '82 was aristocratic. Had it been democratic, like that of '98, its results would have been permanent ... Our struggle must be a democratic struggle ... give the Irish soil to the Irish people and we are content'.[33]

IRB criticism of the Young Irelanders became more intense and sustained with the foundation of the *Irish People* newspaper in November 1863. One of the main motivations behind its founding was to counter the Young Ireland opinions of newspapers such as the *Nation*. IRB leaders such as Stephens and Luby used their new paper to attack all aspects of Young Ireland's political record, especially their faint-heartedness, claiming that this had been the primary cause of the abject failure of their insurrection in 1848 and had subsequently frightened them from any further insurrectionary attempts. They had then compounded their failure by attempting to blame those whom they had led so ineptly:

> In order to screen themselves from the reproach due to their subsequent desertion of the national cause (a defection with hardly a parallel in history) they slandered the people continually, affirming them to be a worthless, cowardly people for whom it was useless to struggle any longer. This pitiful game they played till others proved the falseness of their assertions; proved that they, and not the people, were wanting.[34]

The paper often denounced the moral force policy of Daniel O'Connell as degenerate and unmanly, but argued that 'O'Connell deserves less blame than those Young Ireland leaders who broke from his guidance and turned back again to the same dreary road. We can find no excuse for these. Once having made open profession of the true faith, they should have clung to it to the last, like the men of '98.'[35] In a sharp dig (aimed primarily at Fr John Kenyon), Luby attacked the Young Irelanders as mere 'Aspirationists … the sworn enemies of every practical effort', noting that 'the Aspirationist … gains the reputation of the patriot on very convenient terms'.[36]

The *Irish People* argued that it was the IRB who were the true successors of the national tradition handed down by the United Irishmen and Thomas Davis, while the surviving Young Irelanders had turned their backs on the struggle. In particular, Charles Gavan Duffy's farewell editorial in the *Nation* after the failure of the Tenant League and the Independent Irish Party in the mid-1850s, in which he claimed that there was 'no more hope for the Irish cause than for the corpse on the dissecting table', was frequently invoked as evidence that he and his fellow Young Irelanders were fair-weather patriots who had given up on their country.[37] Duffy's observation allowed them to claim that the IRB had breathed new life into a moribund movement.[38] Rather than encourage this revival of the national spirit, the IRB leadership claimed that the Young Irelanders had tried to thwart it, and that in charging the IRB with political recklessness and hostility to religion they had become no better than O'Connell's henchmen, who had laid similar charges against the Young Irelanders in the days of the old Repeal Association.[39]

Even by the highly polemical standards of Irish nationalist newspapers of the period, the *Irish People* was often distinguished by its severity of tone towards nationalist elder statesmen. Scoffing at William Smith O'Brien's self-appointed role as counsellor to the nation, the *Irish People* dismissed his advice as 'senile' and noted that 'Mr O'Brien has written much – books, pamphlets, letters; but we do not think that the most partial critic could say that he has ever, in one line, soared above mediocrity, if even he has ever reached it.' John Martin, another widely respected figure, was dismissed as an 'old fogey' and readers were reminded that 'a fool frequently makes a more mischievous public character than a rascal'.[40] Young Irelanders such as Thomas D'Arcy McGee, who had repudiated their earlier nationalist views, or those such as Michael J. Barry or John O'Hagan, who had taken official positions, were singled out for particular abuse, and their apostasy was used to discredit the Young Ireland movement as a whole.[41] Reviewing a work on 'The Young Irelanders of '48', the *Irish People* argued that it 'will suggest to our readers the melancholy reflection that some of the most fiery apostles of the national faith of freedom have apostasised … and have become the brazen propagandists of a political heresy which may be profitable but is … as adverse to the opinions of their unbought youth as it is lucrative to the greedy sordidness of their corrupt maturity'.[42]

The struggle between Young Ireland and the IRB was never simply one between constitutional nationalism and physical-force nationalism.[43] Even moderate Young Irelanders drew much of the inspiration from the Grattanite Volunteer tradition of 1782, and during the invasion scare of May 1859 the *Nation* exhorted its readers to organise and procure arms, while John Martin wrote and published several letters welcoming a French invasion as the surest way of securing Irish independence.[44] But differing attitudes to political violence did aggravate the tensions between the two groups. While the Young Irelanders refused to discountenance physical force (which would have involved repudiating their past and smacked of a degenerate O'Connellism), they usually spoke of physical force in theoretical terms and warned of the dangers of popular revolt.[45] The IRB on the other hand maintained that physical force was morally superior to constitutional politics, which they claimed was 'inglorious' and taught 'falsehood, and bluster; lip loyalty and heart-treason; makes the people neither manly rebels, nor good subjects'. Armed rebellion for them was not a last resort, but their preferred means of achieving Irish independence. In fact they maintained that independence achieved without the shedding of blood would clearly be of less value than that achieved through struggle and heroic sacrifice, and that even a failed insurrection was better than successful agitation.[46]

There was little surprise that moderate constitutionalist Young Irelanders such as Smith O'Brien and Gavan Duffy should be wary of an insurrectionary organisation, but many Fenians continued to hope for a lead from those such as John Mitchel, who had preached the fieriest of revolutionary gospels in 1848 and restated his contempt for parliamentary politics and his hopes for the destruction of the British empire in his later writings. Mitchel even went so far as to refer to himself as 'the father of Fenianism'[47] and agreed to become financial agent for the Fenian Brotherhood in Paris after his release from a Union jail in October 1865. However, he soon became disillusioned with the organisation's factionalism and moribund conspiracies, resigning his position in June 1866 and moving back to New York.[48] In February 1867 an attempt was made to unite the opposing factions of the Fenian Brotherhood under Mitchel's leadership, but he declined. He stated that he had no wish 'to take and knit up the two ragged fag ends of an organisation originally rotten and now all tattered and torn, and to wear the patched up thing as a robe of honour', and openly declared his contempt for commissioning generals into a phantom army or engaging in the fiction that an Irish republic had already been established.[49] However, he stressed that his opposition to Fenianism did not mean that he in any way opposed physical force or the methods of the more extreme elements of Fenianism: 'The Irish have the clear right to strike at England anywhere or anyhow, in Canada, in Ireland, in London, by steel or gunpowder or firewood. But I hold that those who undertake such warfare at present, whether civilised or uncivilised, must perish and perish in vain.'[50]

In October 1867 Mitchel founded a newspaper in New York, the *Irish Citizen*, in which he published a series of letters outlining his main criticisms of Fenianism. Firstly, he claimed that it was 'established upon a wrong and false basis by that wretched Stephens' who had deluded Irish and American Fenians about the strength of the movement in their respective countries. Moreover, its plan to mount an immediate insurrection against England, using American forces and arms, was fatally flawed: while England and America were at peace, such efforts would contravene American law and would never be allowed by the American government. Until England was at war, there was no point in calling on people to donate money that would be squandered in secret conspiracy; it was best that Irishmen should join their local militias and wait for their opportunity. And if in the meantime 'the enormous sack of gas' called Fenianism should collapse beneath the weight of its factions, pretensions and delusions, then Ireland would be none the worse.[51]

For most other Young Irelanders, their criticisms of the IRB centred on the organisation's conspiratorial ethos and its desire to dominate or manipulate other national movements.[52] Having frequently been at the sharp end of Fenian invective, the two Sullivan brothers denounced the IRB reflex of dismissing all criticisms of the organisation as 'felon-setting', and its tendency to attack fellow Irishmen, lay and clerical, who opposed it in any way, rather than directing its fire at the British govern-ment.[53] John Martin was also strongly critical of the methods of the IRB and claimed that one of his main reasons for setting up the National League in January 1864 was simply to save Ireland 'from the dangers and evils of this Fenian craze'.[54] In the face of IRB opposition and public apathy the National League did not fare well, but at its lowest ebb in June 1865 Martin still insisted on keeping it alive for at least another six months in the hope that 'the Fenian delusion will probably be by that time at an end, and the best of the Fenians must turn to rational means and measures'.[55]

V

Relations between the Young Irelanders and the IRB had reached a low ebb by the middle of the decade, but they were improved by subsequent events, such as the arrest of leading Fenians and the suppression of the *Irish People* by the British government in September 1865. Not only did this silence the most trenchant critic of the Young Irelanders, but it also provided an example of heavy-handed coercion against which both sides could unite. Editorials in the *Nation* were severely critical of the government, and the manly bearing in court of IRB leaders such as Luby and John O'Leary was a cause of pride to all nationalists. The deposing of James Stephens as IRB leader after his repeated postponements of action in 1865 and 1866 also served to remove a figure whose autocratic and conspiratorial ways were bitterly resented by other nationalists, and further contributed to the thaw in relations between the IRB and Young Ireland. The events of 1867 brought about even greater convergence. Although the *Nation* deplored the IRB rising of that year, it praised those involved for their courage and idealism, and noted with some pride that in no cases had they committed any outrages or seized private property, and that these 'rebels' were 'in other respects, remarkable for their orderly, peaceable and virtuous habits'.[56]

The failure of the 1867 insurrection also had the effect of tempering IRB criticisms of the revolutionary incompetence of Young Ireland. The IRB, after all, had had many years to plan a rising and also had the assistance of a cadre of veteran American officers, yet their showing was scarcely better than that of the inexperienced and unprepared Young Irelanders in 1848. The *Nation*, however, avoided any crowing, and argued that the fact that decent men were driven to insurrection simply showed how intolerable Ireland's position was and stood as an unanswerable argument for self-government. Within weeks of the rising John Martin was calling for an amnesty for all political prisoners, and months later he led the Dublin demonstration in December 1867 to commemorate the deaths of the three 'Manchester Martyrs'.[57] Nationalist indignation at the Manchester executions proved a powerful unifying force. After demonstrations commemorating the executed men, John Martin and A. M. Sullivan among others found themselves charged with seditious assembly; both were acquitted but Sullivan was later convicted of sedition for articles written in his *Weekly News* and served some weeks in prison in spring 1868. This did much for his standing with militant nationalists, as did the publicity that his newspaper gave to the ill-treatment of Fenian prisoners in English jails in 1868–9.

His brother, T. D. Sullivan earned much gratitude from Fenians for his publication of Fenian speeches from the dock, a work which effectively endorsed their actions and placed their sufferings squarely within the tradition of the United Irishmen and Young Irelanders that had gone before them.[58] He was also much admired for commemorating the 'Manchester Martyrs' with the stirring 'God save Ireland' – a song which became immensely popular among Fenians and the unofficial anthem of nationalist Ireland. A. M. Sullivan noted that 'the distinction between Fenian and non-Fenian nationalists seemed to disappear, and the national or popular element came unitedly and in full force to the front'.[59] It was all a long way from accusations of 'felon-setting'.

Reports of the harsh treatment of Fenian prisoners and the growth of the amnesty movement in 1869 provided further common ground for both groups, with John Martin and A. M. Sullivan playing leading roles in the Amnesty Association. Moreover, as R. V. Comerford has noted, the English press and politicians increasingly described almost all nationalist activity, including amnesty agitation, as 'Fenian', and this lumping together of diverse nationalist factions reinforced the unifying effect of recent events.[60] Adding to the British government's inadvertent efforts to unite nationalists, the Catholic Church played its part too. In December 1869 supporters of the Amnesty Association proposed John Martin as an independent national candidate in a by-election in Longford. In a bitterly fought and often violent contest he was opposed by the Catholic clergy and defeated, but local Fenians had formed the core of his most committed supporters and their efforts helped to wipe away the memory of earlier factional disputes.[61] The bonds forged here were of considerable importance and Young Irelanders who were elected to parliament as home rulers in the 1870s, such as Martin, Denny Lane, and P. J. Smyth, often benefited significantly from Fenian support.[62] Indeed, it can be argued that this *rapprochement* laid some of the foundations for the increasing convergence of constitutional and Fenian politics from the later 1870s onwards. Although differences persisted throughout the 1870s and beyond on the best means of achieving self-government and the form that it should take, these were rarely infused with the bitterness that had pervaded the quarrels of the early 1860s.

By the time the main players in these events had got around to writing their memoirs, the heat had gone out of old battles, and most were willing to pay tribute to the other as sincere nationalists who had laboured in their own way for the sake of their country. T. D. Sullivan noted that

> With all its faults and mistakes the Fenian movement was a great manifestation of national feeling. Sympathy with it was widespread as the Irish race; it attracted to itself a multitude of warm-hearted young Irishmen, inspired them with high hopes, set before them a noble ideal, and filled them with a splendid enthusiasm.[63]

John O'Leary regretted the severity of some of the *Irish People*'s attacks upon Young Irelanders such as O'Brien and Martin, and maintained: 'I do not think now that we took sufficiently charitable views of the motives and conduct of these gentlemen.'[64] In later life it was O'Leary who intro-duced the young W. B. Yeats to the literary works of the Young Irelanders, and the term 'Young Ireland' enjoyed a new popularity in the 1880s and 1890s as the title of various newly founded nationalist literary and political societies, many of which had a strong IRB influence.[65]

It is in the nature of nationalist political movements to stress conti-nuity and harmony rather than disunity and suspicion, and most later nationalists would look upon the Young Irelanders and the Fenians as manifestations of the same spirit at different stages of development; Patrick Pearse, for example, praised the Young Irelanders for expounding the ideals of Irish nationalism, and the Fenians for their efforts to put these ideals into practice.[66] Others, however, were more inclined to distinguish between the two, most notably Arthur Griffith who, although an IRB member in his youth, never overcame his reservations about militaristic secret societies lacking a clear agenda. Griffith, who drew so much of his inspiration from the well of Davis and Mitchel, clearly preferred the open defiance and educational initiatives of Young Ireland to the conspiratorial activities of the IRB.[67] Although the Young Ireland influence on Fenianism was undeniable, the latter was a rather more unruly child than most Young Irelanders would have wanted. Their relationship was a complex one, and was often fraught with strains, discord and consid-erable bitterness. Class, generational and personal differences all played their part, and were exacerbated by significant divergences as to how Ireland's independence should best be secured. In their disagreements between open and conspiratorial methods and between constitutionalism and political violence, the relationship between Young Ireland and the IRB prefigured the main tensions that would continue to trouble Irish nationalism up to the achievement of independence and beyond.

NOTES

1. E. R. R. Green, 'The beginnings of Fenianism', in T. W. Moody (ed.), *The Fenian Movement* (Cork: Mercier Press, 1968), pp. 11–22; Owen McGee, *The IRB: The Irish Republican Brotherhood, from the Land League to Sinn Féin* (Dublin: Four Courts Press, 2005), pp. 18–27.
2. John O'Leary, *Recollections of Fenians and Fenianism*, 2 vols (London: Downey, 1896), vol. i, pp. 2–3, 50–1, 79; Jeremiah O'Donovan Rossa, *Rossa's Recollections, 1838 to 1898: Memoirs of an Irish Revolutionary* (Shannon: Irish University Press, 1972, 1st edn, 1898), p. 172; T. D. Sullivan, *Recollections of Troubled Times in Irish Politics* (Dublin: Sealy, Bryers & Walker, 1905), pp. 6, 128.
3. Gary Owens, 'Popular mobilisation and the rising of 1848: The clubs of the Irish Confederation', in L. M. Geary (ed.), *Rebellion and Remembrance in Modern Ireland* (Dublin: Four Courts Press, 2001), pp. 51–5.
4. Owens, 'Popular mobilisation', p. 56.
5. Anthony M. Breen, *The Cappoquin Rebellion, 1849* (Thurston: Drecroft, 1998).
6. R. V. Comerford, *The Fenians in Context: Irish Politics and Society 1848–82* (Dublin: Wolfhound Press, 1985), p. 18.
7. Desmond Ryan, *The Fenian Chief: A Biography of James Stephens* (Dublin: Gill & Son, 1967), pp. 17–19; Marta Ramón, *A Provisional Dictator: James Stephens and the Fenian Movement* (Dublin: UCD Press, 2007), pp. 23–5, 40–3, 67.
8. O'Leary, *Recollections*, vol. i, p. 71; Ryan, *Fenian Chief*, pp. 67–72, 96, 102; Brendan Ó Cathaoir,

John Blake Dillon, Young Irelander (Dublin: Irish Academic Press, 1990), p. 144; Ramón, *Provisional Dictator*, pp. 79, 84–5.

9. James Quinn, *John Mitchel* (Dublin: UCD Press, 2008), p. 37.
10. O'Leary, *Recollections*, vol. i, pp. 9–10; John Savage, *Fenian Heroes and Martyrs* (Boston: P. Donahoe, 1868), p. 47.
11. *Nation*, 25 Jan. 1869; Ramón, *Provisional Dictator*, pp. 84–6, 90, 102.
12. Ryan, *Fenian Chief*, pp. 111, 222.
13. O'Leary, *Recollections*, vol. i, p. 95.
14. Quoted in Ó Cathaoir, 'John O'Mahony (1815–1877)', *The Capuchin Annual* (1977), p. 184.
15. *Nation*, 19 Apr. 1862; Ramón, *Provisional Dictator*, p. 79
16. *Nation*, 30 Oct. 1858; see also A. M. Sullivan, *New Ireland: Political Sketches and Personal Reminiscences*, 2 vols (London: Low, Marston, Seale & Rivington, 1878), vol. i, pp. 201–2.
17. Alexander M. Sullivan, *The Phoenix Societies in Ireland and America, 1858 and 1862*, 2 vols (Dublin: A. M. Sullivan, 1862), vol. ii, p. 24.
18. Ramón, *Provisional Dictator*, p. 108.
19. Sullivan, *Phoenix Societies*, vol. ii, p. 25; see also *Nation*, 23 Mar. 1861.
20. John Martin, *Letters on the National Question* (Dublin: N. Harding, 1863), p. 48
21. Sullivan, *Phoenix Societies*, vol. ii, p. 29.
22. Séamus Pender, 'Luby, Kenyon and the MacManus Funeral', *Cork Historical Society Journal*, 2/56 (1951), pp. 59–60.
23. Ibid., pp. 63–4.
24. James Stephens to John O'Mahony, Dublin, 25 Feb. 1862, quoted in Joseph Denieffe, *A Personal Narrative of the IRB* (New York: Gael Publishing Co., 1906), pp. 169–72; on the McManus funeral see also Ramón, *Provisional Dictator*, pp. 112–23.
25. *Irish People*, 27 Feb. 1864; see also Comerford, *Fenians in Context*, pp. 87–9.
26. 'Abuse of Speech', *Irish People*, 27 Feb. 1864; see also 'Deeds not words', *Irish People*, 16 Apr. 1864.
27. Sullivan, *New Ireland*, pp. 247–50; P. A. Sillard, *The Life and Letters of John Martin* (Dublin: J. Duffy & Co., 1893), p. 167.
28. Sillard, *John Martin*, p. 174; Sullivan, *Recollections*, p. 98.
29. O'Leary, *Recollections*, vol. i, p. 242.
30. John Rutherford, *The Secret History of the Fenian Conspiracy: Its Origin, Objects and Ramifications* (London: C. Kegan Paul & Co., 1877), pp. 56–7.
31. 'By-issues and humbugs', *Irish People*, 19 Dec. 1963; 'A retrospect', *Irish People*, 16 Jan. 1864.
32. 'Modern Antiques', *Irish People*, 9 Jan. 1864; '29th February', *Irish People*, 5 Mar. 1864.
33. 'Gentility in Ireland', *Irish People*, 27 May 1865; 'Democracy', *Irish People*, 11 June 1864.
34. 'Fruits of the American war', *Irish People*, 26 Dec. 1863.
35. 'The Fenian Brotherhood', *Irish People*, 19 Nov. 1864.
36. Thomas Luby to unknown correspondent, Luby Papers, National Library of Ireland, MS 331, ff. 99–100, f. 27; 'Aspirationists', *Irish People*, 2 Apr. 1864.
37. *Nation*, 18 Aug. 1855.
38. 'The corpse on the dissecting table', *Irish People*, 8 July 1865.
39. O'Leary, *Recollections*, vol. i, pp. 178–9; 'A retrospect', *Irish People*, 16 Jan. 1864.
40. 'Mr Smith O'Brien', *Irish People*, 12 Mar. 1864; 'February 22nd', *Irish People*, 27 Feb. 1864.
41. 'A political pack of fools', *Irish People*, 27 May 1865.
42. Review of *The Young Irelanders of '48* by John Lemoinne, *Irish People*, 10 June 1865.
43. Comerford, *Fenians in Context*, pp. 89–90.
44. John Martin, *Correspondence between John Martin and William Smith O'Brien Relative to a French Invasion* (Dublin: John O'Daly, 1861).
45. See, for example, John Martin to O'Neill Daunt, 18 Sept. 1865, O'Neill Daunt journals, NLI, MS 3042, 1370.
46. 'No more agitation humbug', *Irish People*, 30 Jan. 1864; 'The Irish priests and the people', *Irish People*, 14 May 1864.
47. *Irish Citizen* (New York), 27 Feb. 1869.
48. Mitchel to John O'Mahony, Paris, 10 Mar. 1866, quoted in Denieffe, *Recollections*, p. 220; *New York Daily News*, 10 July 1866, reprinted in the *Nation*, 14 July 1866.
49. *Irish Citizen* (New York), 18 Jan., 22, 29 Feb. 1868.
50. Mitchel to Mortimer Moynahan, 28 Jan. 1867, quoted in William D'Arcy, *The Fenian Movement in the United States 1858–86* (Washington, DC: Catholic University of America Press, 1947), p. 226.

51. *Irish Citizen* (New York), 22, 29 Feb., 24 Apr. 1868. In private letters Mitchel was even more scathing about Fenianism: see, for example, Mitchel to John Martin, 28 Mar. 1868?, Belfast Central Library, F. J. Bigger collection, Z 314(5)-1. See also Quinn, *Mitchel*, pp. 77–80.

52. Cato (P. J. Smyth), *Irishman*, 14 Jan. 1865.

53. Sullivan, *Phoenix Societies*, part ii, p. 24; Sullivan, *New Ireland*, p. 238; Sullivan, *Recollections*, p. 47.

54. John Martin to O'Neill Daunt, 18 Sept. 1865, O'Neill Daunt journals, NLI, MS 3042, 1370.

55. John Martin to Miss Thomson, June 1865, cited in Sillard, *John Martin*, p. 178.

56. 'Consider it well', *Nation*, 16 Mar. 1867.

57. *Nation*, 13 Apr. 1867; Sillard, *John Martin*, pp. 182–92; McGee, *The IRB*, pp. 42–3.

58. T. D. Sullivan, *Guilty or Not Guilty: Speeches from the Dock or Protests of Irish Patriotism* (Dublin: 6 Lower Abbey St, 1867); this went through numerous subsequent editions.

59. Sullivan, *New Ireland*, pp. 292–3.

60. Comerford, *Fenians in Context*, p. 152.

61. Emmet Larkin, *The Consolidation of the Roman Catholic Church in Ireland, 1860–1870* (Dublin: Gill & Macmillan, 1987), p. 665.

62. Comerford, *Fenians in Context*, p. 217; Maura Cronin, 'Denny Lane', *Cork Historical Society Journal*, 100 (1995), pp. 11–12; Maura Cronin, 'Denny Lane', *Cork Historical Society Journal*, 101 (1996), pp. 144–5.

63. Sullivan, *Recollections*, p. 128. A. M. Sullivan also praised James Stephens as 'one of the ablest, most skilful, and most dangerous revolutionists of our time'. *New Ireland*, p. 274. Old Fenians also praised the Sullivans for their devotion to Irish nationalism; see, for example, John Denvir, *The Life Story of an Old Rebel* (Dublin: Sealy, Bryers & Walker, 1910), p. 150 and John Devoy, *Recollections of an Irish Rebel* (New York: Charles P. Young, 1929), pp. 39–40.

64. O'Leary, *Recollections*, vol. ii, pp. 21–2, 227. See also John O'Leary, *Young Ireland: The Old and the New* (Dublin: Young Ireland Society, 1885), pp. 5–8, 11–14.

65. McGee, *The IRB*, pp. 84–5, 229–30; R. F. Foster, *W. B. Yeats: A Life. I: The Apprentice Mage 1865–1914* (Oxford: Oxford University Press, 1997), pp. 43–4, 115.

66. Patrick Pearse, 'From a hermitage' and 'The sovereign people', in Desmond Ryan (ed.), *Collected Works of Pádraic H. Pearse: Political Writings and Speeches* (Dublin: Maunsel & Co. Ltd, 1917–22), pp. 204–5, 371.

67. Patrick Maume, 'Young Ireland, Arthur Griffith and republican ideology: The question of continuity', in *Éire-Ireland*, 34/2 (1999), pp. 155–74 and Patrick Maume, *The Long Gestation: Irish Nationalist Life 1891–1918* (Dublin: Gill & Macmillan, 1999), pp. 85–8.

2

National Brotherhoods and National Leagues: The IRB and its Constitutional Rivals during the 1860s

Marta Ramón

I

Fenianism is most commonly described as a purely revolutionary move-ment devoted to the establishment of an Irish republic by physical force. Beyond these simple postulates, Fenian ideology is considered to have been imprecise at best, non-existent at worst. Certainly there are grounds for these assumptions; partly due to the movement's own hetero-geneity and the priority given to the objective of independence over its actual form, the IRB's leaders never formulated an official political doctrine, and as a result many of the subtler elements in the Fenian system of beliefs have tended to go unnoticed.[1] This has influenced modern historiography in a number of ways. On the one hand, the lack of an explicit political programme may have contributed to sparking the well-known debate between those who see membership of the IRB purely as a decision to engage in revolution and those who argue for the importance of the recreational factor.[2] On the other hand, the centrality of physical force to the IRB's historical image has overshadowed the movement's more complex political behaviour and occasionally led to simplification, especially as regards to its relationship with other sections of Irish nationalism.

According to the classical formulation, Irish nationalist politics during the first half of the 1860s was dominated by the confrontation between the revolutionary and the constitutional approaches to Irish independence, a conflict based on differing attitudes to physical force. While the Fenians stood for revolutionary purity and the idea of the republic, and despised constitutional politics as a useless and dangerous diversion from the 'true path', moderate nationalists were content to pursue self-government within the limits of the British constitution and dreaded the Fenians as the anti-Christ who threatened to bring bloodshed, irreligion and social anarchy.

However, political attitudes on both sides were not always so clear-cut, and their relationship was rather more nuanced than this characterisation suggests. IRB recruits or soon-to-be recruits took part enthusiastically in moderate initiatives such as the Papal Brigade of 1860 and the National Petition campaign of 1861,[3] while moderate nationalists had no qualms about the occasional use of physical-force language, whether as a rhetorical flourish or as a means of pressuring the government.[4] Up until 1867, Fenian leaders periodically discussed the possibility of enlisting the support of more advanced nationalists from the constitutional ranks, while the moderates themselves never lost hope of winning IRB recruits over to the constitutional side, or at least establishing some kind of *modus vivendi* with the organisation. These attempts at *rapprochement* failed, although for more complex reasons than their disagreement over physical force. A closer look at Fenian–moderate relations during this period may shed some light on the less obvious aspects of Fenian ideology and raise a new hypothesis about the source of IRB appeal, an appeal positioned somewhere between the recreational and the purely revolutionary. It is suggested here that the confrontation between the IRB and constitutional nationalists was not merely one between advocates and opponents of evolution, but between two conflicting approaches to political activism: whereas the moderates favoured a top-down model in which a nationalist élite worked on behalf of a body of supporters, the Fenians represented a bottom-up model where the rank-and-file were given an active role and a sense of responsibility for their collective actions. This chapter will argue that the IRB's significance as a forum for grassroots politics was central to its development as a mass-republican movement.

II

In order to explain adequately the process leading to the establishment of these two opposing approaches to political organisation, it is necessary to begin in 1847, when Young Ireland seceded from the Repeal Association and established the Irish Confederation. The Repeal Association was designed as a strongly centralised political machine at the service of O'Connell's efforts in parliament. Leadership was concentrated in O'Connell himself, and grassroots involvement consisted mainly of monetary contributions and participation in the organisation of the occasional monster meeting. In an attempt to depart from this top-down model and regenerate the Repeal cause as they saw it, Young Ireland set out to foster individual political activity and shared leadership through a network of semi-autonomous Confederate clubs. Thomas D'Arcy McGee explained their objectives:

> that instead of one centre of agitation, Ireland should have a thousand – that instead of one committee we should have many – that instead of having public opinion under the absolute dictatorship of a Dublin meeting or a Dublin majority, we should have a political union of several free and independent agencies.[5]

These clubs were bound together through a central Confederate council of thirty-nine members where chairmanship was taken in rotation.[6] However, democratisation was far from complete. The council, which had been assembled from the most prominent of the original seceders from the Repeal Association, was invested with the crucial power to 'add to their numbers'.[7] This provision meant that the leaders were entitled to admit new members at their own discretion and without reference to the opinion of the clubs. There were legal reasons for this, particularly the Convention Act of 1793 which prohibited the election of delegates to national assemblies, but it was also an indication of Young Ireland's essential lack of political radicalism. Members of Confederate clubs were given plenty of opportunities for political activism, but leadership remained the preserve of traditional, self-appointed élites.

This situation was to change due to the combined effect of the Famine, the 1848 revolutions and John Mitchel's 'public conspiracy' to incite the Irish population to rebellion. Mitchel's increasing disagreements with Charles Gavan Duffy and other moderate members of the Confederate council led him to resign from the *Nation* at the end of 1847, and from the council the following February. Free from restraints, his *United Irishman* proceeded to promote not only republicanism and the annihilation of the landlord system, but also social egalitarianism and an understanding with the English Chartists.[8] In a letter to his own Confederate club written shortly before his trial in May 1848, Mitchel addressed what he saw as the main defect in the Confederate structure:

> Now, to insure safe and rapid progress, the Confederation absolutely needs a more efficient executive head ... The Council is at present, and always has been, a clique or close borough, and the practice of adding at pleasure to its own numbers has a tendency to make it become continually more and more of a clique, and less and less independent and effective ... constituted as the Council is, arranged as all its proceedings are, in a select circle of gentlemen no bold forward movement is to be expected.
>
> I mean, in short, that the Confederates, the Clubs, the *people* in some form should actually elect the members of the Council – say for six months, and not by any means suffer it to add to its own numbers.

Of course, this would violate the 'convention act', which I consider an additional argument in favor of the thing I suggest.[9]

Mitchel's practical suggestion was not taken up but his radicalism found an eager following, especially among the Dublin clubs, and led to the emergence of two different strands within the Confederation: Mitchel's democratic republicanism and Gavan Duffy and Smith O'Brien's conservative liberalism. After the failure of the 1848 insurrection these two strands continued their separate development into the opposing camps that were to confront each other during the 1860s. Late in September 1849 Charles Gavan Duffy summoned 'the most influential members of the national party' to meet at the *Nation*'s office. This meeting ultimately led to the foundation of the Irish Alliance, a strictly constitutional organisation which eventually took control of the emerging tenant-right movement and provided the basis for the Independent Irish Party of the 1850s.[10] The radical Mitchelites meanwhile gathered in the Irish Democratic Association (IDA), a network of Chartist-oriented clubs who disdained parliamentary politics, despised the Irish Alliance for its 'genteel' tendencies and encouraged the working classes to break their traditional dependence on predetermined élite leadership.[11] The inaugural address of the IDA to the Irish people laid out its programme in the following terms:

> It is time that the people of Ireland should occupy a prominent position in the assertion of their liberties; that the artisan and peasant should think for themselves, and that the workman and labourer should be taught the necessity of self-reliance, in any attempt made to better their present degraded and abject condition ... we cannot desist from what we deem a solemn duty in warning you against being misled by interested parties, who would fain persuade us that our rights are to be obtained by their exertions in Parliament, and that the election of those men calling themselves Repealers whilst soliciting suffrages, and afterwards following in the wake of the Minister ... is the road to liberty. 'Tis time this illusion should be dispelled.[12]

By mid-1850 the IDA had collapsed and been forced to merge with the Irish Alliance. During the brief months it was in existence, however, it served to consolidate Mitchelite republicanism and, as Maura Cronin has pointed out, act as a bridge between the Irish Confederation and the later IRB.[13] In 1858 the IRB was founded by former members of the radical sections of the Irish Confederation, some of whom (like T. C. Luby) had also been members of the IDA.[14] These early IRB founders adhered to Mitchel's doctrine, not only its advocacy of physical force but also its social egalitarianism and grassroots approach to politics. They also embraced the IDA's emphasis on working-class self-reliance and opposed the concept of 'trusted leadership' which formed the basis of the O'Connell–Gavan Duffy constitutional tradition.

That said, in the case of the IRB this was as much a question of principle as of necessity. When laying the groundwork for the official foundation of the IRB in March 1858, Stephens followed the predetermined channels and started by appealing to J. B. Dillon and A. M. Sullivan for support.[15] They declined, and the IRB was left to fend for itself. After the Phoenix arrests in October 1858, mutual distrust hardened into opposition and IRB emerged as a democratically oriented secret society that vowed to follow the revolutionary path exclusively and that denounced the 'demoralising' constitutional methods employed by its adversaries. Still, if the Fenian leadership repudiated constitutional action, they fully acknowledged the potential advantages of support from its most influential proponents. It was just a matter of finding the right political partner, and in 1860 a candidate came forward: Daniel O'Donoghue, also known as The O'Donoghue of the Glens.

The O'Donoghue is one of the most intriguing figures within the constitutional ranks. Between 1853 and 1885 he had a fluctuating political career: a few years of glory as the leader of the Irish MPs at Westminster, followed by a long descent into oblivion from 1865 when he abandoned his Tipperary seat for the more economical borough of Tralee and outraged his former constitutional associates by becoming a supporter of the Whigs.[16] In 1860, however, he was still at the peak of his popularity. T. D. Sullivan explained why in a revealing portrait: 'He was one of the "old stock", a grand-nephew of O'Connell, young, handsome, of fine physique, and of prepossessing manners; also he was owner of a considerable property – just the man to become a popular favourite.'[17] At this time O'Donoghue was the leading public figure in the National Petition movement, a massive campaign to collect signatures in favour of self-government that gave young men all over Ireland, IRB recruits included, an eagerly welcomed opportunity for political activism.[18] Once this petition was rejected in London, as was fully expected by all involved, O'Donoghue intended to return to Ireland and use the momentum to launch a new nationalist organisation. In May 1861 he met John Mitchel in Boulogne to discuss the possibility of Fenian co-operation for what Mitchel described to John O'Mahony as 'an organisation looking to revolution, foreign aid and more or less directly preparing for that, though for the moment within the forms of the law'.[19] Late in 1860 P. J. Smyth had put forward his own plan of organisation, by which – according to the usual 'trusted leadership' constitutional procedure – 'the leading Nationalists in a conference may choose twenty-one men of known character and integrity, and then submit them to the people for approval or disapproval'.[20] The correspondent to the *Irishman* who reported on this plan, however, incisively pointed out that in order to be a truly elective process the number of candidates ought to be larger at least than the number of places to fill on the council; otherwise the people would merely be submitting to a decision already made.

Young Ireland's efforts to develop individual political activism had borne some fruit since 1847, and the National Petition campaign had already galvanised young nationalists in a different direction than intended either by O'Donoghue or P. J. Smyth. In January 1861 Thomas Neilson Underwood, a lawyer from Strabane who had been connected to the Tenant League during the 1850s, suggested that the National Petition network should be used as the basis for a new body called the Friendly Sons of Saint Patrick, that would be in charge of organising simultaneous banquets to discuss 'the Irish difficulty' on the upcoming St Patrick's Day.[21] The initiative received an enthusiastic response, and on 9 March the *Irishman* announced that this project was to be followed by the establishment of a permanent organisation called the National Brotherhood of Saint Patrick (NBSP).

The NBSP's first stated principle was 'the promotion of cordial Union ... amongst Irishmen of every creed and class', but its very foundation created a source of discord in nationalist politics. Initially A. M. Sullivan had been cautiously supportive of the banquet project, but he suspected the organisers' intentions, and his suspicions were rudely confirmed when he learned that he was to be excluded from the list of speakers at the Dublin event, an embarrassment that was only averted through the intervention of The O'Donoghue and G. H. Moore. At the banquet itself, Sullivan could perceive the black hand of the Fenian Brotherhood, from the phoenix figure displayed over the chairman's seat to the toast reluctantly entrusted to him: 'To the men who in *Europe* and *America* signalise the "genius of our race"'.[22] The foundation of the NBSP at the banquet came to him as a disagreeable surprise. In his view, T. N. Underwood's initiative had the potential to mislead the Irish people into thinking that *the* national organisation which the moderates had been trying to set up for years was finally afoot. As he pointed out, however, the moderates themselves were conspicuous by their absence:

> Not a single man known and trusted by the country joined the organisation. Smith O'Brien did not join; John Martin did not join; The O'Donoghue did not join; George H. Moore did not join; John B. Dillon did not join; P. J. Smyth did not join; out of two or three thousand Irish Priests, not five joined – could such an affair be a National Organisation? To compensate for all these, however, there remained Mr Thomas N. Underwood, the amiable but unknown young gentleman from Strabane.[23]

A cynical mind could suspect that the greatest objection posed by all these great names was that the initiative had not been their own. However, there were more important reasons why the NBSP did not conform to the moderates' ideal of a national organisation. Ever since the late 1840s, as previously noted, Irish nationalist organisations had been usually structured around a central committee of, in Sullivan's phrase, 'known and trusted leaders', with power to add to their numbers, supported by local branches whose main task was to advance the policies proposed by the committee. Instead, the NBSP leadership was elected by ballot, and the Brotherhood itself was structured as a loose network of nationalist reading rooms with no specific programme to advance, and with only a nominal link to the Dublin parent branch. The only obliga-tion shared by the branches was the organisation of simultaneous St Patrick's banquets every 17 March. Members could attend the meetings and use the facilities of any branch besides their own, and local branches were expected to correspond with one another independently from Dublin.[24] In a subtle nod towards illegality, the rules of the Brotherhood were accompanied by the general maxim that 'A member of the National Brotherhood of St Patrick, by learning the use of arms, does not forego any of his Social Rights.'[25]

All these features left Sullivan's 'known and trusted leaders' with little room for manoeuvre, but they were exactly what appealed to the new generation of IRB recruits – young urban males from the artisan and shop-assistant class – who joined the NBSP *en masse* and provided the IRB with a foothold into open political activism. In the process, they also put an end to the unquestioned monopoly of middle-class élites over the management of nationalist self-expression.

In about March 1861 the Fenian Brotherhood in San Francisco launched a project to bring the remains of the Young Irelander Terence Bellew MacManus to Ireland for a ceremonial reburial. The following May the NBSP called a public meeting and set up an Interment Committee to take charge of the Irish side of the arrangements.[26] This committee became the instrument by which the IRB managed to secure control of the funeral arrangements and, for the first time, exclude con-stitutional nationalists from the organisation of a public nationalist event.[27] This is not to say that the exclusion was complete and deliberate from the outset; rather, it was the result of the committee's refusal to hand over the reins to the moderates, a stance that met with determined encouragement from James Stephens. The contest for control revolved mainly around the oration to be delivered over the grave at Glasnevin cemetery. Initially Fr John Kenyon, Smith O'Brien and John Martin were asked in turn to do the honours, but they all declined. John Martin tried to compensate for his own refusal by securing The O'Donoghue as a speaker instead, but this only managed to offend the committee.[28] Fr

Kenyon eventually agreed to speak, only to be turned down again when it was revealed that he intended to deliver what the Fenians termed an 'aspirationist' address, praising nationalism as an unattainable ideal rather than a practical goal.[29] The day before the funeral the moderates attended an extremely tense committee meeting and made a last-ditch effort to gain control of the arrangements, but they were repulsed. On 10 November 1861 MacManus's body was taken to Glasnevin cemetery at the centre of a massive funeral procession. At the grave, Captain Michael Smith, a member of the Fenian delegation from San Francisco, read an oration written by James Stephens himself which, among grandiloquent references to MacManus's 1848 record and his supposed revolutionary constancy, preached to the Irish people 'the great, the essential virtue of self-reliance'.[30]

The MacManus funeral has been the subject of contrasting assessments by historians such as Leon Ó Broin, for whom it demonstrated the IRB's 'formidable' strength,[31] and more sceptical critics such as R. V. Comerford, who warn that 'almost the only incontrovertible interpretation that can be put on the affair is that large numbers of people were in the mood for a public spectacle'.[32] I would argue that the funeral was indeed a major event in Irish history, not on the grounds of its nationalist significance, which remains very much a matter of subjective interpretation, but because it broke with the 'trusted leadership' model in force since O'Connell's time, substituting it for grassroots political activity. In the words of Richard Pigott:

> On the whole it was really a most remarkable display, not only because of its dimensions and respectability, but also because it was organized by the people themselves, not only without the aid of the ostensible leaders of public opinion of the day and the Catholic clergy, but really in opposition to them.[33]

Just three weeks after the funeral, the moderates saw their chance to regain lost ground. On 8 November the arrest of two agents of the American Confederacy on board the British mail steamer *Trent* caused a diplomatic crisis, and the resulting prospect of an Anglo-American war presented the moderates with the opportunity to stir up public opinion and establish a more amenable nationalist organisation than the unmanageable NBSP. According to the usual procedure, A. M. Sullivan, P. J. Smyth and Alderman James Plunkett sent out a circular, summoning representatives of all sections of nationalism to a preliminary meeting on Friday 29 November. According to Sullivan, even members of the NBSP, the National Petition Committee and the MacManus Interment Committee were invited; according to James Stephens, none of the 'really active' members were.[34] This preliminary meeting resolved to call a larger public meeting at the Rotunda on the following Thursday, 5 December.

In a similar fashion to the scheme suggested by P. J. Smyth the previous year, the core of the moderate plan was the proposal of a resolution at the public meeting to the effect that 'the Chairman, Secretary, proposers and seconders of resolutions' should form a committee to invite 'leading Nationalists' to design the new organisation, and then submit this design to a new public meeting for approval. As Stephens complained to O'Mahony, the 'Chairman, Secretary, proposers and seconders' were people of their own choosing, as would be the 'leading Nationalists' subsequently invited to draw up the plan of organisation.[35] For the second time in less than a month, the IRB was prepared to frustrate the moderates' initiatives in order to sustain the NBSP's position. On 5 December the Rotunda was carefully packed with IRB members. In the course of the meeting, Luby approached the moderate leaders and announced that his party intended to present an amendment to their resolution. This simple step, perfectly legitimate according to procedure, was enough to sabotage the moderate plan. Faced with the prospect of a debate, and perhaps a riot by the unpredictable secret society men, the moderates were forced to drop the resolution altogether.[36] In due course, Jeremiah Kavanagh, one of the members of the MacManus delegation from San Francisco, stood up and moved

> that a chairman, two secretaries and a Committee of twenty-one members ... be chosen by a majority of voices at this mass meeting to take into consideration the *advisability* of carrying out an organisation in the present state of affairs at home and abroad.[37]

After a chaotic on-the-spot election manipulated by the IRB section of the audience, a committee was assembled with The O'Donoghue as nominal chairman but with Fenians outnumbering the moderates by almost two to one.[38] Not surprisingly the moderates, who included P. J. Smyth and G. H. Moore, resigned from the committee almost immediately afterwards, and the Fenians simply let the scheme die out.[39]

III

At this point it is time to return to The O'Donoghue, the rising political star of the moment and the Fenians' most likely ally within the moderate camp. Unfortunately for O'Donoghue, his recent scheme to set up 'an organisation looking to revolution and foreign aid, within the forms of the law' with potential Fenian support had ended in failure, owing to a lack of enthusiasm on the part of other members of the 'national party'.[40] But the NBSP and the IRB had introduced a new sense of excitement into nationalist politics – however unwelcome for the constitutionalists – and the opportunities to redirect this excitement into more appropriate channels were not yet exhausted. The last two months of 1861 formed a crucial period in Fenian–moderate relations, not only on account of the MacManus funeral and the introduction of IRB sabotage into nationalist meetings, but because, paradoxically enough, an agreement had never looked so likely. Nor was this interest only evident on O'Donoghue's side. In a letter written at the height of the MacManus hostilities, Stephens informed O'Donoghue:

> The committee are convinced that *your* motives in coming to the meeting alluded to [on 9 November] were patriotic; on the other hand, we are as fully convinced that the motives of F. Kenyon, Mr John Martin, to say nothing of such parties as Mr James Cantwell, &c., were as censurable as yours were laudable ...
>
> With regard to what you have been told about the Committee and the 'control of a mysterious individual', your informants must know little about us, or have some questionable motive for what they have said. *We* look on every man who says we belong to a *secret society* as an *enemy*; not that we are opposed to secret societies, *where needed*, but because the motive of the man who so speaks of us *must* be *bad*. Neither we nor the mysterious 'individual' belong to a *secret society* ...
>
> What we, then, including the mysterious individual, *really* are shall be made known to you the first time you give us the pleasure of a meeting.[41]

In the course of the Trent meeting, Luby made an appointment with O'Donoghue to meet Stephens the following day. And so it was that in early December O'Donoghue found himself as the chairman of a committee dominated by the IRB and about to discuss an understanding with Stephens.

Unfortunately for both, perhaps, 1861 was not 1879, and this early 'new departure' never got off the ground. According to the two main accounts of the interview, Stephens wanted O'Donoghue to join the IRB before giving him access to secret information about the organisation; O'Donoghue declined to join, and instead asked Stephens to prove the IRB's strength by assembling ten thousand men for him to inspect.[42] It seems likely that what lay behind this battle of wills was an attempt by both to make the other the auxiliary partner in their agreement. A few days later O'Donoghue withdrew from the Trent committee, and the idea of a Fenian–moderate collaboration was shelved for the time being. Over the next few months, perhaps in a last attempt to attract Stephens' radical followers over to the moderate side, O'Donoghue tried to ingratiate himself with the NBSP by defending it against clerical condemnation and denying accusations that it was a secret society.[43] This stance, however, did not last very long. Perhaps because results were not forthcoming, he finally abandoned his ambiguity. By mid-1863 he was squarely on the moderate side and trying to set up a counter-organisation to the NBSP.

It was at O'Donoghue's insistence that John Martin decided to brave the general apathy among the 'national party', and he began a new attempt to launch a constitutional organisation in the summer of 1863.[44] The goal this time was as much to agitate for self-government as explicitly to offer a 'respectable', middle-class dominated alternative to Fenianism. In the course of a series of letters published in the *Nation*, Martin outlined an organisation designed as 'a microcosm of the nation, wherein every loyal Irish citizen is entitled by right to speak and vote, and is bound by duty to take his stand and act his part', but whose 'founders and patrons' would be 'men who are known and trusted by the country ... men whose education, social standing, political experience, and patriotic reputation qualify them for receiving and retaining the confidence of their fellow countrymen'.[45] On 1 August, Martin launched an appeal for newspaper editors and nationalists in general to call a public meeting in order to found this new organisation. By the end of the month he had to admit that his call had been premature, but his project received an important boost when the Synod of Irish Catholic Bishops that had convened in Dublin in early August issued the following resolution:

ON UNLAWFUL SOCIETIES
Several bishops having represented to the meeting that a society exists called the Brotherhood of St Patrick, having for its object the support and defence by arms of what is called in the oath of member-ship the Irish Republic, or proposing to itself other such illegal ends ... it is resolved to condemn all such associations; and the assembled bishops do hereby condemn them and the publication of any defence of them under any pretext.[46]

This resolution put the NBSP in a very delicate position. Accusations of illegality had been raised against it for some time,[47] but institutional condemnation by the Church gave its opponents an incontestable argu-ment to push for its dissolution or its incorporation into John Martin's new organisation.[48]

The latter organisation, known as the Irish National League, was launched on 21 January 1864 by the usual constitutional procedure: a meeting of 'influential nationalists' was convened by private circular, and out of this meeting emerged a 'provisional committee'.[49] This provisional committee was then nominated as the ruling body of the Irish National League, 'with power to add to its number'.[50] The first version of its rules, issued in February, contemplated the establishment of local committees of the League, but after submission to J. B. Dillon for legal supervision the new version of the rules published in April provided only for the appointment of individual officers to communicate with the League in Dublin.[51] The League was not designed as a nationalist network in the style of the Irish Confederation or the NBSP, but merely as an assembly of notables gathered together to guide and stimulate public opinion. The leaders summarised their programme as

> the enrolment in a public association of those who agree with them for a manifestation to England and the world of the real political sentiments ... of the Irish people, and the organising of public meetings, and the preparation of documents, for the purpose of operating upon opinion at home and abroad.[52]

Barely a month later they received their first opportunity. On 15 February Dublin Corporation voted to pay a compliment to Queen Victoria and erect a statue of the deceased Prince Albert on College Green. The *Nation* immediately denounced the intended 'desecration' of the emblematic nationalist spot, and called a public meeting on 22 February in order to force the corporation to transfer the honour to Henry Grattan.[53] Once again the IRB proceeded to sabotage this meeting, although this time their method was far less civilised than three years before. While The O'Donoghue was speaking, hecklers from the Fenian section of the audience shouted 'put out Sullivan'. After the organisers instead called for a cheer, the Fenian party started a riot, stormed the platform and finally forced Sullivan and O'Donoghue to escape through a side door.[54] On 27 February the *Nation* denounced the rioters as the same party that had broken up the Trent meeting in 1861, and claimed that their real target this time was the newly founded Irish National League. A new meeting was scheduled for the following Monday, 29 February.

On the eve of this second meeting J. B. Dillon and The O'Donoghue met John O'Leary and C. J. Kickham to negotiate the terms on which the Fenians would allow the event to take place without disruptions.[55] There was no agreement, but Sullivan put a number of security measures in place, from admission by ticket to police vigilance, and he succeeded in keeping the rioters out.[56] Immediately afterwards The O'Donoghue put in place arrangements for the establishment of a 'Citizens' Meeting Volunteer Guard', evidently intended as a counter-Fenian force, but which soon evoked references to the Volunteers of 1782.[57] The scheme, however, did not get very far, and the Irish National League stood alone against the recurrent disruption of their meetings by Fenian bands.[58]

IRB sabotage, however, was only one of the League's problems. After the initial enthusiasm surrounding its foundation, support stagnated and began to decline. A police report on 8 June 1864 stated that the League had less than 300 members.[59] A further report noted that its meetings did not seem to be growing in importance.[60] Except in the case of Australia, where John Martin counted 1,130 new followers in November 1864,[61] every yearly report complained of a lack of support, a situation which eventually brought about defections among the leaders themselves. By 1867 The O'Donoghue had abandoned the executive committee.[62] Finally, early in 1868, the League ceased its activities.

John Martin's biographer blamed the League's failure on the people's apathy towards constitutional methods in the midst of the Fenian revolutionary excitement,[63] but revolution was not the only source of IRB appeal, nor the only reason why the National League had found itself at a dead end. The very structure of the League was an important contributing factor. By ruling out the establishment of local branches and limiting its programme to the deliberations of its ruling committee, the 'known and trusted leaders' of constitutional nationalism left little scope for activity to the subscribing members, beyond showing their support at meetings and buying the committee's publications. The NBSP, on the other hand, offered a far more stimulating environment to its rank-and-file. Through the NBSP reading rooms, members could organise lectures, concerts, dances and, occasionally, massive events like the MacManus funeral.[64]

On the other hand, the lack of an immediate goal may have a destructive effect on the morale and enthusiasm of any organisation, and this was true in the case of the Irish National League, the NBSP and certainly the IRB, as James Stephens was well aware. In 1864, in an attempt to re-energise the movement and boost financial contributions from the Fenian Brotherhood, Stephens made the fateful proclamation that 1865 – at the latest – was to be the revolutionary 'year of action', throwing the movement into a frenzy of preparations. This indirectly spelled the end for the NBSP. After the explicit condemnation of the Brotherhood issued by the Catholic bishops in August 1863, and the launch of the *Irish People* newspaper as an official Fenian organ the following November, the NBSP had lost much of its usefulness as a front organisation. The call for a 'year of action' pushed revolution to the forefront and forced IRB members to lay aside the less militaristic pursuits of the NBSP. In the summer of 1864 James Stephens gave explicit instructions for the members to withdraw from the organisation.[65] After this, its numbers declined steadily, and by the spring of 1865 it had become extinct.

IV

Both the Irish National League and the NBSP died away without practical achievements to boast of, but they remain significant as an embodiment of the complex nature of the Fenian–moderate relationship and the new culture of grassroots activism which had begun to animate Irish nationalist politics since 1847. If the IRB rank-and-file was not attracted to the organisation merely as a vehicle for social fulfilment, neither was their attention solely focused on the revolution ahead. Especially in Dublin, participation in the NBSP and opposition to moderate-sponsored initiatives like the Irish National League provided Fenian recruits with a forum for public political expression, if mainly in the shape of protest. In 1869, however, the Amnesty Association finally provided Fenians and constitutionalists with the perfect common ground.[66] The failure of the Fenian rising removed the immediate threat of revolution, and the defeated Fenian prisoners could be safely celebrated as the unselfish heroes that the stagnant 'national party' needed to reinvigorate itself and Irish public opinion. The IRB might naturally be expected to go along with any attempt to help its imprisoned members, but the Amnesty campaigns also provided them with their most successful public platform yet. The moderates supplied the public voice and the ability to apply political pressure to the government, while the Fenians supplied the grassroots structure required to organise petitions and monster meetings. This combination of élite parliamentary politics and popular activism was exactly the strategy that C. S. Parnell would later come to exploit to the full.

NOTES

1. For a treatment of Fenian ideas see Mary Leo, 'The importance of the Fenians and their press on public opinion in Ireland, 1863–70' (M.Litt. thesis, TCD, 1976) and, more briefly, Marta Ramón, *A Provisional Dictator: James Stephens and the Fenian Movement* (Dublin: UCD Press, 2007), pp. 151–8.
2. John Newsinger, *Fenianism in Mid-Victorian Britain* (London: Pluto Press, 1994); R. V. Comerford, *The Fenians in Context* (Dublin: Wolfhound Press, 1998, 1st edn 1985).
3. For an account of moderate campaigns during the late 1850s and early 1860s see Comerford, *Fenians in Context*, pp. 58–66.
4. See, for instance, Peter Gill's speech at Ormond Stile, *Nation*, 10 Oct. 1863.
5. *Irish Felon*, 15 July 1848, quoted in Gary Owens, 'Popular mobilisation and the rising of 1848: the clubs of the Irish Confederation', in L. M. Geary (ed.), *Rebellion and Remembrance in Modern Ireland* (Dublin: Four Courts Press, 2001), pp. 52–3.
6. Richard Davis, *The Young Ireland Movement* (Dublin: Gill & Macmillan, 1987), p. 121.
7. *Nation*, 24 June 1848.
8. See, for instance, *United Irishman*, 26 Feb. 1848.
9. *Nation*, 3 June 1848.
10. For a report of the foundation meeting see *Nation*, 24 Nov. 1849. See also J. H. Whyte, *The Independent Irish Party, 1850–59* (Oxford: Oxford University Press, 1958).
11. See, for instance, 'Leadership', in *Irishman*, 19 May 1849.
12. *Irishman*, 9 March 1850.
13. Maura Cronin, *Country, Class or Craft? The Politicisation of the Skilled Artisan in Nineteenth-Century Cork* (Cork: Cork University Press, 1994), p. 156.
14. *Irishman*, 9 March 1850.
15. John O'Leary, *Recollections of Fenians and Fenianism*, 2 vols (Shannon: Irish University Press, 1968, 1st edn 1896), vol. i, p. 71; *Nation*, 19 April 1862.
16. Comerford, *Fenians in Context*, pp. 102–3, 187.
17. T. D. Sullivan, *Recollections of Troubled Times in Irish Politics* (Dublin: Sealy, Bryers & Walker; Gill & Son, 1905), p. 148.
18. For an account of the campaign see Comerford, *Fenians in Context*, pp. 63–5.
19. John Mitchel to John O'Mahony, 8 May 1861, cited in Joseph Denieffe, *A Personal Narrative of the IRB* (Shannon: Irish University Press, 1969, 1st edn 1906), pp. 164–5.
20. *Irishman*, 5 Jan. 1861.
21. Ibid., 26 Jan. 1861.

22. *Nation*, 26 April 1862.
23. Ibid.
24. See, for instance, Pat Walsh's letter to J. P. McDonnell, n.d., National Archives of Ireland, Fenian Briefs, box 6, file 24.
25. For a complete list of the rules of the NBSP, see the *United Irishman and Galway American*, 8 August 1863.
26. *Irishman*, 25 May 1861.
27. The standard account of the funeral is given in L. R. Bisceglia, 'The Fenian funeral of Terence Bellew McManus', *Eire-Ireland*, 14/3 (Fall 1979), pp. 45–64.
28. J. Kelly [James Stephens] to 'Brother' [John O'Mahony], 16 Dec. 1861, National Library of Ireland; Margaret McKim Maloney Collection, O'Donovan Rossa Papers, New York Public Library, NLI MF P.740.
29. Ibid. Luby Papers, NLI, MS 331.
30. John O'Leary, *Recollections of Fenians and Fenianism*, vol. i, pp. 168–9.
31. Leon Ó Broin, *Fenian Fever: An Anglo-American Dilemma* (New York: New York University Press, 1971), p. 3.
32. Comerford, *Fenians in Context*, pp. 78–9.
33, Richard Pigott, *Personal Recollections of an Irish National Journalist* (Dublin: Hodges, Figgis & Co., 1883, 1st edn 1882) p. 115.
34. *Nation*, 3 May 1862; James Stephens to John O'Mahony, 25 Feb. 1862, cited in Denieffe, *A Personal Narrative of the IRB*, p. 174.
35. James Stephens to John O'Mahony, 25 Feb. 1862, cited in Denieffe, *Personal Narrative of the IRB*, p. 174.
36. O'Leary, *Recollections of Fenians and Fenianism*, vol. i, pp. 175–6.
37. *Freeman's Journal*, 6 Dec. 1861, author's emphasis.
38. Ibid.
39. *Nation*, 14 Dec. 1861.
40. *Irishman*, 12 Oct. 1861, in Comerford, *Fenians in Context*, p. 85.
41. 'James Stephens' draft letter to O'Donoghue', NAI, FB, box 1.
42. Charles Gavan Duffy, *My Life in Two Hemispheres*, 2 vols (Shannon: Irish University Press, 1969, 1st edn 1898), vol. ii, p. 256; Luby Papers, NLI, MS 331. See also James O'Connor, 'Fenianism Photographed', Christmas number of the *Irishman*, 1874.
43. See The O'Donoghue to W. Smith O'Brien, Thursday 13 March 1862, Smith O'Brien Papers, NLI, MS 447/3268; *Nation*, 5 April 1862, cited in John Moloney, 'The National Brotherhood of St Patrick and the rise of Dublin Fenianism, 1858–1865' (MA thesis, University College Galway, 1976), p. 63; *Tablet*, 5 April 1862, cited in Oliver P. Rafferty, *The Church, the State and the Fenian Threat, 1861–75* (New York: St Martin's Press, 1999), p. 27.
44. P. A. Sillard, *The Life and Letters of John Martin* (Dublin: James Duffy and Co., 1901), pp. 170–1.
45. *Nation*, 12 Dec. 1863.
46. Ibid., 19 Sept. 1863.
47. See Moloney, 'National Brotherhood of St Patrick', pp. 59–63.
48. See, for instance, *Nation*, 3, 10 Oct. 1863.
49. *Nation*, 23 Jan. 1864.
50. Ibid., 27 Feb. 1864.
51. Ibid., 23 April 1864.
52. Ibid., 30 Jan. 1864.
53. Ibid., 20 Feb. 1864.
54. Ibid., 27 Feb. 1864; Comerford, *Fenians in Context*, pp. 101–2.
55. John O'Leary, *Recollections of Fenians and Fenianism*, vol. ii, pp. 8–9.
56. A. M. Sullivan, *New Ireland* (Philadelphia: J. B. Lippincott & Co., 1878, 1st edn 1877), pp. 342–6.
57. *Nation*, 5, 12 March 1864.
58. See NAI, Fenian police reports, box 2, nos. 53 and 67, and Sullivan, *New Ireland*, p. 339.
59. Report of 8 June 1864, NAI, Fenian police reports, box 2, no. 24.
60. Report of 20 June 1864, NAI, Fenian police reports, box 2, no. 30.
61. Sillard, *Life and Letters of John Martin*, p. 170.
62. Ibid.
63. Ibid., p. 182.
64. For a sample of NBSP activities see NAI, FB, box 6.

65. Report of 25 July 1864, NAI, Fenian police reports, box 2, no. 26. For a detailed account of the demise of the NBSP see Moloney, 'National Brotherhood of St Patrick', pp. 77–82.
66. For an account of the Amnesty campaigns see Owen McGee, *The IRB: The Irish Republican Brotherhood from the Land League to Sinn Féin* (Dublin: Four Courts Press, 2005), pp. 40–5.

3

The *Irish People* and the Disciplining of Dissent

Matthew Kelly

I

The *Irish People* was *the* newspaper of Irish Fenianism. It was published weekly from 28 November 1863 and had offices at 12 Parliament St – 'within a stone's throw of Dublin Castle gate'.[1] It was run by James Stephens, T. C. Luby, Jeremiah O'Donovan Rossa, Charles Kickham and John O'Leary. By 1865, it had a circulation of some 8,000: low but not insignificant. Worried that 1865 would indeed be the 'year of action', Dublin Castle found a pretext to shut it down, raiding its offices and seizing the presses and other property, including many documents, on 15 September 1865. The following day Luby, Rossa and O'Leary were arrested, marking the close of one phase in the Fenian movement and precipitating the end of Stephens' 'provisional dictatorship'.

The *Irish People*'s significance stemmed in part from the broader newspaper-reading context. Long identified as one of the key agents of modernity, newspapers thrived in mid-Victorian Ireland, benefiting from rising literacy and, arguably, came to rival the priest's pulpit as the primary shaper of popular *mentalités*.[2] They provided a heady diet of politics, entertainment and practical advice, functioning as political and literary reviews, lifestyle magazines *avant la lettre* and commercial directories, packed with advertisements for products, local services and medical quackery. Many were owned by the local big man, who might act simultaneously as publican, grocer, creditor and newspaper proprietor. Despite this localism, the Irish press was not entirely parochial.[3] Local newspapers with low circulations subscribed to press agencies and carried syndicated reports on international events, to which leader writers responded as worldly citizens, adept at identifying the relevance of foreign affairs to Ireland. The 1857 Indian 'mutiny', the Italian question, French politics, the 1863 Polish insurrection, the US Civil War and any number of imperial conflicts and foreign-policy encounters came under scrutiny. Her Majesty's Irish subjects were potentially very well informed and for any young man in a hurry, hungry for information and opinion, the weekly arrival of the national paper was an exciting event, fuelling his bid for status and prestige within the community. Scattered evidence suggests that people gathered together to hear newspapers read aloud and the reader became a source of intelligence about the world, playing an intermediary role, adding a further mediating layer to the many determining what people could know of the world.

Though newspapers have been used by Irish historians as a source for the reconstruction of events and sometimes of attitudes, their contribution to the social or cultural dynamic – in other words, how they were used – needs also to be understood.[4] With this in mind, the *Irish People* is a particularly appropriate subject for study: it had a very strong sense of purpose in the wider newspaper-reading context. In some respects this is a statement of the obvious: the *People* was founded as a propaganda sheet and was ceaselessly – perhaps tediously – didactic. But as an oppositional newspaper, dissenting from almost all aspects of the status quo, whether fingered as Irish or English, it brought an unusual self-consciousness to its purposes. It actively sought to create a new Irish man, someone able to think differently about the world, someone modern and liberated from the strictures that kept him enslaved: he would, to use the *People*'s own favoured description, be 'enlightened'. In this arduous process of mental rewiring, the newspaper's role was disciplinary, guiding its readers and keeping them on task. This purpose was reflected in the repetitive nature of the *People*'s content, with its continual harping on a limited number of themes.

Despite its separatist politics and advocacy of armed revolution, the *People* was not an underground or clandestine newspaper and, though never in rude financial health, was generally available where there was demand.[5] Until the final crunch came in 1865, priestly opposition posed a far greater threat than the Castle authorities. Indeed, there was little political censorship of the press in mid-Victorian Ireland, and the authorities took the view that shutting down seditious newspapers, which were plentiful, was more trouble than it was worth; nationalist invective was treated as a safety valve for Irish passions rather than a genuine threat to the security of the state. The *People* was distributed by professional agents, who added it to a wider portfolio of newspapers, and by amateurs, who adduced their work as evidence of their commitment to Fenianism. According to the police, pamphlets on revolutionary themes were also sent out with the newspaper to Fenian agents, circulated locally, and then returned.[6] In letters to 12 Parliament St, would-be agents like Denis Gilmartin of Templederry, Tipperary, introduced themselves, telling of frustrated young Fenians unable to get their hands on the newspaper, while professionals, boasting of their experience and contacts, suggested local distribution rights be transferred to them. A continual problem was the newspaper's late arrival, with agents frustrated when crucial Saturday trading was missed. Darby O'Grady, agent in Newcastle West and frequent correspondent, claimed he could have shifted eight dozen copies if only they had arrived on time – one woman helped him out by buying a dozen. Worse than the commercial loss was the ammunition late arrivals provided his political enemies, who crowed that he had been cowed into submission by Archdeacon O'Brien.[7]

Accurate circulation figures do not survive, though A. M. Sullivan noted that the *People* 'swept all before it amongst the Irish in England and Scotland, almost annihilating the circulation of the *Nation* in many places north and south of the Tweed', but he also reckoned that in 'many places' in Ireland the *Nation* (Ireland's leading nationalist newspaper) 'drove it totally from the field'.[8] Papers seized by the authorities in September 1865 gave some indication of its distribution, an undated list naming almost one hundred newsagents in receipt of the newspaper.[9] Their orders ranged between a single copy and the 600 copies sent to 40 Roches St, Limerick. Some 750 went to Cork, including 260 to O'Leary at 36 Great Georges St, who sent them on in smaller packages to further agents. Sizeable numbers were also received by single agents in Waterford (100), Tipperary (100), Carrick on Suir (100), Kanturk (100) and Ballina (63). O'Leary was one of several woman agents; others included the Limerick agent and agents in Clonmel (90), Waterford (12), Queenstown (40), Cashel (12), Nenagh (20) and, in England, Leeds (30). Newspapers were also sent to other centres of Irish migration, including Glasgow (60), Liverpool (250), Bolton (24), Birkenhead (36) and Sheffield (84). Sullivan claimed the newspaper's distribution substantially reflected 'where Fenian and non-Fenian Nationalism prevailed',[10] and these figures confirm that the movement was most vital in urban Ireland and Britain – though ninety copies were divided between two rural locations in Co. Mayo – and that in some locations purchasing the *People* was routine for a significant number of the population. The newspaper might be delivered on a Saturday with the week's 'messages' or picked up in person: buying the newspaper, depending on the circumstances, could be a public act of defiance or a secretive act of conspiracy.

Pioneering content analysis of the *People* by Marta Ramón convincingly demonstrates that the *People*'s polemic, though predicated on a consistent set of aims, did not show much evidence of sophisticated political or economic thinking or analysis. This was particularly the case with regard to the central question of land.[11] A complimentary way of thinking about the significance of the newspaper is suggested by an older commentary on Fenianism. In his *Political Violence in Ireland*, Charles Townshend notes that the 'relentless grimness of Fenian rhetoric was established at the outset, and came to form a mental outlook almost entire of itself', arguing that Fenianism's power 'resided as much in rhetoric as in facts'.[12] Roy Foster echoed this point, concluding that 'above all, Fenianism created a mentality',[13] and that from 'the 1860s being a Fenian was a mode of life in Ireland in the same way being anti-clerical or republican was in provincial France'.[14]

What, then, was this Fenian *mentalité*? Plainly the answer to this question must be foundational to any understanding of Irish nationalism, but addressing it has become pressing owing to the problematising of the use of the term 'Fenian'. In particular, historians have begun to examine what the term itself signified in mid-Victorian political discourse. Breandán Mac Suibhne and Amy Martin argue that for British commentators the Irish Fenian existed as 'a terrifying phantasmatic counterpoint to the newly defined ethically masculine working-class citizen'. The idea of the Fenian, they suggest, served 'as the limit of the state's frontier of citizenship and as a rationalization of its monopoly on violence'.[15] Owen McGee takes a similar view, suggesting that the term Fenianism was 'coined' by Tories 'by 1864' and then taken up by antagonistic clergymen as a means of traducing any form of lower-class Catholic political activism. Consequently, McGee does not use the term to describe any Irish nationalists.[16] This is a questionable decision, first, because there is evidence of IRB men at the time casually referring to themselves as Fenians and being familiar generally with the idea that they represented a 'Fenian spirit' and, second, because the term is unproblematically a staple of IRB memoir literature.[17] Not only, as McGee recognises, did its widespread use heighten the IRB's profile, but some Fenians and their fellow-travellers enjoyed the term's notoriety, increasingly identifying with the defiance and menace it signified.[18] More than this, it is my contention that contemporaries recognised the distinction between the use of the IRB to identify a specific organisation and the adjectival use of Fenian to identify a nationalist attitude.[19]

Fenianism, then, was the spectre haunting British politics in the 1860s and beyond, and like communism, Fenianism too needed its Marx and Engels to explain its cause, a task which fell to the *Irish People*. A close reading of the newspaper reveals that Fenian ideas, often reduced by historians to simplified assertions of core separatist principles, evolved in particular contexts. For example, in September 1864 the *People* asserted that 'no conquered country ever regained its independence peacefully'.[20] At first glance a predictable example of Fenian rhetoric, this claim formed part of a more developed argument. In this case, the *People* was addressing the idea, proposed at the time by The O'Donoghue and John Martin, that through constitutional methods Ireland might achieve a 'liberal constitution' similar to those conceded 'to Canada and the Australian colonies'.

The *People* rejected the analogy, arguing that there was a fundamental difference between these 'remote British colonies' and 'countries like Ireland reduced to subjection by conquest'. The new dominions, the *People* argued, would quite naturally seek a measure of self-government *within* the empire because they were *of* the empire. There was no fundamental difference between those settlers and the English themselves; the same reasoning was found in slightly later pro-imperial arguments about a Greater Britain. Contextualised as part of a political debate, it becomes evident that the Fenian belief that Ireland was a 'conquered country' formed part of a more finely calibrated argument than the phrase, quoted in isolation, might suggest.

II

At the heart of the *People*'s polemic was its conviction that the Irish people's faith in the righteousness of the national cause was at best inconstant. Rather than seeing Fenianism as the successor to a fine nationalist tradition, the past was often treated contemptuously, with Smith O'Brien's attempted 1848 insurrection depicted as a national embarrassment rather than a focus for celebration. The sacralising of '98, '48 and '67 would be the work of later articulators of the Fenian ideal who, faced with the failures of the IRB, developed ways of finding victory in successive defeat.[21] By contrast, the Fenians of the 1860s felt they represented a departure and one of the constant reference points for the *People* was the change of attitude in Ireland brought about since 1858.[22] This immediately foregrounds one of the peculiarities of the newspaper: 1858, the year in which the Irish national faith experienced a renaissance, was also the founding year of the Irish Republican Brotherhood. The IRB was never mentioned by the newspaper, and the term Fenianism was only used when discussing the American Fenian Brotherhood or scoffing at priestly condemnation of 'so-called Fenians'.[23] Ireland's renaissance was dated to the beginning of an organisation which it refused to mention in print. Indeed, the *Irish People* scorned the idea that it was Fenian and was dismissive of the suggestion that it was interested in secret societies. It preferred to associate itself with 'quiet work', which, as will be shown, was more than just a euphemism for secret society.

In part, this ambiguity was common sense. The IRB was a secret, oath-bound underground organisation dedicated to revolution and the establishment of a fully independent Ireland. And the *People* lambasted 'felon-setters', those who, in their news stories, casually identified others as Fenians, exposing them to the possibility of arrest.[24] Any discussion of secret societies, which risked indicting any fellow Irishmen, was thought an act of collaboration, underhand and potentially treasonous.

Consequently, Ireland's 'enlightenment' was attributed to very oblique causes rather than the exertions of an organisation: 'Mysteriously a spirit passed over the mind of the country, fortunately once more ripe enough to hail with welcome the creed of manhood, and far and wide a quiet voice of truth was heard, stirring to their depths the souls of men.'[25] As this intimates, all was not quite obscure: the timing could be explained. By 1858, a decade after the last Irish revolutionary attempt, which allegedly failed owing to the pernicious influence of O'Connell, enough time had passed for the emergence of a new generation of Irish nationalists uncontaminated by O'Connellism.

Concerns that the break was not quite so decisive are suggested by the repeated attacks the newspaper made on O'Connell. Occasionally prepared to concede his stature as a political leader, the *People* was unremittingly and repeatedly critical of his politics. First and foremost, O'Connell's 'great crime' was to have persuaded the Irish people that 'Liberty is not worth the shedding of a single drop of blood.' Many editorials, written from a number of starting points, eventually returned to this notion, which was denounced as 'the basest, cowardliest lie ever uttered by human lips'.[26] It was never left in question as to who the culprit was: 'This degrading creed ... was preached ... by one whom the Irish people well nigh worshipped as a god'.[27] O'Connell's second great crime was to make the clergy 'all-powerful' and, though the priests 'never could be good leaders in any revolutionary movement', the 'no-drop-of-blood doctrine made them infinitely more unfit for leadership than if that coward creed had never been heard of'.[28] A properly free people would not 'submit to clerical interference with their temporal concerns'. That the Irish did so was a manifestation of the degradation, debasement and demoralisation that were key motifs in the *People*'s polemic. It was a mark of the abject dependency of the Irish people that they had abdicated responsibility, giving up their independence of mind to the priestly caste.

Opposition to revolutionism and subservience to the priests in political matters had allowed the prominence of what they most despised: 'agitation'. Agitation was the stuff of 'pseudo' patriots, the platform speakers, petition organisers, committee men and, above all, parliamentarians. Parliamentary agitation taught 'falsehood and bluster, lip-loyalty and heart-treason'. In sum, agitation was insincere, leaving nationalists neither true to themselves nor to their supposed English allies; it made 'the people neither manly rebels, nor good subjects'.[29] By contrast, to reject agitation in favour of revolutionary preparation would restore dignity to Irish masculinity, and it is clear that ideals of manliness, so central to mid-Victorian politics, had been internalised by its Fenian critics. Significantly, the *People* did not present Irishmen as the feminised subjects of British rule. Ideas of degeneration and enfeeblement were common but quite distinct from feminine qualities – if Ireland must be a woman penetrated by the imperial oppressor, then Ireland's liberation could only come about when the Irish male was restored to his rightful role as defender of the feminine. Feminine purity was a matter for chivalric celebration and protection: the inadequate Irish male was more eunuch than woman.

'Agitation' embodied further negative qualities, chief among them being hypocrisy and the use of – or susceptibility to – empty, deceptive rhetoric. Seeking the redress of grievance through the parliamentary system necessarily meant compromising on first nationalist principles. This diminished Ireland's inherent dignity, extended legitimacy to the political system of the oppressor, and, most fundamentally, undermined Ireland's very claim to nationhood. The following – a comment on a debate on Irish land legislation – leaves no doubt as to the *Irish People*'s opinion of the Irish people's elected representatives.

> In strains of the most lugubrious, mock-heroic patriotism, did some of the most notorious of those apostles of humbug, called Irish members, mourn over the flight of the oppressed and persecuted people whom they have so effectually misrepresented in a foreign legislature; and for whom to this hour they have never done anything, except deceive and betray them. Each, as a matter of course, was ready with some little peddling proposal of his own about 'compensation for unexhausted improvements', or some other sublime sham of a similar description, which would help to prepare the hustings, when he shall come forward once more and ask the people, with unblushing brow, to authorize him to sell himself and his country in the oppressors' Parliament.[30]

The *People* condemned Irish MPs as 'political traders and grievance mongers' and 'sentimental and theorizing patriots'.[31] Irish nationalists had to guard against their susceptibility to high-blown political rhetoric, a sign of weakness. Rhetoric was negatively contrasted with organisation, planning and action. Speech-making lent self-promoting men patriotic credentials, Irish nationalism becoming a thing of words rather than action and, consequently, a sham. The year 1848, therefore, was criticised for its 'editorial inanities', with the public 'served up weekly as a treat' impractical revolutionary plans, complete with a 'stimulating seasoning of melodramatic horrors'.[32] Disillusionment, which stymied Irish nationalism in the 1850s, set in when men had finally 'perceived that a foolish bray was not the lion's roar'. Listening to a speech or singing a song, the *People* insisted, did not inflict damage on the British connection. Under the heading 'Abuse of speech', the paper editorialised in December 1863:

> There was a melancholy doctrine preached in Ireland some years ago ... that out-spokenness, even to the extent of treason, was the only

effective means of achieving independence. Almost everything it was possible to say (in the treason-felony line) was said, and almost everything it was desirable to do was left undone. With our present experience it is hard to realise the fact that at any time men believed it possible to overthrow the English government by leading articles.[33]

Morale-boosting editorial excess posed a more subtle danger. It risked convincing the Irish that their achievements were greater than the reality, allowing them to loll complacently in an imaginary parallel universe. Lacking a metropolitan self-assurance, Ireland had become a self-deluding place of 'exaggeration, bombast, and make-believe',[34] riddled with 'prating' (a favoured word) about 'Celtic bravery and Celtic virtue'.[35] More than this, the *Irish People* riffed on, John Bull was unaffected by words, however stinging they might be: 'England lets us have our say, and cares little about our enmity while we confine ourselves to words.'[36] Irish eloquence could not hurt – or even rouse – the ineloquent English, and it was vital the Irish did not evaluate their enemy by their own standards. Nor should they underestimate the cleverness of the English: free speech in Ireland, which the *People* admitted existed, served to disguise the reality of England's oppression of Ireland, which was – so they alleged – as great as that experienced by the Poles at the hands of the less subtle Russians.[37] 'Weakness alone is ever wordy', they concluded; the Irish would become strong when they became silent; they must become more like their powerful enemy if ever they were to defeat it.

This need for a new seriousness of intent, or 'earnestness', which would overcome passivity, reflected the *People*'s concern – to use anachronistic terms – that Irish nationalists achieve agency, realising their capacity for self-determination.[38] Demoralisation reflected a lack of faith in their objective capabilities; 'enlightenment' would bring about a fundamental change in Ireland's existential condition, overcoming the pervasive dependency culture. To this end, they objected to nationalists 'weakly' trusting to 'PROVIDENCE', condemning as 'aspirationists' those nationalists who declared themselves committed to an independent Ireland, possibly to be achieved through revolution, but who saw no possibility of it being brought about in the near future.[39] It was a position the *People* found worthy only of mockery and they easily rendered their opposition absurd:

> Then some fine day or other, in some few hundreds or thousands of years, when the skies fall perhaps, or when half England is swallowed up by a monster earthquake, or deluged by an abnormal spring-tide, or something else curious and not to be anticipated happens, POSTERITY might suddenly find England grown weak enough and Ireland grown strong enough to admit of another great effort to win Irish independence.[40]

In short, to rely on 'providence' or 'posterity' was to deny the possibility of Irish agency.

The force of these objections stemmed in part from their revulsion at self-aggrandisement: 'Your aspirationist, where he succeeds in getting people to swallow his cant, gains the reputation of a patriot on very convenient terms.' Cant, like humbug, was a key idea. Picked up from John Mitchel, who used it continuously, but deriving from Carlyle and other British critics, it is an ugly piece of polemical shrapnel which ricochets through Fenian polemic like no other. Those self-identifying as disinterested truth-tellers used the word *cant* to describe the compromises of mainstream politics on both sides of the Irish Sea. In Carlyle's or Mitchel's polemically agile hands it signalled scorn for the liberal universalism which provided a soothing carapace for the hypocritical rapacity of imperial Britain. Among the Fenians it similarly signified the hypocritical pieties, dressed up as high principle, which people who got on subscribed to. If an alertness to cant was the special preserve of the man who put truth before self-interest, accepting marginality, the purpose of the *People* was to ensure that all the Irish developed the critical capacity needed to see through cant, thereby rendering the marginal mainstream and purifying the body politic.

Such loftiness posed the *People* a particular problem. They had to resist close commentary on conventional politics, the stock-in-trade of the nationalist press, which had ensnared their nationalist opponents in the trap British politics set. To comment on British policy was to evaluate it, and to evaluate was to play a role in the political process, thereby implying that effective intervention might bring some good for Ireland. Any such engagement necessitated compromise; such short-termist calculations would represent a betrayal of faith, with demoralisation the inevitable outcome. When the *People* did permit a little ideological slippage in this direction, devoting an occasional densely written column or two to parliamentary proceedings, the editorialist worked to expose the shortcomings of Irish MPs rather than comment on the debate.[41]

An especially risible example of cant was provided by the delusional hopes of 'the French Party'. No such party existed in a formal sense, but the Irish nationalist affinity for France became a central component of nationalist polemic in the mid-Victorian period, providing one of its preferred ways of articulating Irish difference from the British. The basic gist is that tremendous hopes were invested in the likelihood of a French intervention in Ireland. The Second Empire under Napoleon III was characterised by rather credulous Irish nationalists as liberal, anti-imperial and therefore fundamentally at odds with the despotic and monarchical empire-states of Europe, whose interests had been secured by the Vienna Settlement of 1815. The supposed ideological incompatibility between the French state and the rest of Europe meant war was inevitable and the *Nation* newspaper, in particular, dedicated a great deal of space to speculating on how the Napoleonic impulse would bring about the reorganisation of Europe on the basis of nation-states, with French liberation of Ireland the inevitable outcome.

The *People* was distinct but not unique in dismissing this armchair strategising. Placing hope in the French was judged a 'pernicious doctrine', at odds with all principles of 'national self-reliance'. Under the right circumstances, the French could be welcomed as an auxiliary force but not as a liberating force; a French landing in an Ireland unprepared to fight its own war would be a French conquest.[42] Wolfe Tone, they argued, was able to attract French support because the United Irishmen had already got Ireland into a state of military readiness. Above all – and this is perhaps what was most striking about their critique – the French party were thought to be labouring under the delusion that Ireland was counted among the nations of Europe. On the contrary, separatists argued, Ireland had not earned this recognition and, what is more, did not deserve it. Since the Union, 'agitation' demonstrated that the ancient traditions of Irish nationhood had withered and European nationalists no longer had reason to take Ireland into account. The *People* unfavourably contrasted the Irish with the Poles, who rebelled against Russian rule in 1863: 'To obtain even the bare sympathy extended to her, Poland has had to trust to herself alone through ten months' deadly struggle with her colossal foe!'[43] The *People* went on: 'We neither have the sympathy of foreign nations, nor do we deserve it; and most certainly we shall never gain it until we travel on the same road as Italy, Poland, Hungary, and all the peoples that have either gained their freedom, or struggled bravely for it.'[44]

It was not simply that the Irish would only attract sympathy or aid when they were prepared to act without that aid, but until Ireland gave such a clear expression of its distinctive nationhood it was not, in effect, a nation. Nation was performance, requiring continual re-enaction and nations could die, the *People* recognised; or, as was the case with the Poles, against all the odds and without any of the trappings of state, a nation could live. The absurdity of the French party's hopes was that they relied on Ireland having a status – as a European nation – it had yet to earn. Like many nationalist newspapers, the *People* was infuriated by the complacent view of Ireland presented to the world by *The Times* – or *The Thunderer*, as they habitually called it. In particular, they were aghast that *The Times* could argue, only a decade after the horrors of the Famine and the failures of '48, that Ireland now showed no resentment of the English connection nor had any reason to. Consequently, Fenians increasingly believed that revolutionary action was the only way Ireland could represent itself to the world, bypassing England's mediation and overcoming its subaltern

status. This provides an intriguing twist on the classic post-colonial argument that colonised peoples can only know the world through the categories
of the colonial power.[45]

Ireland's inability to self-represent had further ramifications. As a consequence of Irish nationhood going unrecognised, Irish suffering could
not be dignified before the world as a manifestation of a self-conscious
collectivity. For these reasons, and like other nationalist newspapers at
the time, the *People* resented anti-slavery campaigners. Again, their
polemic reflected the Carlylean influence:

> If the dusky African is forced to labour, not for himself, but for another,
> he must be clothed, and fed, and cared for; but the white slave of the
> Anglo-Irish aristocrat must toil on, in cold, and hunger, and naked-
> ness, to fill the coffers of those whose hearts are hard as the nether
> millstone, and whose greed is as insatiable as the ocean or the grave.[46]

As this suggests, a central aspect of the *People*'s argument was class-based
and though a schematic Marxism is not to be found in the newspaper,
much of their argument chimed with English radicalism. Who, then, comprised the Irish people in whose name the paper was dedicated? Most
significant is that the 'Irish people' were distinguished from the middle
and the upper classes. The 'higher classes', on the whole, were a lost
cause, because they were 'not Irish but English', but the middle classes
were more problematic, throwing up a more complex challenge: 'The
middle classes in all countries are more selfish and less chivalrous than
those above or those below them. Yet, leagued with the masses, they are
a great power. Leagued with the oppressor they are a formidable barrier
between the people and liberty – an insuperable barrier, until the people
become enlightened.'[47]

And, in Ireland, the middle classes had become separated from the
'masses' – more normally referred to as 'the people' – thanks to Catholic
Emancipation, which Fenians consistently argued was a piece of class
legislation rather than a reform that benefited all. The year 1829, they
believed, saw the government buy the loyalty of the Catholic middle class,
thereby separating them from the mass of the people who benefited little
from the 'barren victory':

> The 'respectable Catholics' have obtained emancipation. This has
> placed the well-to-do members of that great community, such as peers
> and judges and bishops, 'mimbers' and magistrates, and even Poor
> Law guardians, on a level with their neighbours. So, taking Earl
> RUSSELL'S advice to the English reform party, they 'rest and are thankful'.
> True, the people perish, but the priest levite pass by, and look after
> their own concerns.[48]

By beginning with the assumption that the middle class had to provide the foundations of the movement, O'Connell's campaign for Catholic Emancipation embodied the fundamental problem with all agitations. If all political demands had to be compatible with the middle-class material interest in the status quo, then any movement inevitably became riddled with cant and humbug. However, if 'the people' could demonstrate their unquestioned commitment to Irish independence, it would be in the interest of the middle classes to align themselves with the majority, overcoming their 'criminal apathy'. Self-reliance, therefore, was class independence, a claiming by 'the people' of their national birthright, unsullied by middle-class self-interest.

And the *People* could be at its most entertaining when exposing the delusions and snobbish susceptibilities of the middle classes. In January 1864 it turned its attentions to the 'Modern Antiques': 'We do not like modern-antique chieftains and chieftainry; on the contrary we have a mortal antipathy to them, and this simply because they are not realities, but shadowy humbugs … they are lies and like all lies mischievous.' Scathingly referring to characters like Muddlepate Flimsy O'Flummery, the *People* went on: 'In the name of common sense away with Ollamh Fodhlahism. Let us be Irishmen of our own century and all will be right; but if we want to delight our enemies, let us pin our faith to … such as pretend to modern-antique chieftainship.' And if a real Irish chief were to find himself in contemporary Ireland?

> He would be long sorry to style himself, at this time of day, the O'DONKEY of the Bogs, the O'FLUMMERY DUN, or the Prince of BOGINFIN. He would prefer being called plain Jack or Tom O'Neill or O'Byrne. He would be and act like a true Irish patriot of the 19th century. He would, in a word, be always, under all circumstances, a man of the living time.

The Fenian, then, was modern, un-nostalgic and resistant to comforting but outmoded notions of social order. He understood that those who treated Ireland like a dressing-up party were indulged by enemies keen on whatever made Ireland appear ridiculous.

The *People*, however, never talked about the working classes and the newspaper was highly ambiguous on the question of whether the fulfilment of its agenda would bring about a socioeconomic levelling of the classes. If the middle classes were to adhere to the faith of 'the people' they would become a part of 'the people', apparently without giving up their privileges. What the newspaper did argue, however, was that the Irish had ceased to be an 'aristocratic people': there was no '*Irish* aristocracy now'. 'Irish' was placed in italics to emphasise that there was an aristocracy *in* Ireland, but thanks to its behaviour it could not be thought of as a part of the Irish people. Such ideas were informed by historical analysis: 1782 and the achievement of an Irish parliament was judged to be aristocratic, whereas 1798 was democratic. Though it claimed 1782 would have led to a more lasting settlement had it been democratic – built on the weight of popular opinion – it did not address the question of why '98 was and did not. More pertinent for the newspaper was that after 1798 the Irish aristocracy ceased to be a part of the Irish people because it abandoned nationalism. And though the 'real Irish gentry' were the dispossessed who – following Swift – are 'to be found in the lanes of Dublin',[49] implying that in a genealogical sense the real Irish gentry is Catholic, the aristocracy in Ireland was excluded from Irishness not by its religion but by its actions, its loyalty to the British connection. To be Irish, therefore, was a form of national voluntarism, determined by an adherence to a set of ideals rather than blood or ethnicity. Evidently, Fenianism, like almost all nineteenth-century nationalisms, was an amalgam of romantic and civic values.

Consequently, egalitarianism was not inherent to Irishness but had been forced upon it by the peculiarities of Irish history: 'The Irish people have become democratic by necessity. They had nothing for it but to desert the cause of their country or depend upon themselves alone.'[50] In this usage, democratic does not straight-forwardly refer to electoral procedure but to social structure. The higher classes had opted out of Irishness – or, in the case of the middle class, had a hypocritical relationship with Irishness – thereby flattening *Irish* social structure. Class self-interest rather than religious identity was the motive force here, which, in Davisite fashion, left the door open for the non-Irish of Ireland to eventually become – as 1782 seemed to promise – Irish. Consequently, the newspaper explained, 'Our struggle must be a democratic struggle. The liberty we shall win must, in the first instance at least, be democratic liberty. What shape it will ultimately take let time determine.' An Ireland based on a clear social hierarchy – by their definition, an aristocratic Ireland – remained a legitimate possibility. Ultimately, it really was very simple: 'Give the Irish soil to the Irish people, and we are content.'[51] Some months later, its position was given direct expression: 'We do not contemplate Ireland Catholic or Protestant; we contemplate her free and independent; and we extend the hand of love and fellowship to every man of every class and creed who could labour to make her so.'[52]

None the less, when the mood took it, the *People* admitted Irish realities, albeit in quite surprising ways. Despite the 'undeniable spread of enlightened ideas … a frightful amount of religious intolerance' prevailed. Despite the million men in Ulster thinking '*patriot* and *Papist* are synonymous', Ulster Protestants 'are Irishmen like us', the *People* was convinced, 'and like us are suffering because of the fearful condition of our country'. And here follows a key, if ambiguous, claim: 'They enjoy no peculiar privileges, and are of the same mixed race which exists in every quarter of the island.' It is not clear if this is a reference to biological descent, suggesting that no one on the island was of pure Irish blood, or whether it simply meant that though the people of Ireland are of many different backgrounds all are Irish if they choose to be. Either way, by arguing that calm reason – rather than coercion – would win around Ulster Protestants, civic ideals were again foregrounded.

Equally striking in this passage was the critique of the '98 movement. Recognising that the Protestants of Ulster were the 'originators of the rebellion of '98', and though arguing that 'few, if any' Protestants were killed in '98 'simply because of the creed they professed', the movement none the less 'savoured too much of sectarianism'. '98 was not based on the 'broad principles of religious toleration', so it 'must end in confusion and defeat'. Again, the point it emphasised is how improved Irish attitudes were in the present and that the *People* now could 'see the all-damning blight of religious intolerance surely and steadily stealing away like night mists before the rising sun'; it knew they were on 'the true path, and that sooner or later it must lead' them 'to liberty'.[53]

Reading the *Irish People* helps illuminate one of the most contentious questions in modern Irish historiography, literary criticism and so on: namely, how Ireland's relationship with Britain should be defined, which tends to resolve into the question 'was Ireland a colony?'[54] In a series of excellent interventions – which none the less do not satisfactorily resolve the question – Joe Cleary has demonstrated how much of the historiography of pre-Union Ireland readily situates the relationship in a colonial paradigm, while the historiography of post-Union Ireland tends not to.[55] One of the approaches Cleary queries is the tendency of historians to use the categories that were used by people in the past to make sense of that past. In short, Cleary suggests, just because the Irish did not readily resort to describing themselves as colonised does not mean they were not. To a degree, this debate, which sees the New Historicism pitted against a neo-Marxist post-colonialism, remains unsatisfactory because little historical work showing sensitivity to the language of colonialism or imperialism in nineteenth-century Ireland has been done. It is not yet known whether Irish nationalists habitually thought within these categories, and before this has been established a little wariness might be shown when broaching the post-colonial argument that whether they did or did not should not inhibit *our* identification and analysis of the objective and representational colonial realities of the relationship.

David Fitzpatrick, cogently arguing that there were colonial aspects to the Union, has categorised three main ways of thinking about Ireland in relation to Britain in the nineteenth century. The first was that it was an integral part of the United Kingdom; the second is that it was a backward sub-region of the UK; and the third is that it was a colony. This scheme is helpful because each view roughly coincides with one of the main political traditions of the period, respectively unionism, devolutionism and separatism.[56] The editorials of the *Irish People* confirm at least part of Fitzpatrick's schema: these separatists thought Ireland governed by 'imperial oppressors' whose aim was to 'extract everything which men deem valuable out of this land, which in mockery they are accustomed to call "the sister island"'. Moreover, the 'landocracy' in Ireland could only be maintained through 'Imperial protection', without which, and faced by the 'national will', they would be 'as worthless chaff before the driving storm'. The 'landocracy', then, is a dependent imperial class, 'the "territorial magnates" of the British empire'.[57] In so far as it goes, this is clear enough, but further nuance comes from its distinction that, though a people under imperial control, they were not a colonised people because, despite their 'enslavement', Ireland remained – just about – a distinctive nation. In contrast to the 1890s and early 1900s, a consciousness of imperialism as a process of cultural penetration had not yet developed. For example, the *People* raged against emigration, which it considered a symptom of an exploitative imperial economy, but it had very little to say about the Irish language and did not celebrate the west as a repository of authentic Irishness; as previously suggested, the true Irish were moderns.

Whether Irish nationalists identified with non-white colonised people – as opposed to white settler colonists seeking self-government, as in Canada, New Zealand, Australia or South Africa – is also elucidated by the *People*'s polemic. Commenting on the land question, the *People* argued that Ireland's experience was the universal experience of people under English rule:

> Deprived of their own property, there is nothing left them but to go forth and lay hold upon that of others. The Red men of America have learned this to their cost, and so have the dusky millions of India, as well as the gallant Maories of New Zealand, who are now being shot down like dogs by the 'Christian' settlers from England, whose progress of invasion they have the bravery to resist.[58]

Crucially, this system of 'royal robbery and aristocratic extortion' had 'flourished so long and so luxuriantly in England' that it had reduced 'the mass of her agricultural labourers to a state of semi-serfage'.[59] By this reasoning, native Americans, Indians, the Maoris, the Irish and the English 'people' were all in the same boat. Like much of the nationalist press in the 1860s, the *People* judged English liberties illusory, a way of masking a political system orientated around the interests of the landed aristocracy, which the empire had extended, globalising a system which divided people into 'two castes or classes': 'millions of poor and patient toilers producing all the wealth, in the other a few thousand idlers consuming it'.[60] Fundamentally exploitative, the whole system was based upon the 'rights of property', which, held up as a moral absolute, really reflected class interests. True liberation could only come when the newly 'enlightened' Irish began to think outside of these English categories, overcoming the instincts of deference and mental dependency characteristic of their oppression. By bringing about its own liberation, Ireland's actions would have a domino effect, beginning the global unravelling of this class-based imperialism and, in the process, also liberating the English people.

III

The state's case against Luby, Rossa and O'Leary was derived in part from the content of the *Irish People*. On this basis, Charles Barry, Her Majesty's Counsel, judged Fenianism especially threatening for it was not merely 'some theoretical scheme of regeneration' to be brought about 'by substituting one government for another'. Instead, Fenianism 'partook of the character of socialism in its most pernicious and most wicked phase'. John Lawless, acting for the defence, was quite right to argue that the *People* had not advocated the assassination of priests – also claimed by Barry as a part of Fenianism's revolutionary plans – but, as this analysis of the *Irish People* suggests, he had a weaker case against Barry's claim that the 'lower classes were taught to believe that they might expect a redistribution of the property real and personal of the country'.[61]

This radicalism, however, was possibly less significant than the *Irish People*'s ambition to remake the Irishman, rendering him a freer-thinking, more autonomous individual. The very vitality of the organisation, in the face of overt and aggressive clerical opposition, indicates some measure of its success. As Superintendent Daniel Ryan observed, contemporaries in provincial Ireland could identify the Fenian by his decision to wear a beard (a powerful indicator of masculinity in Victorian Britain), his rejection of conventional habits of deference, and his challenging attitude – 'a stern look in the eye will cause a man who is not up to this mark to look some other way'.[62] Though not to be exaggerated, and apparently weaker in more isolated country districts, this performative aspect of Fenianism was very significant. It was further evidenced through an aspirational liking for things American. 'In a word,' Ryan remarked, 'everything republican in Society is practised by the Fenians and in Yankee fashion, as far as can be by those who were never in Yankee land.'[63] Selling or buying the *Irish People* was another manifestation of this challenging attitude and reading – or hearing another read – the *Irish People* helped to keep the Fenian on task, reinforcing his sense that he was part of a collective and strengthening his determination to dissent. The many letters the office received, some of which survive among the papers seized by the authorities, convey, with a vividness the newspaper does not, the sense of shared endeavour the newspaper generated. It stimulated among Fenians a keenness to give expression to their views, whether on the Union, land or the Church, and an expectation that the editors would enter into discussion – complaints followed when they failed to engage with or notice a letter in the newspaper. Supporters sent in communications (reports of local doings), stories, songs and little polemical screeds containing much armchair strategising. Sensitivity for the beauty of Ireland was particularly evident and in several cases the pattern followed saw the writer jolted out of his reverie by a sudden sign indicating that Ireland was not in the possession of the Irish.[64] The reams of patriotic verse submitted tell the same story; though harshly judged by O'Leary, they testified to the urge of a literate readership to give expression to their patriotic feelings.[65]

Though the *Irish People* made a mockery of the IRB's secrecy, it was significant as 'an admission by Stephens that the political context in which he was functioning was too sophisticated for the unaugmented efforts of a secret society to hold sway'.[66] Fenian sympathisers have clung to the notion that an IRB insurrection, staged in 1865, had considerable chance of success. Most work on the IRB leaves this in doubt and it is notable that it took the arrival of a significant number of battle-hardened Irish-American soldiers to make 1867 remotely feasible. Perhaps the impossible standards the *People* set accounted for its limited appeal, but by allowing Fenians to imagine themselves a part of something greater than their individual selves, it helped the movement achieve that extraordinary 'intensity' in its – albeit unsatisfactory – heyday. It also bequeathed Irish separatism a set of core ideas, none of which were original, but which were propagated with a rigour and consistency they would not again receive until *Irish Freedom* began publication in 1910.[67]

NOTES

1. A. M. Sullivan, *New Ireland: Political Sketches and Personal Reminiscences* (Glasgow: Cameron & Ferguson, n.d., 8th edn), p. 249.
2. On this 'revolution' see ibid., pp. 17–18.
3. The organising theme of K. Theodore Hoppen, *Elections, Politics and Society in Ireland, 1832–1885* (Oxford: Oxford University Press, 1984).
4. The key study is Marie-Louise Legg, *Newspapers and Nationalism: The Irish Provincial Press, 1850–1892* (Dublin: Four Courts Press, 1998). An interesting discussion on the later period is Michael Wheatley, *Nationalism and the Irish Party: Provincial Ireland 1910–1916* (Oxford: Oxford University Press, 2005), pp. 17–21.
5. A small pocket book from late 1863 recorded twenty-five loans made to the newspaper of between 25 shillings and 15 pounds. National Archives of Ireland, Fenian Briefs, box 1, doc. 300.
6. Charles Beggs, 'First steps to Irish liberty' and 'Military resources of Ireland' were noted on 12 Sept. 1864. NAI, Fenian police reports, box 2, Dublin Metropolitan Police reports, 1864–5.
7. All letters from NAI, FB, carton 5, envelope 17.

8. Sullivan, *New Ireland*, p. 249; R. V. Comerford, *The Fenians in Context* (Dublin: Wolfhound Press, 1998, 1st edn 1985), p. 109.
9. NAI, FB, carton 5, envelope 18. Some 500 subscribers in the US are also listed, mainly individuals.
10. Sullivan, *New Ireland*, p. 249.
11. Marta Ramón, *A Provisional Dictator: James Stephens and the Fenian Movement* (Dublin: Four Courts Press, 2007), pp. 151–9, in particular pp. 154–5.
12. Charles Townshend, *Political Violence in Ireland: Government and Resistance since 1848* (Oxford: Oxford University Press, 1983), pp. 28, 35.
13. Roy Foster, *Modern Ireland 1600–1972* (London: Penguin, 1988), p. 393.
14. Roy Foster, *Paddy and Mr Punch: Connections in Irish and English History* (London: Penguin, 1993), p. 272.
15. Breandán Mac Suibhne and Amy Martin, 'Fenians in the frame: photographing Irish political prisoners, 1865–68', *Field Day Review*, 1 (2005), pp. 117–18.
16. Owen McGee, *The IRB: The Irish Republican Brotherhood from the Land League to Sinn Féin* (Dublin: Four Courts Press, 2005), pp. 13–14, 33–7.
17. Police records suggest an Irish-American newspaper, The *Fenian Spirit*, circulated in Ireland; correspondents with the *Irish People* referred to themselves as Fenians and provincial informers likewise. See seized letters and police reports in FB and DMP reports (NAI). Memoir literature includes John O'Leary, *Recollections of Fenians and Fenianism* (London: Downey & Co., 1896) and Mark Ryan, *Fenian Memories* (Dublin: M. H. Gill, 1945).
18. McGee, *The IRB*, p. 37.
19. Such a distinction is implicit to much later use of the term; for an explicit example see M. J. Kelly, *The Fenian Ideal and Irish Nationalism, 1882–1916* (Woodbridge: Boydell & Brewer, 2006), p. 108.
20. *Irish People*, 10 Sept. 1864.
21. See Kelly, *Fenian Ideal*, p. 61 and elsewhere for examples of this thinking.
22. For example, *Irish People*, 19 March 1864.
23. *Irish People*, 14 May 1864; Comerford, *Fenians in Context*, pp. 110–11.
24. For example, *Irish People*, 12 Dec. 1863.
25. Ibid., 5 Dec. 1863.
26. Ibid., 16 Jan. 1864.
27. Ibid.
28. Ibid., 4 June 1864.
29. Ibid., 30 Jan. 1864.
30. Ibid., 2 July 1864.
31. Ibid., 2 Jan. 1864.
32. Ibid., 9 July 1864.
33. Ibid., 26 Dec. 1863.
34. Ibid., 9 July 1864.
35. Ibid., 28 Nov. 1863.
36. Ibid., 21 May 1864. 'In Ireland there are a greater number of people than perhaps in any other country who can string words together in a more or less grammatical shape, and in no other country is the temptation to explode in speech so strong.'
37. The *Irishman* and the *Nation* were prone to similar claims.
38. *Irish People*, 16 Jan. 1864: 'Human beings who lack earnestness are like creatures without souls. Their whole nature is dwarfed and more or less debased. For them life has neither true aim nor holiness. No elevating sense of duty is felt by them.'
39. Ibid.
40. *Irish People*, 2 April 1864.
41. Ibid., 2 July 1864.
42. In a report dated 20 June 1865, a Co. Down policeman overheard two Fenians discussing the organisation's prospects. They claimed 120,000 members and that help would come from France and the United States: NAI, DMP reports.
43. *Irish People*, 2 Jan. 1864.
44. Ibid., 30 Jan. 1864.
45. Joe Cleary, '"Misplaced ideas"? Colonialism, location, and dislocation in Irish studies', in Clare Carroll and Patricia King (eds), *Ireland and Postcolonial Theory* (Cork: Cork University Press, 2003), p. 23.
46. *Irish People*, 11 June 1864. In the same issue there is a dig at Quakerism: 'For all – whether

Quaker or Catholic – who hold it criminal to fight for freedom, we feel either contempt or loathing; contempt for the former, and loathing for the latter. Such a belief is part of the foolish religion of the Quaker, but it is only the creed of cowards or traitors among the Catholics.'

47. *Irish People*, 26 Mar. 1864.
48. Ibid., 11 June 1864.
49. Ibid.
50. Ibid.
51. Ibid.
52. Ibid.
53. Ibid., 25 June 1865.
54. Terrence McDonagh (ed.), *Was Ireland a Colony? Economics, Politics and Culture in Nineteenth-Century Ireland* (Dublin: Irish Academic Press, 2005).
55. Joe Cleary, 'Amongst empires: a short history of Ireland and empire studies in international context', *Éire-Ireland*, 42/1–2 (Spring/Summer 2007), pp. 11–57.
56. David Fitzpatrick, 'Ireland and the empire', in Andrew Porter (ed.), *The Oxford History of the British Empire: The Nineteenth Century* (Oxford: Oxford University Press, 1999).
57. *Irish People*, 11 June 1864, 2 July 1864.
58. Ibid., 9 July 1864.
59. Ibid.
60. Ibid., 16 July 1864.
61. Barry's further claim that the *People* promoted the idea 'that the law by which any man possessed more property than another was unjust and wicked' was considerably less plausible, as A. M. Sullivan comments in his *New Ireland*, p. 260. Barry's submission for the prosecution and the Lawless affidavit can be found in NAI, FB, box 1.
62. NAI, DMP reports, 19 Aug. 1864; Comerford, *Fenians in Context*, pp. 111–12.
63. In the same report, Ryan reported one informer's description of Stephens as wearing 'a straw hat and white vest and looks like a Southern planter Yankee'.
64. For example, see 'H.' on Killiney Bay on regatta day (Aug. 1865) or the rhapsodic account of the west of Ireland written by 'A Galway Boy' (16 April 1865) in NAI, FB, carton 5, envelope 5.
65. NAI, FB, carton 3, envelope 6. 'Garryowen is sufficiently patriotic', goes one scribbled appraisal, 'but entirely unpoetical'.
66. Comerford, *Fenians in Context*, p. 98.
67. Kelly, *Fenian Ideal*, pp. 187–204.

II
POPULAR POLITICS AND
GRASSROOTS FENIANISM

4

Permanent Revolutionaries: The IRB and the Land War in West Cork

Frank Rynne

I

Founded on 21 October 1879, the Irish National Land League (INLL) was a compact between revolutionary nationalists, or Fenians, and Parnell's parliamentary followers which officially sought to create peasant proprietorship in Ireland.[1] In practice the Land League combined the 'land question with the question of national independence' and allowed for a resurgence of the revolutionary secret society, the Irish Republican Brotherhood.[2] The Land War tested the efficacy of the Fenian organisation at the grassroots, an aspect of the movement which historians often marginalise or ignore. There is an inherent difficulty in proving Fenian or Irish Republican Brotherhood activism when members were true to the oath of secrecy that membership demanded and because, notwithstanding informers and infiltrators, a great deal of the organisation's business remained secret.[3] This chapter centres on Ballydehob in West Cork and examines a suspected cell of IRB men. The secret revolutionary organisation had operatives who remained members for life. During the Land War, 1879–82, they publically advanced a political cause of tenant rights under the control and direction of the County Cork IRB.

II

In June 1880, Clan na Gael's John Devoy noted that the Irish National Land League 'made it possible to keep alive a national movement in the future'.[4] For Devoy and his contemporaries the 'national movement' meant Fenianism or advanced nationalism. Two months after Devoy opined on the benefits that Fenianism would derive from the Land League, the first branches of the INLL were established in West Cork. In 1888, at *The Times*/Parnell Special Commission, RIC Sergeant Lang stated that Ballydehob, a tiny village in West Cork, was in 1880 and 1881 'the political centre of the West'.[5] He did not elaborate on what kind of politics the village was the centre of, be it nationalist/Fenian or constitutional. However, the statement does imply that Land League activities in West Cork were led by the Ballydehob branch. An examination of the operation and activities of the Ballydehob branch of the INLL reveals that it was organised and managed by a small cadre who exerted an influence on their community disproportionate to the small membership the branch had during most of the year it was operational. Events at Ballydehob served as the catalyst for what amounted to an open insurrection in West Cork in June 1881. Proving that someone in the Land League was in fact a Fenian organiser or operative relies on the assessment of the circumstantial evidence. In many cases several small clues such as the language used in speeches, personal connections and police intelligence may combine to make it possible to conclude that that someone was an IRB man.

Chartered in 1620, Ballydehob was in the barony of West Carbery in Cork's West Riding and was part of the Skull Poor Law Union.[6] Ballydehob is 9 miles west of Skibbereen and 10 miles east of Clonakilty. During the famine of 1822 Richard Griffith was commissioned to build a road through the Mizen peninsula allowing the authorities easy access to an area reputed to harbour 'Whiteboys, smugglers and robbers'.[7] In 1823, six years before they were introduced in London, police were stationed in Ballydehob.[8] The district was severely affected by the Great Famine and in 1846 was 'even more wretched than Skibbereen', the 'cradle of revolution'.[9] In 1880 the district was again in a deprived state with incidents of nakedness due to poverty being reported in Skull.[10]

The Mizen peninsula had strong connections with the nascent Fenian movement. It was in Skibbereen in May 1858 that the chief organiser of the 'Organisation', James Stephens, came across a revolutionary body known as the Skibbereen Literary and Phoenix Society.[11] Ten years earlier Stephens and other Young Irelanders had secured the assistance of Skibbereen solicitor McCarthy Downing in effecting their escape to France.[12] Among the members of the Phoenix Society who embraced the Fenian cause were Jeremiah O'Donovan Rossa and Mortimer Moynihan. By the end of 1858 the Phoenix Society in Skibbereen had been infiltrated by Daniel Sullivan (Goula).[13] McCarthy Downing acted for members following their arrest and at their 1859 Cork trial.[14] However, the police failed to identify men from Ballydehob reported to have been 'involved in the Bantry and Skibbereen Societies'.[15] John Devoy believed the Phoenix trials, which centred on Skibbereen, were a boon for the nascent revolutionary movement and 'instead of frightening the young men of Ireland, really advertised the movement and helped in its recruiting'.[16] It is notable that the Phoenix men of Ballydehob were not identified by the police despite their placing an informer in the society.

The first public steps to establish a branch of the Irish National Land League in Ballydehob were taken by a sixty-year-old Ballydehob man, Richard Hodnett, who had a small shop and was agent to several small properties.[17] Hodnett had witnessed 'the first death' of a worker from hunger when he acted as an overseer on relief works near Ballydehob in 1847.[18] On 28 August 1880 he attended a meeting of the Cork Land League which was the controlling branch for the county, to seek approval for inaugurating a branch at Ballydehob.[19] Hodnett told the meeting he had just returned from London where he had spoken to Parnell about the need for a Land League branch in western West Carbery and that he had been 'expecting for some time that they would have formed a branch in Skibbereen but there was some underhand influence at work there that prevented them'.[20] Hodnett assured the gathering that a branch could be formed at Ballydehob and implied that the League would advance from there.[21] It is not clear what had prevented the formation of a branch in Skibbereen, but with Ballydehob to the fore the Land League quickly took root in West Carbery, and the following day held its inaugural meeting in neighbouring Clonakilty.[22] Constable Stringer described the speakers Edward Farrell, chairman of the Cork Land League, and J. O'Brien, a Cork publican, as being 'Nationalist'.[23] The speeches urged tenants to join the Land League and to take over no land from which a tenant has been evicted, but they also condemned oppression and tyranny. J. S. Enright, a farmer from Ballincollig, said: 'When they became educated, they combined as one man and wiped the petty tyrants off the face of the earth.'[24] Mr Murphy, secretary of the Dunmanway Land League branch, concluded his speech with the words: 'Go on in your masses, dense, resolute, strong to war against treason, oppression and wrong.'[25] The speakers' assertions, reminiscent of revolutionary France, combined an advocacy of tenant rights with the aspiration to liberty.

John O'Connor, MP, giving evidence before *The Times*/Parnell Special Commission in 1889, stated that the word *nationalist* in the early 1880s meant 'men of Fenian opinions and proclivities'.[26] He was in a position to know as he was one of the 'principal Nationalists of Cork', secretary of both the Irish Republican Brotherhood in the county and the County Cork Land League as well as IRB supreme council member P. N. FitzGerald's right-hand man.[27] At the Special Commission he lied about his IRB involvement in the early 1880s, stating he had 'dropped out of the body' but that he recruited active IRB men into the Land League.[28] He had met John Devoy, who later noted that O'Connor, J. C. Flynn and P. J. Sheridan were among the IRB men who had initially denounced the 'New Departure' but became prominent later in the Land League.[29] In

1881 O'Connor's smuggled prison correspondence was reported to Devoy as part of an IRB report from T. H. Ronayne.[30] O'Connor was one of at least four committee members of the Cork Land League the authorities believed were advanced nationalists or Fenians. The aforementioned chairman, Edward Farrell, and committee member Frank Harris held meetings in October 1880 with IRB supreme council member C. G. Doran and James Redpath, an American Fenian supporter and journalist who was noted for making 'violent' speeches against the government.[31] Committee member John Heffernan from Blarney was reported to be a 'land agitator' who also made 'advanced' violent speeches against the government.[32] The term *advanced* referred to 'advanced nationalist', which was synonymous with Fenianism and Fenians who were 'sympathetic to Parnell'.[33]

III

On Sunday 12 September Richard Hodnett chaired the inaugural meeting of the Ballydehob branch, held in the village's chapel yard.[34] The local parish priest, Revd John Murphy, though invited to chair the meeting, did not attend but he sent a letter urging the people towards 'moderation'.[35] Reports varied on the size of the meeting, with *The Times* reporting it was 'not large' but that it included strong farmers and a solicitor, Patrick O'Hea. The police reporter Jeremiah Stringer estimated 2,500 people attended, while the *West Cork Eagle*, whose chief correspondent was a relative of O'Donovan Rossa's, reported 'immense crowds'.[36] Patrick O'Hea asserted that landlordism had drained 'the life blood out of Érin'.[37] He referred to his being in London 'a little more than a fortnight ago' where he was 'present in the House' when John Dillon's speech was being debated.[38] He reported to the meeting the substance of Dillon's controversial remarks that he would like to see 'six hundred thousand farmers of Ireland ... banded together' and 'in possession of a rifle'.[39] 'We want them' was the response of one member of the audience.[40] Edward Farrell suggested ostracising rather than 'tarring and feathering' anyone who took over a farm from which a tenant had been evicted.[41] A voice shouted: 'No, but we'll cut his ears off.'[42] John Heffernan stated that 'wherever landlordism raised its unholy head it should be stuck down'.[43] Richard Hodnett, who chaired the meeting, declared its objective was to show the 'English Government and the world at large the disadvantages of the present system of landlordism in Ireland'.[44] Though emphasising national distinctions in his speech, he made no overt separatist statements.

Edward Farrell said Hodnett was 'leading the land war here against the enemies of your homesteads', that 'there is a great deal of work for the young men to do', and that Cork would stand against tyranny.[45] While endorsing Hodnett he also stated that Irishmen have 'no country to fight for, but let us have a cause and a country to fight for, and we will do it'.[46] Hodnett, aware that 'the police in all the outlying parts were brought in to enjoy the oratory', ended the meeting with four lines from Oliver Goldsmith's 'The Deserted Village'.[47] From the beginning the Ballydehob Land League intertwined the idea of land reform with separatist rhetoric, tenant rights with the denunciation of tyranny, while calls for non-violence were met with uncensured calls for violence.

Hodnett's suggestion to the Cork Land League that the movement would spread through West Carbery from Ballydehob proved well founded. On 26 September a land meeting attended by a reported 10,000 people – 'surpassing any gathering of the kind' held in Cork – was held in Skibbereen.[48] The meeting was advertised by a large poster bearing Thomas Davis' watchword in bold print, 'Ireland for the Irish', and other slogans including 'Skibbereen to the Front' and 'God Save Ireland'.[49] The latter phrase, which appeared on most Land League posters, was the unofficial national anthem and a Fenian marching song made famous by T. D. Sullivan's composition commemorating the Manchester Martyrs executed following the 1867 Fenian rescue in which a policeman was killed.[50] This revolutionary poster urged the men of the Carberies to aspire to freedom and defy government of the few:

> Men of the Carberies assemble in the Numbers and Strength of your Manhood! Show that you have the spirit and aspirations of Freeman, and that you are determined no longer to be ground down under the Oligarch's sway.[51]

The purpose of the meeting was declared to be: 'To consider the position of the IRISH PEOPLE with regard to THE LAND OF IRELAND'.[52]

The meeting commemorated and celebrated rebellion and republicanism in music, banners and song. Skibbereen hotelier Patrick Spillane's band played rebel tunes such as 'The Rising of the Moon'.[53] The slogans that adorned carts and buildings included 'God Save Ireland', 'Land for the People', 'Ireland for the Irish', 'The Husbandman Must Partake of the Fruits', 'Unity is Strength' and 'Faith and Fatherland'.[54] The speeches merged the tenants' cause with IRB republicanism by including references to the 1798 rebellion, 'raising the flag of Vinegar Hill', the end of landlordism and the soon-to-come fall of the 'oligarchy'.[55]

T. W. Moody noted the dilemma that Michael Davitt faced in trying to balance his role as a tenants rights advocate with his membership of a secret revolutionary organisation: 'The incompatibility between his public inculcation of moral force with his secret approval of supplying tenant farmers with the means of using physical force was never resolved.'[56] The

founding of the Land League in West Cork was followed, on Sunday 17
October, by a gun attack near Skibbereen on the landlord Samuel
Hutchins which left his driver mortally wounded.[57] By the month's end,
the earl of Bandon had called a meeting of the county's magistrates which
passed a resolution demanding the suspension of the Habeas Corpus Act
and the provision of twenty extra police while further warning the
lord-lieutenant to be prepared to send troops to Bantry, Bandon,
Skibbereen and Dunmanway.[58] In November, *The Times* reported that
extra police were needed due to 'the disturbed state of the district'.[59] The
early phase of the Land War indicated that threats could be supported by
physical force.

Meetings of the Skull Poor Law Board of Guardians and Extraordinary
Presentment Sessions brought local landlords face to face with Richard
Hodnett. His questions caused one magistrate, Richard Notter, to lose
his temper and declare his hope that poor people 'will get powder and
ball before long'.[60] Within two weeks, Notter's words appeared on threatening notices signed 'Rory Jnr' that were posted in the district.[61] The
'West Cork Shooting Gallery', armed with Enfield rifles and Notter's
'powder and ball', warned landlords to charge no more than the Griffith's
Valuation, which was a key demand of the Land League.[62] The notices
appear to have had the desired effect, though whether it was from fear of
reprisals, genuine adherence to the Land League or merely tenants using
threats as an excuse to withhold rent is unclear. On 8 December, at the
fair in Ballydehob, tenants refused *en masse* to pay rent in excess of their
valuation and withheld payment when this demand was refused by the
landlord's agents.[63] The following day three locals who worked for landlords – Richard Daly, Henry Allen and Thomas Allen – received notices
signed 'Rory of the Hills' ordering them to 'join the League'.[64] Though
the *nom de guerre* Rory of the Hills was originally associated with
Ribbonism, in 1880 it was closely associated with attacks on landlords, as
well as Fenianism and Irish republicanism.[65] IRB supreme council president Charles Kickham's 1857 ballad 'Rory of the Hills' (which referred to
Wolfe Tone, pike-making and freedom) was a popular Fenian song.[66]

IV

Clifford Lloyd, resident magistrate (RM) for the Kilmallock and
Kilfinane districts in Co. Limerick, continually raised the concern that
various branches of the Land League 'abrogate to themselves and exercise the functions of a Government and of our Courts'.[67] Weekly public
meetings of the Ballydehob Land League provided a forum for local tenants to seek redress of disputes.[68] The Ballydehob Land League issued
summonses on headed stationery and failure to attend or agree to this

arbitration resulted in boycotting.[69] On 24 January 1881 the chief secretary of Ireland, W. E. Forster introduced a bill for the Better Protection of Person and Property in Ireland (PPP). The attempt to usurp government functions by Land League courts was cited by Forster as one reason for the introduction of the bill on 24 January 1881 along with the activities of Fenians, the Ribbon society and *mauvais sujets*.[70] He noted that a 'large number of Fenians ... have taken advantage of the present condition of the country'.[71] On 5 March, prior to the Poor Law elections, the lord-lieutenant, Lord Cowper, proscribed eleven baronies in West Cork, including West Carbery, under the provisions of the Protection of Person and Property Act (1881), which allowed for the suspension of *habeas corpus*.[72]

In 1878 Davitt told American nationalists that constitutionalists should be challenged whether they were Poor Law Guardians or MPs 'in an alien Parliament'.[73] Two years later he boasted to John Devoy that the Land League 'carry on the government of the country from 39 Upper Sackville St.'[74] In March 1881 the voters of Skull returned thirteen Land Leaguers to the Board of Guardians of Skull Poor Law Union, gaining control of a local taxing body. Richard Hodnett, who had been a guardian for many years, was elected by the board members as chairman, defeating an appointee to the board and Justice of the Peace George Swanton.[75] Swanton and his father Robert were the principal targets of the Ballydehob branch.

In a show of defiance at their district being proscribed, a 'monster meeting' was held at Ballydehob on 30 March.[76] Richard Hodnett introduced the guest of honour Anna Parnell, sister of Charles Stewart, and head of the Ladies' Irish National Land League.[77] Her speech sought to reassure the tenants that they would not suffer financially by supporting the League:

all the money of the Land League is in the hands of trustees ... men who would not allow an evicted tenant to suffer if he continues to live according to the teaching of the Land League ... the people in America would subscribe as much money as would keep the tenants for five years ... [78]

When she mentioned the application of the Coercion Act, Richard Hodnett asserted loudly enough to be heard by the reporting policeman: 'We are ready.'[79]

John O'Connor spoke after Parnell. Admitting his Fenian past, he linked that past with his present Land League activities, stating: 'I shouldered my rifle in '67 and am prepared to associate and organise every association to benefit my country.'[80] He praised Hodnett as the local leader but was ambiguous about how to deal with land-grabbers. 'I will not advise you to nail his ears to the village pump. I won't tell you to boycott him, but you know how to meet him yourself.'[81] By not endorsing a specific remedy, O'Connor appeared to encourage violence.

The next meeting of the Ballydehob branch was told that Robert Swanton had issued notices for rent at double the valuation.[82] His process server, James Camier, was declared obnoxious to the Land League by Hodnett's daughter Annie; this denunciation was followed on 11 April by an attack on him in his home by seven men with blackened faces who attempted to cut off his left ear.[83] Seizing this opportunity, on 18 April Lord Cowper signed a warrant for the arrest of Richard Hodnett.[84]

On 25 April Hodnett was arrested at his home in Ballydehob. He refused to dress, delaying his removal until a crowd had gathered, while car drivers hired by the police refused to carry them, necessitating their return to Skibbereen on foot.[85] At Skibbereen railway station they were met by a large crowd headed by John O'Connor. O'Connor again alluded to Fenianism, likening Hodnett to Morty Moynihan and Jeremiah O'Donovan Rossa. He blamed 'tyranny on the part of the English Government' for placing Hodnett in a prison cell in 'the cause of good old Ireland'.[86] He declared that the arrest proved that Irishmen needed 'to have the preservation of their Liberties in their own hands'.[87] After eradicating the land system they would 'continue ... efforts for a national independence'.[88] The IRB aim of national independence had finally come to the fore.

V

Following the arrest of Richard Hodnett, the Skull Board of Guardians passed a resolution demanding his release.[89] The Ballydehob ladies' branch declared that those not in the League were 'enemies of the people',[90] while the Ballydehob Land League stated that the 'violation of justice' could be blamed on George Swanton and Richard H. Notter.[91] A monster indignation meeting was held on 8 May in Ballydehob under the slogan 'Freedom for the People! No Compromise!'[92] Henry O'Mahony of the Ballydehob Land League committee, a recently elected Poor Law Guardian, 'spoke violently against the local magistrates including Swanton'.[93] O'Mahony was an American citizen, a successful grocer, publican and farmer.[94] Like many Fenians, he had served in the US Civil War.[95] He came back to Ballydehob in 1873 but returned twice to America, the last visit occurring 'some two years' before the formation of the local Land League branch.[96] In 1877 American Fenians were sent to Ireland to recruit and reorganise the IRB prior to their founding local Land League branches.[97] From 1857 to 1862 O'Mahony was an apprentice cooper in Skibbereen a few doors away from O'Donovan Rossa's shop.[98] During this time Fenians drilled on his father's land at Coomnageha.[99] He later wrote a memoir of the period at the insistence of his daughter, but made no mention of being involved in either the Phoenix Society or the IRB.[100]

On 19 May George Swanton was fired on while returning home from Skibbereen,[101] and on 1 June a warrant was issued for the arrest of Henry O'Mahony, citing his 'incitement to murder' Swanton.[102] An examination of the incomplete records available, which give details of the reasons for arrest under the PPP Act, shows that 23 per cent were 'Fenians', 'advanced nationalists' or 'members of a secret society'.[103] As O'Mahony was not described as being political before his arrest, he is not included in that 23 per cent.

When ten policemen attempted to arrest O'Mahony on 4 June in Ballydehob, the people of the district forcibly resisted them.[104] Having prior knowledge that he would be arrested, he had asked that it should be effected by a single constable.[105] This foreknowledge also gave him an opportunity to organise resistance. Fifteen hundred people assembled on hearing the chapel bell and horns. They rescued him twice from armed police, who withdrew to avoid loss of life.[106] O'Mahony refused the opportunity to escape on an American ship which was harboured in Skull, declaring that the 'boys of Ballydehob will make it hot' for the Swantons as he set off for Skibbereen at the head of the crowd.[107] He took the train to Cork and proceeded to Limerick gaol with members of the Cork Land League;[108] he later claimed his travel expenses from the government.[109] Having had ample opportunity to flee the country, O'Mahony chose to become a political prisoner. His arrest precipitated popular uprisings in Ballydehob, Skull and Skibbereen.

On 6 June a rumour was circulated that the parish priest at Skull was to be arrested. Horns were blown and chapel bells rung. Three thousand people 'armed with sticks, stones, some few firearms and enormous pikes ... took complete charge of the village'.[110] They stoned the police barracks and the inspector's home but remained under the control of leaders, one of whom was overheard ordering the cessation of an attack on the coastguard station: 'The coast guard have not meddled with us yet, when they do will be the time to meddle with them.'[111] Communication outside the district was impossible as the telegraph wires and poles were pulled down and thrown into bogs leaving Dublin Castle to rely on newspaper reports for intelligence.[112] Navy gunboats – the HMS *Britomart* and HMS *Valorous* – were sent to Skull and the HMS *Orwell* was dispatched to Bantry.[113] An attempt to restore order at Ballydehob by E. B. Warburton, RM, and a company of marines was repulsed by a thousand people. Two officers and several men were injured and the party was compelled to retreat to Skull.[114] On the night of 7 June men in military order marched to the house of Richard Notter and formed a line opposite. Notter commenced shooting on hearing a voice issuing orders 'Halt! Front! Uncase revolvers' and the group withdrew.[115] On 8 June John O'Connor arrived in Ballydehob with an American named Captain Bell, staying one night with the local Land League treasurer before moving on to Skull. Though local police were to report that Bell was not recruiting for a secret society, the RIC in Limerick was informed that he was in Ireland with other Americans 'to increase the number of young men joined in the confederation known as "The Irish Republican Brotherhood" and the "Skirmishing Fund"'.[116]

On 8 June magistrates and justices of the peace, meeting at Skibbereen courthouse, wrote to Lord Cowper requesting reinforcements of 'two hundred military' as the town had been ransacked on the previous night.[117] Railway lines were pulled up near Skibbereen to prevent reinforcements arriving. Men marched in a formation 'four deep' to await troops at the station but were eventually induced to disperse by a local curate.[118] Marines arriving in launches fired on the town, injuring one woman.[119] By 9 June order was restored, but threatening notices continued to appear around Ballydehob. Notter, the Swantons and their agents were placed under a boycott,[120] while on 16 June drivers who worked for the police were severely beaten outside the village.[121] The arrest of locals including Hodnett's son Richard did little to restore order, but rather created further excitement and 'hooting and groaning' at the police.[122] Though he could find no evidence, District Inspector Hume felt these disturbances were 'preconcerted'.[123] The destruction of train lines and telegraph wires, military-style marching, the open bearing of arms and the direct targeting of magistrates, military and police strongly suggest that the IRB was at work. A 'Lady Resident of Skibbereen' wrote to the lord-lieutenant and named Michael (*sic*) O'Hea, solicitor, as one of the leaders.[124] DI Hume, investigating, stated:

> Mr Patrk O'Hea [not Michael] is a solicitor in this town. He is an active member of the Land League, of Republican tendencies, and has been known to say he 'was a Fenian' but in such a way as to imply he has ceased to be one.[125]

At the end of June a report was prepared following suggestions by Mr Plunkett, RM, that in Ballydehob and Skull Fenians were acting with the Land League and were involved in the disturbances. Sub-Inspector Hurley agreed that they were, a conclusion based on the following circumstances:

> at Ballydehob for some time past Mr Henry O'Mahony, a returned American, took a very prominent part in the Land League agitation, and being a man of extreme political views – strongly imbued with revolutionary ideas – the belief is that whilst he ostensibly advocated a reform of the land laws, his real object was to ferment agitation in the interest of Fenianism.[126]

However, as was the case with Ballydehob Phoenix Society members in 1858, other IRB members were not identified. On 30 July George Swanton's father Robert was shot in the head near Ballydehob.[127]

VI

Between its formation in September 1880 and 16 May 1881, the Ballydehob Land League branch recruited only 114 people. Only after Hodnett's arrest did recruiting begin in earnest. On 26 May 141 people joined the branch in a single day, and following O'Mahony's arrest in June, membership grew steadily. The last entries in the membership book on 20 October brought its total number to 1,037.[128] The large land meetings of 1880 and 1881 should have proved sure recruiting grounds for the branch, but it is clear that no effort was made to get people to join the Land League and threatening notices urging specific individuals to join were merely to intimidate landlords and government employees. It may be concluded that the Ballydehob Land League branch wished to remain a small cadre of trusted men until the government directly challenged them by arresting their leader. By 20 June 1881 even the landlord Michael Hergarty, who had threatened the League the previous December, had joined and lowered his rents to the Griffith Valuation.[129]

Hodnett was released from prison on 29 April 1882;[130] three nights later he assaulted a constable at Ballydehob while celebrating Parnell's release.[131] On 5 May, after three cheers were called for Davitt – 'the leader of the Fenians' – following his release from Portland prison, Hodnett declared: 'Aristocracy is rolling and democracy rising up in this place.'[132] On 22 February 1883 Richard Hodnett Jnr was observed at the post receiver at Ballydehob. The next day Richard Daly found a package containing dynamite addressed to the chief secretary for Ireland, Earl Spencer. However, he appears to have aided the perpetrator by destroying the address label, thus making handwriting analysis impossible.[133] A week later Hodnett Jnr was overheard saying the dynamite 'came from across the water'.[134] By March 1883 both Hodnetts were in jail, Richard Jnr awaiting trial for attempting to murder Earl Spencer and Richard Snr under the provisions of the Crimes Act. Richard Daly subsequently received a letter from America threatening his life and the life of 'The Invincibles' approver James Carey.[135]

There is no direct evidence that Richard Hodnett was a Fenian but, in the 1850s, he had been a member of a society that included many Fenians. Some time between 1856 and 1860 Hodnett joined the Ossianic Society, a society for the preservation 'of manuscripts in the Irish language, illustrative of the Fenian period of Irish history with literal translations and notes'.[136] The Ossianic Society was formed on St Patrick's Day 1853, five

years to the day before the IRB.[137] Its publications used the spelling
Fenian (rather than Fianna), which may account for the Fenian move-
ment's adoption of that spelling. On the day the 'brotherhood' was
founded in 1858, James Stephens' Young Ireland commander, William
Smith O'Brien, became the Ossianic Society's president.[138] Among the
early members were James Stephens' brother-in-law and IRB member,
George Hooper, as well as O'Donovan Rossa, Patrick O'Hea and Richard
Hodnett.[139] The New York branch, founded to sustain the Irish branch
financially, used the offices of the *Phoenix* newspaper and counted John
O'Mahony, Colonel Michael Corcoran, Michael Doheny and other leading Fenians as members.[140] Though there is no evidence that an interest
in the Irish language and the 'Fenian period of Irish history' made
Hodnett a Fenian, in its latter days the society was a front for Fenianism.
On the basis of the circumstantial evidence, including his connection to
O'Donovan Rossa through literary matters, Hodnett may have been one
of the Ballydehob Phoenix Society members who escaped police identification in 1858.

There is no doubt that the organising body of the Irish National Land
League in Cork was controlled by active IRB men. Furthermore, it is clear
that Patrick O'Hea and John O'Connor had been IRB men in the 1860s,
though both O'Hea and O'Connor claimed that they were not in the IRB
in the 1880s. As O'Connor was lying, there is no reason to presume O'Hea
was not too. Richard Hodnett and O'Hea were members of the Ossianic
Society, which attracted members of both the Phoenix Society and the
Fenians. As they were both from the same area of the country they are
likely to have known each other personally at that time. Their journey to
London prior to the establishment of Land League branches in West Cork
and their attendance at early land meetings in the county indicates their
close co-operation. The speeches made by O'Connor, Heffernan,
O'Mahony, Farrell, O'Hea and Hodnett, both overtly and by allusion, promoted nationalism and republicanism in opposition to a tyrannical oligarchy. Following the arrests of Hodnett and O'Mahony, insurrections
broke out in West Carbery. Their arrests also prompted the first organised
recruitment into the Land League at Ballydehob and demonstrations
against the government which were clearly insurrectionary displays. The
dynamite incident at Ballydehob and the subsequent letter from America
(intimidating a witness on Richard Hodnett Jnr's behalf) proves an international revolutionary connection with Ballydehob. The area had been
associated with the Young Ireland movement and was also associated with
its successor, the Fenian movement, and radical Land League agitation.
Though Henry O'Mahony never admitted his Fenianism, the fact that the
early Fenians drilled on his father's land while he lived in 'revolutionary'
Skibbereen proves his association with the early movement. If Richard

Hodnett was not Fenian, he certainly had Fenian friends and was a man with Fenian opinions and proclivities.

VII

Recent research has re-emphasised the contribution made by Fenians to successive phases of the land struggle. This chapter has sought to demonstrate that the study of the Land War at a local level helps to illuminate the structure and organisational skills of the Irish Republican Brotherhood. Although there are problems involved in studying a secret organisation at the grassroots, by identifying local IRB men it is possible to demonstrate the strength of the IRB's local networks. It is also possible to trace these circuitries, via local organisers like John O'Connor, directly to the supreme council of the IRB. In the case of the IRB in West Cork, not only did it infiltrate an open movement and contest local elections, but it usurped government functions and took local initiative in steering the Land League in an explicitly militant direction. Late Victorian Fenianism, then, was not a monolith, and a consideration of the IRB at a parish level not only throws new light on its internal workings but also on the development of the new political class born out of the land struggle.

NOTES

1. John Devoy, 'Parnell and the Fenians', *Chicago Tribune*, 24 Mar. 1899, cited in T. W. Moody 'The new departure in Irish politics, 1878–9', in H. A. Croone, T. W. Moody, and D. B. Quinn (eds), *Essays in British and Irish History* (London: Fredrick Muller, 1949), p. 303.
2. T. W. Moody, *Davitt and the Irish Revolution 1848–82* (Oxford: Clarendon Press, 1981), p. 36.
3. Report of Supt John Mallon, 'G' Division, Dublin Metropolitan Police, 2 Dec. 1880, National Archives of Ireland, Irish National League Papers, box 9. This report details information received from a Mr Bernard on the state of Fenianism in Ireland.
4. Frank Rynne, '"This extra parliamentary propaganda": Land League posters', *History Ireland*, 16/6 (2008), p. 39.
5. Evidence of Sergeant Lang, RIC, 6 Dec. 1888, *Special Commission Act 1888, Report of the Proceedings before the Commissioners appointed by the Act*, 4 vols (London, 1890), vol. i, p. 526.
6. Patrick Hickey, *The Famine in West Cork* (Cork: Mercier Press, 2002), p. 14.
7. Ibid., pp. 52–6, 50.
8. Ibid., p. 58.
9. Ibid., p. 161; *West Cork Eagle*, 2 Oct. 1881.
10. *West Cork Eagle*, 6 Mar. 1880.
11. Mr Fitzmaurice (RM) to Lord Naas, 27 Dec. 1858, NAI, Irish Crime Records 16, Fenian Police Reports, box 1; Jeremiah O'Donovan Rossa, *Rossa's Recollections 1838 to 1898* (Guilford, CT: Lyons Press, 2004), pp. 149–50; Joseph Denieffe, *A Personal Narrative of the Irish Republican Brotherhood* (Shannon: Irish University Press, 1969), p. 26.
12. Fitzmaurice (RM) to Naas, 27 Dec. 1858, NAI, ICR 16, Fenian Police Reports, box 1.
13. Jeremiah O'Donovan Rossa, 'The Fenian movement: an account of its origin, progress and temporary collapse', *Brooklyn Eagle*, 14 June 1885.
14. Fitzmaurice to Naas, 27 Dec. 1858, NAI, ICR 16; O'Donovan Rossa, *Rossa's Recollections 1838 to 1898*, pp. 216–29.
15. Sub-inspector Humphreys to RIC Inspector General, 4 Nov. 1858, NAI, ICR 16, Fenian Police Reports, box 1.
16. John Devoy, *Recollections of an Irish Rebel* (Shannon: Irish University Press, 1969), p. 31; F. S.

L. Lyons, *Ireland Since the Famine* (London: Fontana Press, 1973), p. 127; Devoy, *Recollections of an Irish Rebel*, p. 20.

17. Lang, *Special Commission Act*, p. 526; *West Cork Eagle*, 4 Sept. 1880.
18. L. O'Regan, 'Anna Parnell in West Cork', *Southern Star*, 23 Nov. 1991, in Hickey, *Famine in West Cork*, p. 267.
19. 'County of Cork, WR, Crime and Outrage resulting from the Establishment of the Land League at Ballydehob, on 12th September 1880, and continuing until the summer of 1883, showing direct connection between the League and several outrages', p. 1, NAI, INLP, box 10 (hereafter cited as Ballydehob crime and outrage report); *Cork Constitution*, 30 Aug. 1880; *West Cork Eagle*, 4 Sept. 1880.
20. *West Cork Eagle*, 4 Sept. 1880.
21. Ibid.
22. Cressida Annesley, 'Boycott of William Bence Jones', *Journal of the Cork Historical and Archaeological Society*, 99 (1994), p. 6.
23. Report of land meeting, Clonakilty, Co. Cork, Sunday 12 Aug. 1880, NAI, Chief Crown Solicitor's department, Queen v. Parnell papers, 1880–1881, box 4.
24. Ibid.
25. Ibid.
26. Evidence of John O'Connor, 9 July 1889, *Special Commission Act* (London, 1890), vol. iii, p. 666.
27. District Inspectors Office, Cork, 'List of names of those who come under the provisions of the Protection Act', NAI, INLP, box 9; Eoin McGee, *The IRB: The Irish Republican Brotherhood from the Land League to Sinn Féin*, 2nd edn (Dublin: Four Courts Press, 2007), p. 77.
28. Evidence of John O'Connor, *Special Commission Act*, vol. iii, p. 665.
29. Ibid., pp. 664–5; T. H. Ronayne to John Devoy, 24 Sept. 1881, cited in William O'Brien and Desmond Ryan (eds.) *Devoy's Post Bag, 1871–1928*, 2 vols (Dublin: C. J. Fallon & Co., 1848 and 1954), vol. ii, p. 101; Carla King and W. J. McCormack (eds), John Devoy, *Michael Davitt from Gaelic American* (Dublin: UCD Press, 2008), p. 69.
30. T. H. Ronayne to John Devoy, 24 Sept. 1881, *Devoy's Post Bag*, vol. ii, p. 101.
31. Michael Fogerty to Inspector General, 15 Nov. 1880, NAI, Chief Secretary's Office Registered Papers /1881/21817. Forgerty wrote Edmond rather than Edward but noted he was from the Cork Land League.
32. List of persons whose arrest is recommended under the Protection of Person and Property (1881) Act for Cork City, NAI, Protection of Person and Property Act (1881), box 1.
33. Frank Callanan, '"In the names of God and dead generations": nationalism and republicanism in Ireland', in Richard English and Joseph Morrison Skelly (eds), *Ideas Matter: Essays in Honour of Conor Cruise O'Brien* (Dublin: Poolbeg, 1998), pp. 110–14; evidence of John O'Connor, *Special Commission*, vol. iii, p. 666.
34. Report of land meeting, Ballydehob, Co. Cork, Sunday 12 Sept. 1880, NAI, CCS, Queen v. Parnell, box 4.
35. Ballydehob crime and outrage report, p. 2, NAI, INLP.
36. *The Times*, 13 Sept. 1880; Report of land meeting at Ballydehob, NAI, CCS , Queen v. Parnell; *West Cork Eagle*, 18 Sept. 1880; entry for John Eager O'Mahony in Timothy Cadogan and Jeremiah Falvey (eds), *A Biographical Dictionary of Cork* (Dublin: Four Courts Press, 2006), p. 262.
37. Report of land meeting at Ballydehob, CCS, Queen v. Parnell.
38. Ibid.
39. Ibid; *West Cork Eagle*, 18 Sept. 1880.
40. *West Cork Eagle*, 18 Sept. 1880.
41. Ballydehob crime and outrage report, NAI, INLP.
42. Ibid.
43. Ibid.
44. Report of land meeting at Ballydehob, NAI, CCS, Queen v. Parnell.
45. Ibid.
46. Ibid.
47. *West Cork Eagle*, 18 Sept. 1880; Report of land meeting at Ballydehob, NAI, CCS, Queen v. Parnell.
48. *West Cork Eagle*, 2 Oct. 1880.
49. Thomas Davis, 'The history of Ireland', in Thomas Davis, *Selections from his Poetry and Prose* (London: Gresham Publishing Company, 1970), p. 84; Rynne, '"This extra parliamentary

propaganda": Land League posters', p. 40.
50. John Denvir, *The Life Story of an Old Rebel* (Dublin: Sealy, Bryers & Walker, 1910), p. 113; D. J. Hickey and J. E. Doherty, *A New Dictionary of Irish History from 1800* (Dublin: Gill & Macmillan, 2003), p. 306; Rynne, '"This extra parliamentary propaganda": Land League posters', p. 40.
51. *West Cork Eagle*, 2 Oct. 1880; poster for land meeting at Skibbereen, 26 Sept. 1880, NAI, CCS , Queen v. Parnell papers, box 1.
52. Poster for land meeting at Skibbereen, 26 Sept. 1880, reproduced in Rynne, '"This extra parliamentary propaganda": Land League posters', p. 40.
53. Rynne, '"This extra parliamentary propaganda": Land League posters', p. 40.
54. *West Cork Eagle*, 2 Oct. 1880.
55. Ibid.
56. Moody, *Davitt and the Irish Revolution 1846–82*, p. 381.
57. *West Cork Eagle*, 23 Oct. 1880.
58. *West Cork Eagle*, 30 Oct. 1880.
59. *The Times*, 13 Nov. 1880.
60. *West Cork Eagle*, 20 Nov. 1880.
61. Ballydehob crime and outrage report, p. 3, NAI, INLP.
62. Ibid; *The Times*, 1 Feb. 1881.
63. Ballydehob crime and outrage report, p. 3, NAI, INLP; *The Times*, 1 Feb. 1881.
64. Ballydehob crime and outrage report, p. 3, NAI, INLP.
65. *New York Times*, 18 Oct. 1879; Charles Townshend, *Political Violence in Ireland: Government and Resistance Since 1848* (Oxford: Clarendon Press, 1983), p. 23; Seumas MacManus, *The Story of the Irish Race* (New York: Cosimo, 2005), pp. 612–13.
66. MacManus, *Story of the Irish Race*, p. 613.
67. Clifford Lloyd to W. E. Forster, June 6 1881, NAI, CSORP/1881/18837. For Lloyd's account of his work combating the Land League in his roles as resident magistrate and special resident magistrate, see Charles Dalton Clifford Lloyd, *Ireland Under the Land League: A Narrative of Personal Experiences* (London: William Blackwood & Sons, 1892).
68. Richard Hodnett to Martha Daly, 5 Dec. 1880, NAI, INLP, box 8, envelope 36; letter on notepaper of Ballydehob Land League branch from John Collins to A. Bennett, 17 Jan. 1881, NAI, INLP, box 8, envelope 39; minute book of Ballydehob branch of Irish National Land League, NAI, INLP, box 9.
69. John Collins to A. Bennett 17 Jan. 1881, NAI, INLP; Ballydehob crime and outrage report, p. 3, NAI, INLP.
70. *Hansard*, cclvii (1881), c. 1226.
71. Ibid.
72. Memorandum of proceedings in the case of Richard Hodnett, NAI, INLP, box 9.
73. Michael Davitt, *Fall of Feudalism in Ireland or The Story of the Land League Revolution* (Chicago, IL: Sequoyah Books, 2003), p. 129; speech by Michael Davitt, 8 Dec. 1878, from *Boston Pilot*, 21 Dec. 1878, quoted in Davitt, *Fall of Feudalism*, p. 133.
74. Michael Davitt to John Devoy, 16 Dec. 1881, in O'Brien and Ryan, *Devoy's Post Bag*, vol. ii, p. 23.
75. *Thom's Directory, 1881* (Dublin: Alexander Thom, 1881); membership book of Ballydehob branch of the National Land League, NAI, INLP; Liam O'Regan, 'Anna Parnell's 1881 visits and amazing sequels', *Mizen Journal, Mizen Archaeological and Historical Society*, 3 (1995), p. 51.
76. Membership book of Ballydehob branch of the National Land League, NAI, INLP; O'Regan, 'Anna Parnell's 1881 visits and amazing sequels', p. 51; Moody, *Davitt and the Irish Revolution 1846–82*, p. 457.
77. Constabulary report of land meeting held at Ballydehob, 30 Mar. 1881, reported by Sub-Inspector Jacob Ruttle, 5 Apr. 1881, NAI, INLP, box 8, envelope 72.
78. Speech of Anna Parnell, quoted in constabulary report of land meeting held at Ballydehob, 30 Mar. 1881, NAI, INLP, box 8, envelope 72.
79. Constabulary report of land meeting held at Ballydehob, 30 Mar. 1881, NAI, INLP, box 8, envelope 72.
80. Speech of John O'Connor, ibid.
81. Ibid.
82. Memo. of Swanton case from *West Cork Eagle* by Mr Plunket RM, quoting *West Cork Eagle*, 9 Apr. 1881, NAI, INLP, box 8, envelope 71.
83. Ballydehob crime and outrage report, pp. 4–5; *West Cork Eagle*, 9 Apr. 1881; evidence of

James Camier, 5 Dec. 1888, *Special Commission Act*, vol. i, p. 529; Memorandum of Proceedings in the Case of Richard Hodnett, NAI, INLP, box 9.

84. Copy of arrest warrant for Richard Hodnett, 18 Apr. 1881, NAI, INLP, box 9.
85. Evidence of Lang, *Special Commission*, vol. i, p. 526;
86. Ibid; *West Cork Eagle*, 30 Apr. 1881.
87. *West Cork Eagle*, 30 Apr. 1881.
88. Ibid.
89. Ibid.
90. Ibid.
91. Ibid.
92. Ballydehob crime and outrage report, p. 6, NAI, INLP.
93. Evidence of George Swanton, 5 Dec. 1888, *Special Commission*, vol. i, p. 529; membership book of Ballydehob branch of the National Land League, NAI, INLP; evidence of Lang, *Special Commission 1888*, vol. i, p. 526.
94. Henry F. Quirke, 'Diary of a Land League activist', *Skibbereen and District Historical Society*, 4 (2008), pp. 26–7.
95. Interview with Henry O'Mahony's grand-nephew Henry F. Quirke, 15 June 2008.
96. Quirke, 'Diary of a Land League activist', p. 27; evidence of Lang, *Special Commission*, vol. i, p. 527.
97. Edward O'Toole, *Whist for Your Life, That's Treason: Recollections of a Long Life* (Dublin: Ashfield, 2003), p. 28.
98. Quirke, 'Diary of a Land League activist', p. 24.
99. Interview with Henry Quirke, 15 June 2008; Quirke, 'Diary of a Land League activist', p. 24.
100. Quirke, 'Diary of a Land League activist', p. 23.
101. Ballydehob crime and outrage report, pp. 6–7, NAI, INLP.
102. List of Warrants by county and district, Skull, Cork West Riding, NAI, PPP, box 1; *The Times*, 6 June 1881.
103. Memorandum of proceedings for 127 prisoners arrested under the PPP (1881) Act, NAI, PPP, box 1 and box 2.
104. Sub-Inspector A. I. MacDonald, RIC, report on the arrest of Henry O'Mahony, 4 June 1881, NAI, CSORP/1881/21205.
105. Ibid.
106. Ballydehob crime and outrage report, p. 6, NAI, INLP, box 10; *The Times*, 6 June 1881; Report on the arrest of Henry O'Mahony, NAI, CSORP/1881/21205.
107. *The Times*, 6 June 1881; MacDonald, RIC report on the arrest of Henry O'Mahony, 4 June 1881, NAI, CSORP/1881/21205.
108. *The Times*, 6 June 1881; Report on the arrest of Henry O'Mahony, NAI, CSORP/1881/21205.
109. *Hansard*, cclxii (1881), c.983; Quirke, 'Diary of a Land League activist', p. 27.
110. H. W. Cobb to Rear Admiral R. T. Hamilton, 6 June 1881, NAI, CSORP/1881/19291.
111. Ibid.
112. *The Times*, 9 June 1881; Rear Admiral R. T. Hamilton to W. E. Forster, 8 June 1881, NAI, CSORP/1881/19372.
113. Telegram from Admiralty, Queenstown to W. E. Forster, 7 June 1881, NAI, CSORP/1881/19372; *The Times*, 9 June 1881.
114. *The Times*, 9 June 1881; Ballydehob crime and outrage report, p. 8, NAI, INLP.
115. Ballydehob crime and outrage report, p. 8, NAI, INLP.
116. DI Horne's report, 20 June 1881, NAI, CSORP/1881/21028; J. Moore Coffey to Head Constable Clark, 11 July 1881, NAI, INLP, box 9.
117. Chairman O'Donovan to Lord Cowper, 8 June 1881, NAI, CSORP/1881/19372.
118. *The Times*, 9 June 1881.
119. Ibid.
120. Ballydehob crime and outrage report, p. 8, NAI, INLP; James S. Donnelly, *Land and the People of Nineteenth-Century Cork: The Rural Economy and the Land Question* (London: Routledge & Kegan Paul, 1975), p. 276.
121. *The Times*, 18 June 1881.
122. *The Times*, 20 June 1881.
123. Sub-Inspector Hume, constabulary minute, 17 June 1881, NAI, CSORP/1881/20424.
124. 'Lady Resident of Skibbereen' to Lord Cowper, 7 June 1881, NAI, CSORP/1881/20424.

125. Hume, constabulary minute, 17 June 1881, NAI, CSORP/1881/20424. Note: abbreviations from original.
126. Sub-Inspector M. Hurley, constabulary report on Fenianism and the Land League in Ballydehob, 30 June 1881, NAI, CSORP/1881/23544.
127. Donnelly, *Land and the People of Nineteenth-Century Cork*, p. 282; Ballydehob crime and outrage report, p. 9, NAI, INLP.
128. Membership book of the Ballydehob branch of the Irish National Land League, NAI, INLP.
129. Minute book of the Ballydehob Land League branch, NAI, INLP, box 9; John Collins to Richard Hodnett, 20 June 1881, NAI, INLP, box 9.
130. List of warrants issued under Protection of Person and Property (Ireland) Act 1881, Co. Cork, Skull, NAI, PPP, box 1.
131. Sub-Inspector M. Hurley, RIC report on Ballydehob disturbances on 5 May 1882, NAI, CSORP/1882/25572.
132. Ibid.
133. Ballydehob crime and outrage report, p. 12, NAI, INLP; *Manchester Guardian*, 26 Feb. 1883.
134. Ballydehob crime and outrage report, p. 12.
135. *Manchester Guardian*, 10 Mar. 1883; anonymous to Richard Day, 27 Mar. 1883, NAI, INLP, box 8, envelope 40.
136. *Transactions of the Ossianic Society for the Year 1856* (1859), p. vii; *Transactions of the Ossianic Society for the Year 1853* (1854).
137. *Transactions of the Ossianic Society for the Year 1856* (1859); Denieffe, *Irish Republican Brotherhood*, p. 25.
138. *Transactions of the Ossianic Society for the Year 1856* (1859), p. ix.
139. *Transactions of the Ossianic Society for the Year 1853* (1854); *Transactions of the Ossianic Society for the Year 1856* (1859), pp. 334, 330, 335.
140. *Transactions of the Ossianic Society for the Year 1856* (1859), pp. 338–40.

5

Gunfire in Hayes's Hotel:
The IRB and the Founding
of the GAA

Paul Rouse

I

At 2 p.m. on Sunday 1 November 1884, seven men met in the billiards room of Lizzie Hayes's hotel in Thurles, Co. Tipperary. All were there in answer to circulars both published in the national press and distributed privately by Michael Cusack and Maurice Davin, two of the leading figures in Irish athletics. The ambition of the association they founded on that afternoon – the Gaelic Athletic Association – was to take control of Irish athletics, to resuscitate and promote the game of hurling, and to invent, and legislate for, a football game which came to be known as Gaelic football. Despite the pre-publicity, the poor attendance meant that this was not an occasion of glamour or glory. It would have surprised few people if the GAA had disappeared in as low-key a manner as it had been founded – after all, this is what happened to numerous other sporting clubs and organisations founded in that period. In time, the GAA, of course, would thrive to the point where it emerged as the most important sports organisation in Ireland.

From the very beginning, however, it was considered that the GAA was no mere sporting organisation. As the first historian of the GAA, T. F. O'Sullivan, put it in 1916, the men of the GAA founded the association to 'foster a spirit of earnest nationality' and as a 'means of saving thousands of young Irishmen from becoming mere West Britons'.[1] For some, the GAA was founded for a more definite political purpose. A police report written in the mid-1880s by Inspector A. W. Waters of the Royal Irish Constabulary's Crime Branch Special department in Dublin Castle claimed that the GAA had been founded by the Irish Republican Brotherhood. It had done so, he wrote, in preparation for the likely establishment of a home rule government in Dublin. According to Waters, the IRB had hit upon the idea of founding the GAA because of its desire to get 'the muscular youth of the country into an organisation, drilled and disciplined to form a physical power capable of over-awing and coercing the home rule government of the future'.[2]

The backdrop of the 1880s goes some way towards explaining the sense that the GAA was a political body, in whole or in part. This was a decade defined by a struggle for land and freedom. Debates on Irish affairs dominated the House of Commons in London, and the establishment of a home rule parliament in Dublin, led by Charles Stewart Parnell, emerged as a genuine possibility. Republican separatism targeted the very heart of British rule in Ireland with its most important officials in Ireland being murdered while out walking in the Phoenix Park in the summer of 1882. Bound up with this political upheaval was a dramatic battle over land ownership between landlords and their tenants. For month after month, whole swathes of the countryside were in tumult, with newspapers filling their pages with stories of evictions, boycotting and agrarian outrages by secret societies.

Ultimately, the politics of the 1880s and the vivid nature of the reports written by members of the police have influenced various historians to describe the founding of the GAA as a political act, rather than a sporting and cultural one. W. F. Mandle, for example, claimed in the 1970s that the GAA was 'founded, manipulated and sustained, first by the IRB and then by the nationalist movement as a whole'.[3] Mandle tempered this view somewhat in his book, *The GAA and Irish Nationalist Politics, 1884–1924*, but he continued to leave a heavy emphasis on IRB involvement, which he described as 'so influential'.[4] Mandle's work has also influenced books on the IRB, including those by Matthew Kelly and Owen McGee.[5] Historians of the GAA have also been swayed (though not necessarily by Mandle) to lend credence to the notion of the IRB as the key influence in founding the GAA. Marcus de Búrca, for example, had long been sceptical of exaggerated claims of IRB involvement, although acknowledging that the theory that the IRB were the true founders of the GAA had been handed down through the generations. More recently, de Búrca has written that, in the light of the new information (on which more later) which was coming to light, 'far from this theory fading out the further away we move from the 1880s, the more convincing it is becoming'.[6]

This sense that the GAA was somehow the creature of the IRB is shaped by a convergence of explanations, which are, in short:

1. That the IRB had decided to establish a nationalist sporting association in 1883 and that this decision eventually led to the founding of the GAA the following year.
2. That Michael Cusack was – or had been – a member of the IRB. And either knowingly or unknowingly was the front for the IRB in the establishment of the GAA.

3. That at least three or more of the seven men who attended that
   founding meeting of the GAA were active IRB men, and that
   these men – and many more – who developed and then ran th
   GAA at local and national level in the 1880s were involved in the
   IRB.
4. That, by 1887, three years after the GAA was founded, the IRB was
   in complete control of the GAA executive, thereby bringing into
   the open what had actually been the hidden reality all along.

The ambition of this chapter is to examine the strength – or otherwise –
of these four basic explanations.

II

The idea of IRB intrigue in the founding of the GAA begins with the assertion that, following an IRB meeting in June 1883, a sub-committee was
established to consider the idea of establishing a nationalist athletics movement. This sub-committee, chaired by P. N. Fitzgerald, a member of the
supreme council of the IRB, was said to have met in Blackrock, Co. Dublin,
in late 1883. As well as Fitzgerald, others reported as being present include
Patrick Hoctor, James Menton and Jim Boland. Having decided upon the
establishment of a sporting body, they are then said to have approached
Michael Cusack – owner of the most important grinds academy in
Dublin, and sometime journalist and athlete – winning his support for
the plan.[7] This story appears in various forms in the works of W. F.
Mandle, Owen McGee and various historians of the GAA. It cannot,
of course, be proven whether this meeting and subsequent process
happened or not, but its provenance seems more than a little suspect.
    The story of the IRB sub-committee seems to have first appeared in
a newspaper supplement, published in 1934 by the *Irish Press* to celebrate
the fiftieth anniversary of the founding of the GAA.[8] It is not mentioned,
for example, in T. F. O'Sullivan's *Story of the GAA*, published in 1916, or in
any other pre-1934 GAA publication. The author of the article in the *Irish
Press* supplement was Tom Markham, who was chairman of the Dublin
GAA minor board (the section of the GAA in Dublin which organised
players under the age of 18) in 1931. Markham was a civil servant who
was reputed to have been an undercover agent in Dublin Castle for
Michael Collins. It should be noted in passing that this role is entirely
unremarked upon in almost the entire body of literature on the war of
independence.[9]
    Markham's story is repeated in a manuscript written by Kevin Boland,
the Fianna Fáil TD, about his grandfather, Jim Boland, who was chairman
of the Dublin county board on his death in 1893, and who was one of the
IRB men who were supposed to have attended the meeting. Again, this

is problematic. Jim Boland was most likely in America in 1883, having fled there in the aftermath of the Phoenix Park murders of the previous year.[10] He returned to Ireland in 1885 and later became a prominent figure in Dublin GAA circles, while also drawing the attention of the police due to his association with the radical faction of the IRB.

One man who, according to Tom Markham, was supposed to have attended the meeting, but could not have, was Pat Nally. Nally was a leading member of the IRB who was arrested in May 1883 and was subsequently sentenced to ten years in prison following a conviction which was based on questionable evidence. He never left prison, dying in Mountjoy in 1891 in suspicious circumstances, amid allegations of mistreatment. Nally had been an outstanding athlete and had organised the 'National Sports of Mayo' on his father's land at Rockstown House in Balla, Co. Mayo.[11] This sports meeting was a clear rejection of the élitism which so often attended athletics meetings of that time. Nally's action drew the attention of Michael Cusack, and the two went walking in the Phoenix Park in Dublin later in 1879. Twenty years later – in the spring of 1899 – Michael Cusack wrote that his talk with Nally gave him much strength, encouragement and sustenance in his endeavour to establish the GAA. Cusack wrote: 'Great thoughts develop slowly. The two men agreed that an effort should be made to preserve the physical strength of our race.'[12] It must be remembered, however, that this is Cusack as an ageing man, writing about Nally long after the latter's martyrdom. Nally was a remarkable figure – powerful, heroic and beloved of nationalists – and it is eminently reasonable to suggest that his idea of founding a national sports organisation struck a chord with Michael Cusack. None the less, it is a simple fact that more than five more years were to pass after the meeting of Cusack and Nally before the GAA was established. During those five years, Cusack founded and played in a rugby team, extolled the virtues of cricket as the national game of Ireland and continued to play a prominent role in the existing athletics scene in Dublin.

Other fragments of folklore appear to support the idea of republican intrigue in the founding of the GAA. One such fragment recalls that on 15 August 1884 Michael Cusack was reputed to have taken the train to Galway and, in the early evening, joined a meeting of five local men in the home of leading IRB man, John Sweeney, in Loughrea. The men are reported to have confirmed their desire to establish a nationalist athletics association and to have walked 300 yards down the road to the residence of Dr Duggan, the Bishop of Clonfert. Duggan was renowned as a rather exceptional figure among the Irish Catholic hierarchy – he was nationalist, a man of the common people and a man who had supported the tenants of his diocese in their campaigns for land reform. Cusack asked Duggan to become patron of his new association. Duggan declined, saying that his health and advanced years (he was 71) were not conducive to assuming the position. He advised Cusack to go to Thurles and to approach Dr Thomas Croke, the archbishop of Cashel and Duggan's principal ally in the hierarchy, about becoming patron.[13]

There are several problems with this story. The surviving record is an oral one – of which there are several versions. All that is agreed is that a delegation did wait on Bishop Duggan on 15 August 1884 to discuss the setting up of a nationalist athletics or hurling organisation, centred on Loughrea. Against that, there is no agreement over which Galway men attended the meeting or that Michael Cusack even came to Loughrea at that time – and one account which actually does place Cusack in the town says that he chose not to accompany the delegation to meet the bishop. More than that, it is clear that, at least since May 1883 there had been rumours around Dublin that Cusack was about to strike out on his own in organising athletics in Ireland.[14] And in August 1884 Cusack was putting arrangements in place with the great Irish athlete, Maurice Davin, with a view towards establishing the GAA.

The role of Davin in founding the GAA is critical. He wrote the first constitution of the association, wrote the first GAA rules for football and hurling, and wrote the rules by which the GAA organised its athletics meetings. Davin was a large farmer with a river haulage business who was a social conservative. He lived until well into his eighties and left no record of political engagement. He was, instead, devoted to sport. He won numerous regattas, in rowing boats which he had built himself. He won the British amateur athletics championships in the 1870s and early 1880s, and was considered the finest weight thrower in the world. He was also a scholarly, studious man who planned his training in the most meticulous way. Such was his dedication that he kept a special notebook in which he detailed his diet and training and stuck newspaper cuttings of the performances of his competitors.[15] Davin had a track record of organising sports meetings around his home town of Carrick-on-Suir, Co. Tipperary, sometimes in concert with the local gentry.[16]

He had known Michael Cusack – a fellow weight thrower – since the mid-1870s, when both competed and officiated at athletics meetings in Dublin. A letter written by Cusack to Davin on 26 August 1884 emphasises the extent to which the founding of the GAA was motivated by sporting concerns. This letter – one which is clearly part of an ongoing correspondence the rest of which has been lost – sees Cusack cite the importance of having the association in place, with its rules properly drawn up, by the end of 1884.[17] Even allowing for this correspondence, it remains just about conceivable that the GAA was founded by men acting as a front for the IRB. And it is certainly more exciting to view this possibility as real. Perhaps Davin was duped by Cusack, who was acting in concert with the IRB. This, however, would appear to be a triumph of conspiracy over reason. The mundane truth is that, primarily, what was driving Michael Cusack and Maurice Davin was sport and not politics.

III

What would lend the story of IRB intrigue in the founding of the GAA greater credence – and this brings us to the second issue – is the notion that Michael Cusack, if not then a member of the IRB, was at the very least a former member who retained a deep sympathy with his one-time revolutionary colleagues. In his dying years, Michael Cusack did nothing to dissuade people from the belief that he had been a Fenian in his youth. He wrote in 1899, for example: 'I resolved to be a Fenian. In order to be a Fenian, I had to be a hurler.'[18] This and several other statements led Cusack's most prominent biographer – Marcus de Búrca – to note that it seems likely that Cusack had been among those who assembled under the cover of darkness in Corofin to take part in the IRB's failed rebellion of 1867.[19]

This seems most unlikely. Even Cusack himself never claimed to be out in '67. He did hold Fenian sympathies – of that there is no doubt – but it is a misreading to consider him to have been a member of the IRB in any meaningful way. This is because of the sheer weight of evidence which shows how Cusack lived his life. There was a restlessness, an individuality, an outspokenness to everything he did, which renders impractical the idea that he could ever merely be part of any movement – let alone a secret conspiracy. His career in education is a case in point. Through the 1870s Cusack had moved around, year on year, teaching in the élite public schools of Ireland before he established his own grinds school – Cusack's Academy. In the 1880s, nobody in Dublin was more successful than Michael Cusack in preparing students for the examinations that brought entry into the civil service of the British empire. Through his career in the public schools, Cusack had entered the world of codified British sports and he fell in love with that world. He was a particular devotee of cricket. As late as the summer of 1882, for example, he wrote: 'You may be certain that the boy who can play cricket well will not, in after years, lose his head and get flurried in the face of danger.'[20]

There are a lot of ironies contained in that sentence – not the least is the truth that, when it came to losing the head, Michael Cusack was in a league apart. As much as he was capable of extraordinary generosity and vision, he seemed equally incapable of diplomacy and was utterly devoid of perspective in personal exchanges. Overall, he could never be considered an easy man to work with and was, instead, more properly born to serve on a one-man committee. There are many examples of outrageous behaviour. In the year after the GAA was founded, the new association became embroiled in a bitter row with the Irish Amateur Athletic Association (IAAA), which had been formed by existing athletics clubs in response to the arrival of the GAA. Cusack was in his element as he attacked his opponents. At one point, for example, he described the IAAA as a 'ranting, impotent West British abortion'.[21] And when John Dunbar, the secretary of the IAAA, wrote a conciliatory letter to Cusack in the midst of their dispute, Cusack replied to him: 'Dear Sir, I received your letter this morning and burned it.'[22]

The thing about Cusack was that he made enemies within the GAA as easily as he did without. A mere eighteen months after the GAA was founded, he was removed from the association at a special meeting. It has been suggested in various quarters that this was an IRB-led heave, motivated on the understanding that Cusack had outlived his usefulness as a front for the Brotherhood. This is not the case. The GAA was thriving beyond all expectation by the middle of 1886, but Cusack had succeeded in alienating almost every section of the association, thanks to what one Cork GAA club described as 'the unfortunate knack possessed by Mr Cusack in a superlative degree of offending and insulting those with whom he comes in contact'.[23] On top of that, his administrative and organisational shortcomings were on a biblical scale. What is true is that the IRB did then take control of the central executive of the GAA in the summer of 1886. The manner in which the IRB assumed control of the GAA will be addressed later in this chapter but, to conclude on the matter of Cusack's relationship with the IRB, it should be noted that he immediately set about publicly excoriating the IRB men who replaced him at the head of the GAA. In a series of newspaper articles he condemned them as 'a junta of knaves and fools', 'a miserable mischievous traitorous gang' and, more simply, 'bastards'.[24] In return, he claimed he was physically assaulted at least three times, and also had shots fired over his head in the lobby of Hayes's hotel in Thurles.[25]

IV

The basic point is that it is impossible to see Cusack acting in concert with the IRB in founding the GAA – nor do I believe that he acted as their dupe. That is not to suggest that Cusack was not aware of the presence of various IRB men at the founding meeting of the GAA and of the prominence of IRB men in the early activities of a whole host of clubs. In founding the GAA, Cusack courted support from everywhere and this included men who were involved in the IRB. This is the third issue at hand. J. K. Bracken, a leading IRB man in Tipperary, and two other men, John McKay and John Wyse Power, who are also generally cited as Fenians, were present at the founding meeting of the GAA. Over the following months and years they were joined in the upper reaches of the association by other IRB men, such as P. N. Fitzgerald from Cork and Anthony Mackey from Limerick.[26]

The question is: were these men in thrall to sport or to republicanism? That is not to suggest that this is a mutually exclusive divide; of course it is not. None the less, the extent to which these men were motivated by sport is an important matter. They were republicans, but they were also Victorians, and a defining characteristic of Victorian life was the sports revolution that brought the origin of so many modern sporting bodies. The temptation is to look at the GAA in the context of the political upheavals of the 1880s – but the context of the development of modern organised sport is even more crucial. To this end, the engagement of IRB men such as J. E. Kennedy with the GAA cannot be seen as one which saw them simply do the bidding of the IRB. Kennedy was elected as vice-president of the GAA and is seen as a key man in the IRB drive to control the association. However, it should be remembered that his love of hurling predated even the establishment of the GAA. In 1883 he had actually brought hurleys to Dublin for Michael Cusack to help with the formation of a hurling club in the city and had later played in goal for that team. After the GAA was founded he continued to play the game and also refereed matches.

The story of J. K. Bracken is also of note. Bracken was at the founding meeting and was one of the most important figures in establishing the GAA across Tipperary. He was also an active IRB member who regularly featured in police files as a committed revolutionary. On the surface, he seems to epitomise the manner in which the GAA was controlled by the IRB. And yet the lengths to which Bracken went to further the cause of his club, Templemore, are not easily explained by politics. In October 1887, Templemore were playing the semi-final of the first ever All-Ireland Football Championship against the Limerick Commercials. With the game nearly over and the Commercials pushing for a winning goal, a Commercials player found himself alone with the ball in front of the Templemore goals. He was about to shoot the winning score when he was grabbed by Bracken and thrown to the ground. The tackle has always been difficult to define in Gaelic football, but this was a foul – one made considerably worse by the fact that Bracken was actually a match umpire, and not a player.[27] Although Templemore went on to win the match, the Central Council of the GAA ordered that it be replayed on account of Bracken's behaviour and Commercials duly won out, before going on to win the final. I should add here that in the mid-1890s, when the GAA came extremely close to disappearing altogether following lengthy internal disputes, Bracken remained involved, working to organise hurling and football across Tipperary, refereeing matches and serving his club.[28]

But even if IRB men like Kennedy and Bracken, who were active in the GAA, had actually founded and run the association with a purely political purpose in mind, the reality of the GAA's politics was mixed and often moderate. By the beginning of 1887 there were over 400 clubs affiliated to the GAA, so it is scarcely a surprise that the politics of the association should reflect the range of political sentiment within the nationalist community. Many Irish nationalists, after all, were quite content to live within the British empire, even in the polarised politics of the 1880s. In Wicklow, for example, the Bray Emmets GAA club was criticised for flying Union Jacks above the fields during a sports day and for carrying out those sports in a 'thoroughly West British fashion'.[29] The club was also derided for giving the use of their club rooms for unionist meetings and it was alleged that in its politics it was 'a Unionist club'. These allegations were made by a 'Bray Nationalist' who wrote to the *Drogheda Independent* in advance of a proposed match in Drogheda, Co. Louth between the Bray Emmets and the Drogheda Gaelic Club. Upon publication of this letter – and despite the fact that the allegations were unproven – the Drogheda Gaelic Club refused to play the Bray team. It says much for the shades of nationalist opinion within the GAA and the political priorities (or lack of such priorities) of its members that another Drogheda club, the Davitts, were more than willing to play the Emmets. A huge crowd turned out to watch the match, played at Shamrock Lodge a mile outside Drogheda town.[30]

The evident diversity of political allegiance within the GAA is everywhere, even in the names chosen by the clubs. In respect of the apparent political allegiances of members, there were clubs called after republican martyrs, such as Wolfe Tones, Robert Emmetts, Henry Grattans; clubs called after constitutional nationalists, such as Daniel O'Connells and Parnells; and clubs called after saints, such as St Finbarr's and St John's. There were also clubs called after places of work and professions, including the Grocers' Assistants, the GPO and the Commercials. Some clubs simply took the name of the locality in which they were based, for example Cloyne and Moycarkey, while other clubs might have borrowed their names from the lexicon of British public school sport, including Dauntless of Rathmines. In Westmeath the Kinnegad Slashers GAA Club met on Sunday afternoons to play matches among themselves and divided their number into Tories versus Liberals. And, finally, there was the club named after a British prime minister: Gladstonians.[31]

The diversity of political opinion within the GAA was such that, in the summer of 1887, a deputation from the Cork Executive of the association travelled across the Irish Sea to Swansea in Wales to make a presentation to the former British prime minister, William Gladstone. Gladstone may have been unsuccessful in his attempts to introduce home rule to

Ireland, but he was viewed as a hero by many moderate nationalists. The Cork GAA members, in conjunction with the Cork Protestant Home Rule Association, made a presentation to Gladstone of a miniature gold hurley, which he immediately fixed to his watch-chain. They also presented him with a shield bearing the inscription: 'To the Right Hon. W. E. Gladstone, MP, from the Cork County Executive of the Gaelic Athletic Association, 1887'. The shield also carried the Cork coat-of-arms, surrounded by emblems of a wolfhound, a round tower and a harp, and the entire production rested on a spray of shamrocks. Finally, the GAA delegation – at least one of whom was reported to be an IRB man – presented Gladstone with a hurley, a regular match ball and a copy of the GAA rules.[32]

Naturally, of course, even if the IRB did not found the GAA, the success of the association inevitably attracted IRB men, who saw it as a vehicle for revolution rather than recreation. One radical newspaper columnist looked at the hurlers who took the field for the first All-Ireland hurling final in 1887 and proclaimed that he would 'teach them that the goal of their ambition should be the happiness and independence of their native land'. He wrote: 'I could not help wishing that I were at the head of ten thousand such gallant fellows for the short space of one week. What work would I not accomplish for my native land. From Malin Head to Mizen Head, and from Achill to Donaghadee, I would rid the country of slavery.'[33] Making their way to the head of the GAA was an obvious step for any member of an organisation wishing to 'rid the country of slavery'.

V

This leads to the fourth and final issue – the take-over of the GAA by the IRB. At the GAA's second annual convention in Thurles on 15 November 1886, the IRB moved from symbolism to substance as they claimed almost every position of importance in the GAA. All four vice-presidents, all four secretaries and the position of treasurer were claimed by men who were in the IRB.[34] The president of the supreme council of the IRB, John O'Leary, was also invited to join Croke, Davitt and Parnell as the fourth patron of the GAA. The only remaining official of importance who was not in the IRB was the re-elected president, Maurice Davin.

The IRB now controlled the GAA, but what exactly did that control mean and what could the IRB do with the GAA now that it was in control? This was a conundrum which the IRB sought to solve throughout 1887. Police informers were of the view that it was all about men and money. It is a signature tune of the Victorian sports revolution that it generated money through gate receipts. This was an almost entirely new phenomenon and it was one which the GAA benefited from. From the summer of 1886 onwards it was a regular occurrence for several thousands to pay into matches in towns and villages across Ireland. Little of this money came back to the GAA's central committees, finding its way instead into the accounts of local clubs or into the pockets of local entrepreneurs. Reports from Clare and from Kerry record the belief that the GAA became a money-making machine for the IRB. One correspondent, Maurice O'Halloran, wrote from Clare: 'As the cool, moderate people say, "Tis only a swindle for Fenian organisers to make money out of."'[35]

More than money, however, the GAA was seen as a place where the IRB found a fertile recruiting ground. Over the years informants painted vivid (occasionally fanciful) pictures of how GAA players were sworn into the IRB. One informer recounted how, initially, hints are given to a player that the person they are talking to is involved in 'a higher club'. Later, the discussion is moved to talk about various Irish patriots such as Robert Emmet, Lord Edward Fitzgerald or the Manchester Martyrs and 'a close watch is kept on the patient to observe how the bait takes'. Then, if the player appears a suitable candidate, he is plied with drink, to see if he can hold his tongue, or if he is given to blabbing. Finally, if all is well, the candidate is brought to some dark place and asked will he 'join the IRB and fight for the Republic'. And, with that, he is sworn in to the IRB.[36]

It is impossible to quantify how well the IRB did out of the GAA in terms of men and money. Presumably, this is something that varied from locality to locality – something the IRB could have managed without actually taking central control of the association. If the desire was to impose some sort of centralised order on the flow of money and on the recruitment of men, it simply did not happen. Centralised recruitment of men was obviously not an option, and it was not until well into the twentieth century that the GAA successfully centralised its finances.

What the IRB actually tried to do was to take control of the clubs of the GAA by bringing them to the heel of the central executive. They did this in February 1887 at a meeting of the central executive in Wynn's hotel in Dublin. Firstly, they appointed all members of the executive as *ex officio* members of every GAA county committee in the country, with full voting rights. Secondly, they decided that no GAA event could take place in any club in Ireland without the sanction of a county committee. Thirdly, it was ordered that every club that wished to hold an event had to forward a copy of the programme and a list of club officials to one of the secretaries of the association. Fourthly, all members of the police were banned from membership of the GAA and from competing at GAA athletics meetings.[37] The executive added these new rules to the existing constitution, altered several of the old rules, printed up copies and distributed them across the country.

The result was a year of extraordinary discontent. Maurice Davin, the president of the GAA, had not been present at the meeting where these rules were passed and he resigned in protest. Across the country, clubs refused to abide by the new constitution. Two of Dublin's leading athletics' clubs – the Grocers' Assistants club and the Freeman's Journal club – refused to submit to the rule of the executive in the running of their annual sports. The executive responded in a fierce manner. The Grocers' Assistants club was expelled from the association, all members of the Dublin GAA county committee who had supported the Grocers' Assistants were also expelled, and all the athletes who had competed at the sports were suspended for three months.[38] From that moment on, the GAA was divided between those who supported the IRB-controlled executive and those who began to organise against it.

Events came to a head at the GAA's annual convention in November 1887 in Thurles courthouse. More than six hundred men filled the room and they witnessed extraordinary scenes. The meeting was being chaired by P. N. Fitzgerald – a member of the supreme council of the IRB – when the platform was stormed by a Nenagh curate, Fr John Scanlan, who was backed by several other priests. Sticks were brandished as the opposing sides pushed each other around the judges' benches. IRB man Anthony Mackey was reported to have roared out: 'We'll pulverise the priests.' With that, the reporters' table collapsed and men fell to the floor. Order was only restored when Fr Scanlan retreated from the room, followed by around a hundred supporters.[39]

This convention has wrongly been interpreted as a simple battle between priests and republicans for control of the GAA. It was more than that. There was a third group in the room – the representatives of clubs who were there for the simple love of sport. They followed neither the clergy nor the IRB, but were there to vindicate the rights of Maurice Davin, who they wished to see returned as president of the GAA. They numbered more than two hundred men and would have succeeded in seeing Davin re-elected had not the IRB rigged the final ballot. Later, these men refused to join Fr Scanlan in his attempt to set up a rival priest-led GAA, preferring instead to fight for control of the association. Over the following five years, contests for control of the GAA all but destroyed it. Throughout these contests what became abundantly clear was that, although the IRB were skilled at winning control of the central executive of the GAA, they were unable to exercise that control in any meaningful way on the ordinary clubs of the association. When they sought to ignore that reality, the GAA all but collapsed. The nadir was reached in the years after the Parnell split. By 1893, fewer than twenty people were attending the annual convention and most counties in the country were entirely unrepresented. The IRB's attempt to control the GAA in its first decade ultimately ended in failure.

Failure to exercise control did not lead to abandonment of involvement. Through the remainder of the 1890s and on through the revolutionary period, IRB men continued to hold high office within the GAA and retained a certain influence on the running of the association. In the first decade of the twentieth century, for example, a series of rules were put in place which banned all who played rugby, soccer, hockey and cricket from joining the GAA. That ban was later extended to include those who served in the British army. Such rules were opposed by a significant section of the association's membership and it remained the case that those who played Gaelic games were of divergent (or of no) political views.[40] The influence which the IRB appeared to exert at national and provincial levels of the GAA was not often significantly reflected at the local level. Individual members and certain clubs may have held radical republican views, but the GAA as a whole did not – and never could – do the bidding of any political organisation, much less an organisation such as the IRB. More than that, as one leading GAA official complained in 1914, for the vast majority of GAA members, their 'nationalist sentiment begins and ends with the mere practice of kicking a football or striking a hurling ball'.[41] This was a complaint typical of officials who despaired of their failure to radicalise their fellow members. It was further evidence that, instead of being in the vanguard of the revolution, the nationalist sentiment of the GAA fell and rose in line with that of the wider nationalist community throughout its history.

NOTES

1. T. F. O'Sullivan, *Story of the GAA* (Dublin, 1916), p. 1.
2. Report by Inspector A. W. Waters, 11 Nov. 1887, National Archives of Ireland, Crime Branch Special, 126/S.
3. W. F. Mandle, 'The Gaelic Athletic Association and popular culture, 1884–1924', in Oliver MacDonagh, W. F. Mandle and Pauric Travers (eds), *Irish Culture and Nationalism, 1750–1950* (Dublin: Gill & Macmillan, 1983), p. 105.
4. W. F. Mandle, *The GAA and Irish Nationalist Politics, 1884–1924* (Dublin: Gill & Macmillan, 1987), p. 221.
5. See, for example, Matthew Kelly, *The Fenian Ideal and Irish Nationalism, 1822–1916* (Woodbridge: Boydell & Brewer, 2006) and Owen McGee, *The IRB: The Irish Republican Brotherhood from the Land League to Sinn Féin* (Dublin: Four Courts Press, 2005).
6. Marcus de Búrca, 'J. K. Bracken centenary: a reflection', *Tipperary Historical Journal* (2004), pp. 263–4, 263.
7. W. F. Mandle, 'The IRB and the beginnings of the GAA', *Irish Historical Studies*, 20/80 (1977), p. 420; Meelick GAA Club, *Centenary of the First All-Ireland Hurling Final* (Galway: Meelick GAA, 1888).
8. *Irish Press Jubilee Supplement*, 14 Apr. 1934, p. 56.
9. It is included in William Nolan (ed.), *The Gaelic Athletic Association in Dublin 1884–2000* (Dublin: Geography Publications, 2005), pp. 234–5. The Markham Cup, awarded to the winners of the All-Ireland minor football championship was donated after his death in 1939.
10. See David Fitzpatrick, *Harry Boland's Irish Revolution* (Cork: Cork University Press, 2004), ch. 2.
11. Páraig Ó Baoighill, *Nally as Maigh Eo* (Dublin: Binn Éadair, 1998).
12. *United Irishman*, 4 Mar. 1899.
13. Mandle, 'The IRB and the beginnings of the GAA', p. 420; Meelick GAA Club, *Centenary of the First All-Ireland Hurling Final*.
14. *Sport*, 19 May 1883.

15. Maurice Davin notebook, GAA Museum and Archive, Croke Park, Dublin.
16. Séamus Ó Riain, *Maurice Davin: First President of the GAA* (Dublin: Geography Publications, 1994), *passim.*
17. Maurice Davin file, GAA MA.
18. *United Irishman*, 25 Mar. 1899.
19. Marcus de Búrca, *Michael Cusack and the GAA* (Dublin: Anvil Books, 1989), p. 25.
20. *The Shamrock*, 8 July 1882.
21. Mandle, *The GAA and Irish Nationalist Politics*, pp. 21–3.
22. *United Ireland*, 19 Dec. 1885.
23. *Sport*, 27 Mar. 1886.
24. *Celtic Times*, 15 Oct. 1887.
25. *Celtic Times*, 12 Nov. 1887.
26. There is considerable dispute over how many people actually attended the meeting. Many more people claimed later to have been present than were actually listed. There is no conclusive proof that more than the seven people who were listed in press reports actually attended. Even allowing for the fact that up to thirteen people might have attended, it does not change the basic fact that members of the IRB were prominent at the meeting.
27. *Sport*, 29 Oct. 1887.
28. See Nancy Murphy, 'Joseph K. Bracken: GAA founder, Fenian and politician', in William Nolan (ed.), *Tipperary: History and Society* (Dublin: Geography Publications, 1985), pp. 379–93.
29. *Celtic Times*, 8 Oct. 1887.
30. Ibid.
31. For further evidence of the wide range of names given to GAA teams see match reports in the *Celtic Times* and *Sport*, 1886–9, *passim.*
32. *Celtic Times*, 11 June 1887 and *Sport*, 11 June 1887.
33. *Midland Tribune*, 5 Apr. 1888.
34. Mandle, 'The IRB and the beginnings of the GAA', p. 420.
35. Maurice O'Halloran letter, 9 Nov. 1887, NAI, CBS 126/1.
36. RIC Report, 14 Apr. 1890, NAI, CBS 296/S.
37. *Sport*, 28 Feb. 1887 and 5 Nov. 1887.
38. Mandle, 'The IRB and the beginnings of the GAA', p. 429
39. *Sport*, 12 Nov. 1887.
40. William Murphy, 'The GAA and the Irish revolution', in Mike Cronin, William Murphy and Paul Rouse (eds), *The Gaelic Athletic Association, 1884–2009* (Dublin: Irish Academic Press, 2009), *passim.*
41. *Gaelic Athlete*, 19 July 1914.

6

A Period of Nationalist Flux:
The IRB and the Growth of Devlinite Nationalism in East Tyrone, 1902–7

Fergal McCluskey

I

In early 1900, almost a decade after the Parnellite split, the leaders of the Irish Party's three main factions, John Redmond, T. M. Healy and John Dillon, had all declared for unity. However, the impending reunion was not based on meaningful reconciliation, but rather political expediency. As Patrick Maume explains: 'They began a process of reunification of the MPs, led from above, to counter the United Irish League (UIL) threat growing up from below.'[1] Owen McGee goes further, arguing that the United Irish League's creation allowed the 'Catholic political establishment' to reassert 'control of popular political activity in the country. This was done not merely by championing the land question but also by attempting to capitalise upon popular enthusiasm for the 1798 celebrations.'[2]

In a strategy which characterised the constitutional leadership's reaction to a series of indigenous popular organisations, the UIL's early radical and popular platform was modified in order to ensure the maintenance of the Irish Party's power.[3] Maume describes the phenomenon as 'Irish Party "vampirism" – co-opting new organisations, absorbing the activists and leaving the shell'.[4] This process was not as one-sided as it appeared. For example, in western Ireland, continued Fenian-inspired 'agrarian militancy' obliged the party 'to adopt a radical agrarian policy in June 1907'.[5] However, outside Connacht, the UIL was certainly not 'the Land League reborn'.[6] In East Tyrone, the League was largely concerned with registering nationalist voters for the notoriously close electoral struggles against local unionists.[7] As such, positions of authority on UIL executives were divided between the two factions of the old anti-

Parnellite Irish National Federation – the clericalist Healyites and the more populist Dillonite element.[8]

Rather than the land issue, the demand for self-government dominated the local agenda and enthusiasm for the '98 celebrations excited popular nationalist passions: a situation reinforced by the fact that local politics was 'cast in the denominational mould which has characterised them ever since'.[9] Within this distinctively northern context, one shaped by the reality of a significant adversarial loyalist community, a different species of popular organisation emerged – the Ancient Order of Hibernians (AOH). In 1891 the RIC 'pooh-poohed this (largely Parnellite) body' as 'scarcely worth considering', though it added the prophetic caveat that 'in the hands of clever and designing leaders' it 'might even become dangerous'.[10] By 1911 the order was the strongest nationalist organisation in Tyrone, with the county's eighty-five divisions constituting local constitutionalism's backbone.[11] This expansion took place under the stewardship of Joseph Devlin, Board of Erin president from July 1905. However, in a process reminiscent of the transformation of the western UIL, Devlin had responded to an organic growth in Hibernianism, which had its origins in an arc along the western shores of Lough Neagh. Ironically this growth was largely generated by local IRB attempts to use the order to assist the '98 anniversary celebrations, increase membership and propagate the Fenians' 'democratic and republican social ideal' within the wider nationalist community.[12]

It appears Hibernianism was being pulled in opposite directions by two rival ideological groups – but this is not the whole story. This chapter will demonstrate how local Fenians actually contributed to Devlin's eventual ascendancy. It will also attempt to analyse how and why republicanism, after a promising start in terms of gaining a controlling influence, failed to carry local Hibernianism. The key to understanding this lies in an examination of the means by which northern constitutionalism, through Devlin, eventually harnessed the AOH as its chief organ of popular constitutional mobilisation and discipline in the province.

The reunification of the Irish Party coincided with the meteoric rise of 'Wee Joe'. Devlin was an elementary-educated member of the Falls Road working-class community, one-time bottle washer and *Irish News* journalist, whose platform oratory not only earned him the nickname 'Pocket Demosthenes' but the political patronage of John Dillon, MP. These credentials eventually led him to be appointed as UIL secretary in 1902. Like his political mentor, Devlin was obsessed with centralised control. He built his early career on routing Bishop Henry's Catholic Association. Although fundamentally an attack on any independent voice, Devlin's success exploited the language of militant popular nationalism, the growth of democracy and working-class welfarism.[13]

What, then, were Devlin's intentions in harnessing the Hibernian

movement? Owen McGee emphasises Devlin's pivotal role in the establishment of the Belfast United '98 Centenary Association, arguing that he
'revived the sectarian Ancient Order of Hibernians in Ulster with the
clergy's support to counteract the republicans'.[14] As a conclusion this has
definite merit: Devlin manipulated the '98 centenary to garner majority
support within Ulster nationalism, the AOH was the organisational vehicle for this take-over, and the ultimate objective was the consolidation
of the position of the constitutionalist leadership and their moderate
agenda.

However, although Devlin sought to control popular nationalism as
early as 1897, this remained a work-in-progress well into the first half of
the next decade. This was partly because the Irish Party's reunification
had really only papered over the cracks of the Parnellite split. McGee
treats the Catholic establishment as a political monolith. Devlin certainly had several clerical backers, particularly Bishop O'Donnell of Raphoe;
however sizeable elements of the northern clergy were intent on unilat-
eral control of Catholic politics and demonstrated equal antipathy
towards both republicanism and popular Dillonite constitutionalism.
Devlin's genius was to camouflage the contest for control of moderate
constitutionalism as a battle between the forces of democracy and reaction – thus actually generating Fenian support. It was only after he had
cleared the initial conservative hurdle that the AOH was directed against
the northern IRB, the erstwhile supporters of burgeoning Hibernianism.
The politicisation that resulted from the '98 centenary shaped popular
constitutionalism's rhetorical agenda over the next decade; but if, as
Matthew Kelly argues, 'once the political holiday of 1898 was over, most
were happy, stimulated but under-challenged, to return to their constitutionalist homes',[15] it is equally true that any nationalist politician intent
on winning widespread support was forced to tailor rhetoric to these very
turn-of-the-century ideals. Devlin's mastery of northern nationalism lay
in his innate ability to balance *realpolitik* with the appeasement of the
popular mindset – if history 'is nothing but the activity of men in pursuit
of their ends', Devlin did indeed make his own history; but he did not
make it just as he pleased, or under circumstances chosen by himself,
'but under circumstances directly encountered, given and transmitted
from the past'.[16]

A similar process to the Irish Party's vampirism of the UIL took place
in relation to Hibernianism – though the socio-political materials at
Devlin's disposal differed. Hibernianism in the 1890s was essentially a relic
of earlier secret societies with their often ill-defined and contradictory
blend of republicanism, sectarianism and concepts of lower-class social
justice.[17] Throughout the 1890s local republicans had fostered links with
the rural AOH in east Tyrone.[18] In the wake of the local '98 movement,

provincial IRB leader Neal John O'Boyle persisted with the Fenians' traditional policy of infiltration, attempting 'to direct the IRB's new working-class and much more militant following, centred in East Tyrone'.[19] As such, a state of flux existed between 1902 and 1906, where the ultimate control and nature of grassroots northern nationalism had not yet fully settled. From this perspective the long rhetorical shadow cast locally by the '98 centenary celebrations is a logical starting point.

II

The police reported a 'decided stir' in Fenianism by mid-1895, and the local '98 centenary was unequivocally Fenian-inspired.[20] By the height of the '98 movement, the centenary had stimulated a 'considerable increase of activity amongst the old Fenians, and it is beyond doubt that old circles have been reformed'.[21] The release of Fenian dynamitard and Dungannon native Tom Clarke in 1898 further stimulated local republican efforts. According to local Fenian W. J. Kelly, Clarke 'lived on and off in Dungannon' and 'organised some circles of the IRB'.[22]

The IRB did indeed use the centenary to promulgate the Fenian faith. However, the movement's rapid spread led to a loss of Fenian influence, a trend aggravated by the split in the national movement.[23] Added to this, a Devlinite Ulster executive was formed in Belfast as a weapon against the clerical influence of Bishop Henry's Catholic Association.[24] In East Tyrone, predominately Dillonite branches, usually extensions of Hibernian divisions, soon outnumbered Fenian clubs. By the movement's zenith, it had generated considerable popular militancy, but the reality, as Matthew Kelly argues, was that moderate constitutionalists 'dominated the speech-making, and the insurrectionary talk of the preceding months was largely absent from the official proceedings'.[25] The movement was, however, massively popular: the police and both sides of the journalistic spectrum referred to 'enormous crowds', which the RIC stated were entirely composed of 'the extreme section of Irish Nationalism'.[26]

Dillonites may well have restrained the movement's more militant impulses, but their language at least was forced to reflect the advanced sentiment stoked up by the '98 anniversary. The need to placate militant sentiment played a major role in continued constitutionalist support for the movement, despite the fact that constitutionalism's ultimate trajectory did not conform to the expectations implicit in such rhetoric. This divergence between rhetoric and reality left constitutionalism vulnerable to republican attack. On St Patrick's Day 1899, leading Hibernian and Ardboe IRB centre, James Devlin, told a massive Hibernian demonstration in Dungannon that 'if ever the day came when a blow was required to be struck at our old enemy – England – he was sure that the men here around him would strike a blow for freedom'. Stewartstown's J. J. Lowe stated that they were not 'here to celebrate any of the recent victories of Lord Kitchener or any other of England's butchers'.[27] In this respect the IRB leadership's entryist strategy towards the AOH made sense, as republicans could argue that their agenda better conformed to popular sentiment.

At this stage AOH membership was still dominated by small farmers and labourers in the countryside and the working classes in the towns. Local Fenians and Hibernians shared a demographic profile, nascent economic-corporate identity and militant nationalist disposition.[28] By 1903 members of both organisations were involved in the county's thirty-eight UIL branches, with 'most local Fenians also belonging to the AOH and UIL'.[29] In this context local Fenians initiated the 1903 Emmet centenary celebration, an attempt to reignite the grassroots enthusiasm of the '98 commemoration and gain further influence over local Hibernianism. The RIC reported that

> an association known as the 'Emmet Centenary club' was formed in Dungannon on the 1st May believed to be the result of P. T. Daly's visit in March last ... The club was started by IRB men, the intention evidently being to strengthen the 'physical force' party. All nationalists are permitted to attend the meetings ... and efforts are being made to get AOH men to join. This will no doubt be a fresh source of danger to the public peace in Dungannon.[30]

The Emmet club committee had forty-three members. The membership, although predominantly republican, contained several prominent Hibernians.[31] Because of the central Fenian policy of infiltrating the wider constitutional movement, Irish Party patronage of the celebration was actually encouraged. At the December 1903 Emmet rally in Dungannon, the main platform speaker, J. G. Swift McNeill, MP epitomised the trend within the party towards quasi-separatist rhetoric when he declared:

> The aim of the Irish Volunteers, of the United Irishmen, of the men of '98 and '48 and '67 and today of the United Irish League is to win salvation for our native land, to free her from the grasp of ignorant, insolent and rapacious strangers ... The principle of Irish nationality which produces men of the Emmet type and treasures their memory in passionate remembrance is indestructible.[32]

By 1903 a loose popular militant consensus had been formed but its future direction remained unclear. The emerging consensus was also firmly based on a lower-class appetite for popular democratisation. Both movements viewed control of the UIL as a means of subverting local

Healyite influence, a process actively encouraged by Joseph Devlin. However, the popular agents who effectively achieved Devlin's control of Ulster constitutionalism were unaware of the subtlety and cynicism of the party's rhetoric. Indeed, despite the fact that P. T. Daly's policy towards the League was 'one of general courtesy and civility',[33] local Fenian support for Devlin's anti-Healyite campaign may well have relied as heavily on the local demand for democratisation as on the intentions of their leaders.

In this respect the Emmet centenary celebrations in Belfast proved noteworthy. The police stated that 'the secret societies, and the official leaders of the Belfast United Irish League supported by the *Star* newspaper, are strongly in favour of the movement' which was condemned by Dr Henry's Catholic Association.[34] However, P. T. Daly and Devlin's support for the Emmet commemoration served different political objectives. For Daly, it was an effort to instil republican sentiment and attract membership; for Devlin, it galvanised popular support against the rival Catholic Association. Arguably, neither the majority of Fenians nor Hibernians participated in order to consciously fulfil their respective leaderships' objectives. Rather, the commemoration was an articulation of shared militant nationalism, acting as another outlet for popular fraternisation and social interaction.

This may explain why in 1903, at the same time that grassroots Fenians and Hibernians co-ordinated an attack on the UIL's Healyite East Tyrone executive, Devlin was attempting to coax the AOH into the mainstream by seeking 'the countenance of the Roman Catholic clergy', while the Clan na Gael envoy, John T. Keating, simultaneously sought 'to unite the AOH and IRB in opposing the constitutional movement'. The fact that Keating 'failed to carry the AOH with him' greatly contributed to the subsequent breakdown of Fenian–Hibernian relations.[35] However, while political control remained in flux for a further two years, the rank-and-file of the East Tyrone IRB and AOH subscribed to a shared political programme.

III

The Hibernian–Fenian combined attack was predicated on attacking the undemocratic process by which MPs and local UIL councillors were selected. The UIL executives in the East and Mid-Tyrone constituencies were dominated by a coterie of solicitors who carried out registration work, and carried away substantial fees into the bargain, the county inspector noting that 'the UIL is a somewhat tame organisation in this county'.[36]

The Hibernians, on the other hand, were far from tame. The order's

marches, commemorations and penchant for recreational violence made
it the county's most popular and flourishing nationalist institution. There
was significant resentment that when elections arrived the Hibernians
had a disproportionately small voice in the selection of candidates. There
was also a widespread feeling that the middle class used the League to
access political patronage and gain social prestige. In 1902 the popular
nationalist *Ulster Herald* criticised such Leaguers: 'no sooner did they get
in than they rejected their contract and gave up the United Irish League.
They should show that they were not going to assist flunkeyism in this
country, no matter whether it came from clergyman or layman.'[37]

The Hibernians were determined to bend the League to their representative and advanced nationalist will. A succession of local electoral
disputes ensued, with frequently violent exchanges between the
Hibernians and affluent Leaguers.[38] The most decisive case occurred at
Pomeroy in 1902, when leading Hibernian, Irish National Forester and
former Fenian, Terence McGuone challenged the East Tyrone Executive
candidate John Doris, JP.[39] The Hibernian-dominated UIL branch in
neighbouring Carrickmore denounced 'the practical disfranchisement of
the delegates from Creggan electoral division' and the actions of the East
Tyrone Executive 'in arbitrarily refusing to allow said delegates to exercise the right of voting, or have a voice in the selection of a candidate'.[40]
A full-scale faction fight ensued in Pomeroy, with the Hibernians tri-
umphing through a combination of weight of numbers and political
'zeal'.[41] This underlined the fact that if the UIL's national directory
ignored the strength of the Hibernian demand, the chief nationalist
organisation in the county might well be lost to the party.

The year after the Pomeroy faction fight, the Hibernians' Lady Day
procession was deliberately held in the town, Terence McGuone being
elected platform president. The county inspector reported:

> By special and secret arrangements the meeting had the support of
> the IRB in the locality. It was presided over by an expelled member of
> the UIL [McGuone] and was addressed by two members of parlia-
> ment, whose presence at such gathering was so much resented local-
> ly that some withdrew their support from the UIL ... The priests did
> all in their power to prevent the meeting being a success, but large
> numbers of people as already stated attended ... On the 13th August
> some members of the IRB held a meeting in Dungannon and decided
> to support ... the Pomeroy meeting.[42]

Pomeroy signalled the culmination of the Hibernian coup and the presence of the local MP (P. C. Doogan) demonstrated the Irish Party's anx-
iety to bring the potentially volatile Hibernians in from the cold. Terence
McGuone asserted that the Hibernians were not being 'asked to lay down

their flags' and if the Irish Party 'lost the Ancient Order of Hibernians they would lose the Irish cause in Tyrone of the O'Neills' – a point which the party was evidently well aware of.[43] This does little, however, to explain Fenian support for the meeting.

IV

Speaking in retrospect, Denis McCullough claimed: 'The IRB in my time was not wedded or pledged to action in arms only; it was prepared to back any man or movement that had separation from England as its final objective.'[44] As such, its main impulse was organisational, resulting in the formation of new units around existing cells comprised of 'mostly old IRB men', like 'Jack McElvogue and Willy Kelly in Dungannon'.[45] Members of these cells then infiltrated wider nationalist groups.

The absence of land agitation and the power struggle between perceived conservative and democratic factions for control of local constitutionalism, represented by the Hibernian assault on League 'shoneenism', clarified the issue in local Fenian minds. In addition, there was considerable dual membership, as the IRB's clandestine organisation and network of cells had greatly facilitated recent Hibernian growth. In May 1904 the local RIC reported that the Donaghmore Hibernian branch was 'arranged by IRB men' and was 'proof that the latter is working under the cloak of the AOH'. However, the same report noted that at Hibernian meetings in Moy, Killeenan and Donaghmore,

> a letter was read from John Dillon, County Delegate, asking if any IRB men belonged to the branch. This is regarded as indicating an ostensible intention to expel IRB men from the society. The necessity for this is to ward off clerical hostility and be prepared for any representation that may be made at the next synod of bishops at Maynooth.[46]

In fact, Dillon was a prominent Cookstown Fenian. These push-and-pull factors represented by republican infiltration and the desire to gain mainstream respectability characterised the ambiguous position of Fenians within the Hibernians. After all, Dillon was also the county delegate to the Board of Erin.[47] Indeed, he was selected by the board to negotiate a union with the American AOH in 1907, after the American and Irish orders split again in the wake of the failure of the Keating mission of 1903. It was not surprising, then, in an attack on Joe Devlin and the Irish Party's seizure of the Board of Erin, that Clan na Gael's *Gaelic American* absolved Dillon of responsibility.[48]

Up until Devlin's absolute take-over, the order's fusion of democratic and separatist language stimulated Fenian interest. Despite a nominal secular republican ethos, local Fenians were overwhelmingly Catholic and would have had little compunction in tolerating or ignoring the AOH's crude sectarianism. At the 1904 St Patrick's Day demonstration in Coalisland, Dillon assured Cardinal Logue of the AOH's 'faith and father-land' principles: 'We will always live faithful children of the Church, and pray that God may spare him long days to rule over his flock.'[49]

From the IRB's perspective, continued influence within the AOH represented an opportunity to pursue both short- and long-term objectives. At the turn of the century, the northern IRB's old guard attempted to exploit the impetus provided by the '98 commemoration to proselytise among Hibernians. As such, O'Boyle (the IRB's provincial leader) was obliged to placate the militant tendencies of recent converts.[50] By May 1905 the IRB's seventeen East Tyrone cells had received their second consignment of arms.[51] Insurrection may have been off the agenda, but such tokenistic preparations provided a sense of purpose. Moreover, due to the perennial threat of clerical condemnation, the IRB sought to employ the Hibernians as cover. In April 1905, at Devlin's pub in Moneymore, the Antrim, Armagh, Derry and Tyrone cells discussed 'the getting up of IRB halls wherein to meet etc. It is intended to make an appeal for funds in the name of the AOH.'[52]

Essentially, the Hibernians represented another element of the IRB's broader entryist policy: its strategy of securing positions of influence in an attempt to direct broader nationalist movements along republican lines. Referring to the Gaelic League and GAA, Denis McCullough observed that the IRB's 'intensity and honesty of purpose made them invincible in any organisation of which they took control, and for them all roads led to one end'.[53] However, rather than succumbing to Fenian influence, the Hibernians instead became the brotherhood's chief antagonists in East Tyrone. The principal reason for Fenian failure was that a formidable political adversary had very different plans for the Hibernian constituency.

V

The Hibernians' emergence as a force within national politics can be dated to the success of the organisation's chaplain, Fr McKinley, in uniting the movement in Ireland on 4 March 1902.[54] The American and domestic organisations were temporarily unified in the same year. It is interesting that during McKinley's efforts, Joe Devlin was sent to America to secure funding for the ailing UIL.[55] The massive power and electoral influence of the order along its eastern seaboard must surely have impressed the West Belfast ward boss.

Although working at cross purposes, Devlin was certainly aware of the IRB's central role in promoting Hibernianism in Tyrone up until 1905. In

September 1904 the RIC identified tensions between a Hibernian leadership intent on entering the political mainstream and a residual element associated with northern Fenianism, keen to preserve the order's quasi-revolutionary roots. The inspector general reported that the alliance between the 'United Irish League and the Ancient Order of Hibernians appears to be growing more cordial in the North of Ireland. Several members of parliament have recently joined the ranks.' There was an initiative to make the order a 'registered Benefit Society, the object being to obviate by this the hostility of the Roman Catholic clergymen to the AOH owing to its secret character'. Devlin convened a meeting of the Board of Erin in Belfast to discuss these developments; however, 'strong opposition to the new departure was manifested at the meeting by certain sections, and further consideration of the subject was adjourned'.[56]

In Tyrone this movement into the constitutional mainstream was conditioned by the Hibernians' recently won dominance over the local UIL. This development suited Devlin's objectives, since it effectively neutralised the Healyite faction on the local executive. As a result, the *raison d'être* of the alliance with local Fenians had dissolved. In the two years after Pomeroy, radical IRB-aligned Hibernians were squeezed out, as middle-class Catholics assumed increasingly prominent roles in the order and the movement mushroomed across Tyrone: the Board of Erin was transformed into the UIL reborn. The final consolidation of the AOH occurred in July 1905 when Devlin took complete control, fusing the Hibernians with the UIL and adding a constitutional clause linking them to the Irish Parliamentary Party (IPP). The AOH sought further respectability by declaring itself a friendly organisation. Bishop O'Donnell sponsored the removal of the clerical ban, leading to a split between the board and the overtly separatist Scottish section (promoted by Fenian old guard men like Robert Johnson and Henry Dobbyn).[57]

The RIC county inspector's report for October 1905 neatly sumarised the developments of the previous half-decade, noting Hibernianism's rapid growth in the wake of Devlin's presidency that July:

> The AOH has I think in great measure taken the place of the UIL. This society is gaining ground every day and many new branches have been established all over the county. Up to a few months ago the AOH confined itself to Cookstown and Dungannon districts.[58]

By the next month the Board of Erin had fifty-two branches in Tyrone. By the following May the number had risen to sixty-six and by March 1907 there were seventy-nine branches in Tyrone, approximately half of which were situated in the order's East Tyrone birthplace.[59]

There was still residual IRB involvement in Hibernianism, but any prospect of Fenian control over the AOH's ultimate direction appeared increasingly unlikely. In his summation of 1905, the inspector general commented on the situation with regard to IRB–Hibernian relations in the area:

> In Armagh and Tyrone this society [IRB] has acquired much influence amongst the local leaders of the AOH, but the latter, as an organisation, lends its support to the parliamentary party whilst the IRB remains hostile to constitutional agitation ... While awaiting foreign complications they are willing for the present to support any movement which may tend to estrange Ireland from England.[60]

The final statement is pivotal in explaining the breakdown in relations between the IRB and the popular militant AOH. After 1905, the northern IRB's policy changed from 'awaiting foreign implications' to openly contesting constitutional dominance of nationalist politics. It was the emergence of the Dungannon Clubs, with their advocacy of the Sinn Féin policy, and the ascension of notable Clan na Gael members to positions of authority within the American AOH that essentially forced Devlin's hand.

VI

Arguably, Devlin had several aims in assuming control of the AOH. Firstly, his immediate local concern was his dispute with the Catholic Association. Here, following the American model, he employed the AOH in machine politics, routing adversaries at the local government elections. His election as MP for West Belfast in 1906 'crowned his role as the city's nationalist supremo'. This victory, achieved through a combination of staunchly nationalist and welfarist appeals to his largely working-class and Hibernian constituency, was balanced against reassurances to the city's Catholic middle class 'that his demands went no further than this'.[61]

It was a variation on this theme which effectively carried majority Hibernian support in East Tyrone. Devlinism continued to project a separatist image to its grassroots. At Cork in 1909 Devlin argued that 'the revolutionists of the past and the constitutionalists of to-day' were all agreed that 'it was the function of practical and sane Irish patriots to utilise whatever instrument God and progress had given them to forge their way to Irish freedom'.[62] As Michael Wheatley has observed, 'the debate among local nationalists' was 'more about means than ends; should physical force still be employed, or should the "fight" be continued on by constitutional methods?'[63] In March 1908 the Board of Erin's *Hibernian Journal* still confidently proclaimed that 'our national ideal is a free and independent Ireland, subject to no outside control or influence'.[64]

Perhaps more fundamentally, republican failure rested on the sectarian realities of local politics. In the wake of the Board of Erin take-over an existing Hibernian policy of 'invading' Protestant areas was actually intensified. The RIC reported a serious disturbance at the St Patrick's Day demonstration in Stewartstown in 1907.[65] The Devlinite *Ulster Herald* provided a different perspective, sardonically claiming it was changed times in a town where previously 'no nationalist procession dare defile its sacred streets'.[66] In essence, the local Hibernian militant disposition was sated through a consolidated campaign against local Orangeism.

The Board of Erin's dominant position also reinforced communal solidarity and offered attractive social outlets and avenues for fraternal expression through the ubiquitous Hibernian hall and the plethora of politico-religious parades. Such activism had a more bellicose facet and Hibernians were known 'to obstruct the administration of justice by bringing influence to bear on magistrates, when members are concerned at courts and petty sessions'.[67] At a confirmation ceremony in Carrickmore in 1909, Cardinal Logue described the local AOH as 'a pest, a cruel tyranny, and an organised system of blackguardism'. Not only was 'drinking and dancing till the small hours of the morning' taking place in Hibernian halls, but local Hibernians 'endeavoured to compel others to join the order by means of boycotting, threatening ... waylaying and beating persons who did not join'.[68] Across a range of social and political aspects of quotidian life, the individual Hibernian received tangible compensation for his loyalty to the Board of Erin.

Secondly, from Devlin's perspective, Hibernianism's network of social connectivity offered an important outlet for the party's mobilisation of its grassroots supporters as dividends from the land issue grew smaller and smaller. The 1903 Wyndham Act, with its potential to undermine land's centrality to the national question, coincided neatly with Devlin's appropriation of the AOH. Perhaps more importantly, Devlin's dual appointments as UIL secretary and board president brought significant political power, reflected in John Redmond's claim that Devlin was 'the real Chief Secretary of Ireland'.[69] Although Redmond was the United Irish League's nominal president, real power rested with the secretary, appointed by the standing committee, a body more or less controlled by Devlin's mentor, John Dillon. Although coloured by his own resentment and treatment by Hibernians at the infamous 'Baton' convention of 9 February 1909, it is difficult to challenge William O'Brien's assessment that, through the manipulation of Hibernianism, Devlin's AOH

> was soon enabled to spread its network of lodges all over Ulster and over the greater part of Connaught, as well as to meet the branches of the United Irish League on at least equal terms at the conventions for

the selection of Parliamentary candidates, and eventually acquired an actual majority of the Standing Committee who controlled the organisation and funds of the United Irish League.[70]

Thirdly, and more speculatively, Devlin may have sought to exploit the union of American and Irish Orders to boost ailing party funds and strengthen constitutionalism in America. Due to the significant Clan element in the American AOH, early Hibernian ambivalence towards political violence actually helped Devlin's attempts. During his 1901 fundraising mission, Devlin asked his New York audience 'to give our movement a fair chance' despite the presence of 'many men in America who think the means which we are operating to-day … are not sufficiently sharp and decisive'. Devlin continued:

> When equipped with comparative freedom home rule, then would be the time for those who think we should destroy the last link that binds us to England to operate by whatever means they think best to achieve that great and desirable end. I am quite sure I speak for the United Irish League on this matter.[71]

Devlin never gave up his attempts to reconcile the American AOH: Arthur Griffith's *Sinn Féin* subsequently gloated about the defeat of the Board of Erin envoys to the 1906 American convention.[72] Indeed, imitation was the greatest form of flattery. Devlin's use of Hibernianism mirrored American machine politics, adding some credence to his depiction as 'a ghetto boss assiduously cultivating an atavistic sectarian vote' along the lines of the Molly Maguires.[73]

VII

The UIL's emergence and the popular enthusiasm surrounding the '98 centenary the same year forced the constitutional élite to adopt a policy of vampirism to counteract the separatist challenge. However, this was not a one-way process. Joseph Devlin's influence rested on his ability to balance popular demands with the leadership's priorities. Indeed, Tom Garvin argues that the IPP's vampirism of the AOH ultimately affected the character of the party adversely.[74] It was ironic, then, that Devlin's influence over northern nationalism was greatly assisted by the actions and energy of his republican opponents.

A consummate utilitarian, Devlin consistently employed the political tools available to him to achieve the greatest benefit to himself and the party. However, a new generation of advanced nationalists was no longer prepared to continue the traditional Fenian infiltration which Devlin had so skilfully exploited. The formation of the Belfast Dungannon Club on 8 March 1905 marked a new departure in northern republicanism.

Initially, Devlin employed familiar tactics. In December 1905 Tom Kettle visited Belfast 'at the request of Joseph Devlin MP with a view to effecting an arrangement with the members of the Dungannon Club so that a united effort might be made to have a nationalist representative returned for West Belfast … but it is not thought that any agreement will be arrived at'.[75] The pragmatic nature of Devlin's politics always permitted him to at least countenance co-operation, floating the idea of an accommodation with Sinn Féin to John Dillon as late as December 1907.[76] However, as it became apparent that the Dungannon Clubs' open separatist agitation sought to subvert the party's position, Devlin employed the Hibernians against the republican threat as he had earlier set them against Healyite opponents.

The northern IRB's failure to carry the Hibernian movement had two important results. Firstly, it consolidated the Irish Party and Joe Devlin's prominence within it – a position based on strict centralised control and the manipulation of populist rhetoric. The hollowness of such rhetoric was exposed by Devlinite central dictation. Up until 1905, Hibernians had been encouraged to oppose the conservative UIL. After the Board of Erin's victory, independent and democratic selection of candidates was condemned. In 1906 the AOH 'was very anxious to "run" a candidate of their own in opposition to Mr Murnaghan, late Healyite MP for Mid Tyrone', but was 'induced to withdraw its opposition'.[77] At a subsequent election, Dungannon Club organiser Patrick McCartan indicated that rather than siding with the Hibernians (in line with previous IRB policy), younger republicans saw little to differentiate a Board of Erin candidate from a United Irish Leaguer: 'The difference is Tweedledum and Tweedledee but the Hibs are mad at their men for withdrawing.'[78]

Secondly, Fenian failure led to a reassessment within northern republicanism. It became clear to a new generation, centred on Denis McCullough and Bulmer Hobson, that the IRB's traditional tactics were counterproductive and had actually strengthened constitutionalism. The Dungannon Clubs' support for Arthur Griffith's Sinn Féin was, in some measure, an attempt to replace the unsuccessful traditional strategy of 'characteristically ill-coordinated … infiltration, subversion, resistance and association'.[79] However, the new republicanism still recognised the AOH's latent separatist potential, with Seán Mac Diarmada becoming an organiser amongst Tyrone's Hibernians early in 1907. Faced with an overt republican challenge, Devlin was forced to dispel any ambiguity and openly attack the new movement. Mac Diarmada described his own hostile reception: 'The Dungannon club organiser is having some very narrow escapes from the Ribbonmen in Tyrone. They have received secret orders to fight Sinn Féin and they are doing so. Their leaders and national chaplain are very aggressive and often brutal in their opposition.'[80] By the

time of Mac Diarmada's mission, the flux in Tyrone nationalism had well
and truly passed. In the race for popular support, the Sinn Féin policy was
adopted as the new republican vehicle. The problem was that Devlinite
Hibernianism had an established momentum, and the IRB was left playing catch-up in a contest that had begun half a decade earlier.

NOTES

1. Patrick Maume, *The Long Gestation: Irish Nationalist Life, 1891–1918* (Dublin: Palgrave
   Macmillan, 1999), p. 31.
2. Owen McGee, *The IRB: The Irish Republican Brotherhood, from the Land League to Sinn Féin*
   (Dublin: Four Courts Press, 2005), p. 258
3. Philip Bull, 'The reconstruction of the Irish parliamentary movement, 1895–1903', (Ph.D.
   thesis, University of Cambridge, 1972), p. 2.
4. Maume, *Long Gestation*, p. 153. Maume borrowed the phrase from David Fitzpatrick. For 'vam-
   piric' party policy towards the Co. Clare Volunteers, see David Fitzpatrick, *Politics and Irish Life:
   Provincial Experiences of War and Revolution* (Cork: Cork University Press, 1988), p. 88.
5. For Fenian involvement in radical agrarianism in Galway, see Fergus Campbell, *Land and
   Revolution: Nationalist Politics in the West of Ireland* (Oxford: Oxford University Press, 2005), p.
   116.
6. For the argument that the UIL was not 'a semi-revolutionary challenge to the British state
   in Ireland', see Paul Bew, *Conflict and Conciliation in Ireland, 1890–1910: Parnellites and Radical
   Agrarians* (Oxford: Oxford University Press, 1987), p. 79.
7. The party only won the July 1906 East Tyrone by-election by eighteen votes. Brian Walker,
   Parliamentary Election results in Ireland, 1801–1922 (Dublin: Royal Irish Academy, 1978), p. 377.
8. For the factions involved, see Frank Callanan, *The Parnell Split, 1890–91* (Cork: Cork
   University Press, 1992), pp. 175–7.
9. Enda Staunton, *The Nationalists of Northern Ireland, 1918–1973* (Dublin: Columba Press, 2001),
   p. 8.
10. Ibid., p. 10.
11. Michael T. Foy, 'The Ancient Order of Hibernians: an Irish political-religious pressure
    group' (MA thesis, Queen's University Belfast, 1976).
12. McGee, *The IRB*, pp. 348–9.
13. Foy, 'The Ancient Order of Hibernians', *passim*.
14. McGee, *The IRB*, p. 253.
15. Matthew Kelly, *The Fenian Ideal and Irish Nationalism, 1882–1916* (Woodbridge: Boydell &
    Brewer, 2006), p. 129.
16. Karl Marx, *The Eighteenth Brumaire of Louis Bonaparte* (Oxford: Oxford University Press,
    1977), p. 300.
17. The Hibernians' three 'objectives': 'to punish Land Lords; to assist in the gaining of Irish
    Independence by any means and to put down the Protestant Ascendancy'. RIC Crime
    Branch Special précis report, 4 Feb. 1889, National Archive: Public Record Office, Colonial
    Office 904/10. The leadership of Tyrone's seven lodges comprised three fishermen, one tin-
    smith, one shoemaker, one farmer and one 'scutcher'. RIC CBS précis report, 1891, TNA:
    PRO, CO 904/10.
18. For example, the Ardboe Amnesty association was 'undoubtedly a branch of the IRB'. Report
    of the RIC County Inspector, Tyrone, May 1896, TNA: PRO, CO 904/51. After the meet-
    ing several members were involved in a sectarian attack. *Irish News*, 13 May 1896; *Dungannon
    News*, 14 May 1896. Leading Ardboe Fenians were also Hibernians, i.e. IRB centre James
    'Dundee' Devlin and the McConville brothers; Devlin's Fenianism. Statement of Wm J.
    Kelly Senior, Cardinal Ó Fiaich Library Armagh, Louis O'Kane Papers, II.A.35/0001/12;
    Tyrone Courier, 24 Mar. 1898; Thomas J. 'Banba' Martin interview, COFLA, LOK, IV.B.07
    0002); *Tyrone Courier*, 24 Mar. 1898. The AOH upper Ardboe branch contained the majority
    of identifiable local Fenians. *Dungannon News*, 3 Sept. 1896.
19. McGee, *The IRB*, p. 313.
20. Report of the RIC County Inspector, Tyrone, June 1895, TNA: PRO, CO 904/50.
21. Report of the RIC County Inspector, Tyrone, Mar. 1898, TNA: PRO, CO 904/68.

22. Statement of Wm J. Kelly Senior, COFLA, LOK, II.A.35/0001/12.
23. McGee, *The IRB*, pp. 251–5.
24. Veteran Fenian John McElhone of the Stewartstown '98 club denounced the 'few men in Belfast, who have taken the action of forming a central executive in Belfast without the knowledge of the Ulster Clubs, as a body, and we call on all the Ulster clubs to stand shoulder to shoulder with the central executive, Dublin ... and to have nothing to do with the clique of men who are only forming a so called executive in order to carry on a war with the Catholic Association in Belfast'. *Dungannon News*, 11 Nov. 1897.
25. Kelly, *Fenian Ideal*, pp. 116–17.
26. Report of the RIC Inspector General, Aug. 1898, TNA: PRO, CO 904/69; *Belfast News-Letter*, 17 Aug. 1898; *Irish News*, 16 Aug. 1898.
27. The meeting resolved to 'do all within our power to advance the demand for national freedom as foreshadowed by Wolfe Tone and the patriots who followed in his footsteps, and that we shall work persistently to establish true nationality in the country, which should consist of maintaining the principles, and also when necessity arises practising the methods of the glorious heroes of 1798, '67 and '48'. *Dungannon News*, 23 Mar. 1899.
28. There was IRB–Hibernian involvement in the Ulster Labourers' Union. Report of the RIC County Inspector, Tyrone, Feb. 1904, National Archive of Ireland, Crime Branch Special, Inspector General and County Inspectors' Monthly Reports, box 3.
29. Report of the Tyrone County Inspector RIC, Mar. 1903, NAI, CBS, IGCI, box 3.
30. Report of the RIC County Inspector, Tyrone, May 1903, NAI, CBS, IGCI, box 3.
31. *Dungannon News*, 2 Aug. 1903.
32. Swift McNeill was a Protestant and MP for South Donegal, 1887–1918. *Dungannon News*, 10 Dec. 1903.
33. Report of the RIC Inspector General, Mar. 1903, NAI, CBS, IGCI, box 3.
34. Ibid.
35. Report of the RIC Inspector General, Sept. 1903, NAI, CBS, IGCI, box 4.
36. Report of the RIC Inspector General, May 1903, NAI, CBS, IGCI, box 3.
37. *Dungannon News*, 11 Sept. 1902.
38. In 1902, at Mountjoy, the Hibernians attempted to kill a UIL candidate, a mob shooting at 'Yellow' Morris' family and attacking his house with stones; Mountjoy, or Brocagh, is a predominantly Catholic townland near Lough Neagh. *Dungannon News*, 12 June 1902.
39. *Irish News*, 22 Apr. 1902.
40. *Dungannon News*, 24 Apr. 1902.
41. *Dungannon News*, 22 May 1902.
42. Report of the RIC County Inspector, Tyrone, Aug. 1903, NAI, CBS, IGCI, box 4.
43. *Dungannon News*, 20 Aug. 1903.
44. Transcript of radio interview, 8 Mar. 1965, University College Dublin Archive, Denis McCullough Papers, P120/35.
45. Draft of McCullough's statement to the Bureau of Military History, UCDA, DMP, P120/33.
46. Report of the RIC County Inspector, Tyrone, May 1904, NAI, CBS, IGCI, box 5.
47. RIC CBS précis report, 1 Oct. 1905, TNA: PRO, CO 904/117; RIC CBS précis report, 1 Dec. 1905, TNA: PRO, CO 904/117.
48. *Gaelic American*, 4 May 1907.
49. *Dungannon News*, 24 Mar. 1904.
50. RIC CBS précis report, 14 May 1905, TNA: PRO, CO 904/117.
51. RIC CBS précis report, 29 Apr. 1905, TNA: PRO, CO 904/117.
52. John Devlin's pub was in Moneymore, just north of Cookstown. RIC CBS précis report, 26 Apr. 1905, TNA: PRO, CO 904/117; RIC CBS précis report, 29 April 1905, TNA: PRO, CO 904/117. The following month witnessed an 'appeal in the names of the AOH and UIL for funds to build a Hall at Clovenden Loughall, Co. Armagh. Three of the five signatories to the appeal are IRB men'. RIC CBS précis report, 25 May 1905, TNA: PRO, CO 904/117.
53. Statement by Denis McCullough Papers on his role in the IRB, UCDA, DMP, P120/23/12.
54. Foy, 'The Ancient Order of Hibernians', pp. 27–37.
55. McGee, *The IRB*, p. 291.
56. Report of the RIC Inspector General, Sept. 1904, NAI, CBS, IGCI, box 6.
57. A. C. Hepburn, 'Liberal Policies and Nationalist politics in Ireland' (Ph.D. thesis, University of Kent, 1968), p. 835.
58. Report of the RIC County Inspector, Tyrone, Oct. 1905, NAI, CBS, IGCI, box 8.
59. Report of the RIC County Inspector, Tyrone, Nov. 1905, NAI, CBS, IGCI, box 8; Report of

the RIC County Inspector, Tyrone, May 1906, NAI, CBS, IGCI, box 9; Report of the RIC County Inspector, Tyrone, Mar. 1907, NAI, CBS, IGCI, box 11.

60. Report of the RIC Inspector General, Dec. 1905, NAI, CBS, IGCI, box 8.
61. Staunton, *Nationalists*, p. 9.
62. *Freeman's Journal*, 6 Sept. 1909.
63. Michael Wheatley, *Nationalism and the Irish Party: Provincial Ireland, 1910–1916* (Oxford: Oxford University Press, 2005), p. 82.
64. *Hibernian Journal*, Mar. 1908.
65. Report of the RIC County Inspector, Tyrone, Mar. 1907, NAI, CBS, IGCI, box 11.
66. *Ulster Herald*, 30 Mar. 1907.
67. Report of the RIC County Inspector, Tyrone, Mar. 1908, NAI, CBS, IGCI, box 13.
68. *Irish Independent*, 12 May 1909.
69. Redmond speaking at Detroit, *Irish World*, 5 Nov. 1910.
70. William O'Brien, *An Olive Branch in Ireland* (London: Macmillan, 1910), p. 420.
71. *Irish People*, 21 June 1902.
72. *Sinn Féin*, 11 Aug. 1906.
73. Éamon Phoenix, *Northern Nationalism: Nationalist Politics, Partition and the Catholic Minority in Northern Ireland* (Belfast: Ulster Historical Foundation, 1994), pp. 1–10.
74. Tom Garvin, *Nationalist Revolutionaries in Ireland, 1891–1922* (Oxford: Oxford University Press, 1987), p. 92.
75. RIC CBS précis report, 27 Dec. 1905, TNA: PRO, CO 904/117.
76. Joseph Devlin to John Dillon, 20 Dec. 1907, Trinity College Dublin Archive, John Dillon Papers, MS 6729/120; Staunton, *Nationalists*, pp. 11–12.
77. Report of the RIC County Inspector, Tyrone, July 1906, NAI, CBS, IGCI, box 10.
78. Patrick McCartan to Joseph McGarrity, 1 May 1908, National Library of Ireland, Joseph McGarrity Papers, MF P.8186.
79. Kelly, *Fenian Ideal*, p. 134.
80. Seán Mac Diarmada to Joseph McGarrity, 22 July 1907, NLI, JMP, MS 17; Gerard MacAtasney, *Seán Mac Diarmada: The Mind of the Revolution* (Leitrim: Drumlin Publications, 2004), p. 24.

III
THE FENIAN DIASPORA

7

'Cheap as Soap and Common as Sugar': The Fenians, Dynamite and Scientific Warfare

Niall Whelehan

I

Patrick Ford, the editor of the New York-based *Irish World*, often engaged with the more unusual aspects of technological innovation when he called on Fenians to practise 'scientific warfare'. In 1877 one of his editorials envisioned Fenians circling London in hot-air balloons and dropping a cargo of explosives upon targets below. The barracks and artilleries of the British armed forces, Ford predicted, could be wiped out in a matter of days using these methods. This was not imagined as a strategy of terror, but as a progressive form of warfare where precise targets could be effectively hit without the barbarity and loss of civilian life that usually characterised a more polite encounter.

> The ultimate result of this scientific warfare ... will be the utter abolition of all modes of warfare ... aerial bombs – Jove's thunderbolts – will yet be invented with which one man in the clouds may assail fifty thousand below! Ascend in the air in a balloon and throw down showers of such explosives upon an army, and that army will be speedily wiped out. With armies and fleets done away with, international wars are done away with.[1]

Neither was Ford alone among Irish-American nationalists in advocating such measures. In 1884, at a meeting of the Manhattan branch of the Irish National League, 'balloon warfare' was seriously discussed. A few months later, ex-IRB leader James Stephens remarked that dirigible balloons 'manned by desperados' could inaugurate a new form of aerial warfare against the British forces, which would be preferable to the dynamite campaign that was then at its height in Britain.[2]

These declarations read like something from the realms of science fiction and appeared to reflect a marked fanaticism among a small but determined group of Irish republicans resident in the US. Balloons, along with so-called infernal machines (improvised explosive devices) and submarines, were the instruments of 'scientific warfare', a strategy that New York-based Fenians believed to be the means to 'equalise the great and the small ... if weak peoples go to war to wrench back their rights from titanic powers, common sense will suggest that they use such appliances as physical science puts into their hands'. [3]

It is tempting to take Ford's article on 'balloon warfare' and his eulogies on dynamite as colourful indicators of the political extremism of the *Irish World* and a commitment to terrorism. Yet, they were nothing extraordinary in the aftermath of the American Civil War, when technological advances created considerable apprehension and excitement about a society tilting towards the future. In the late nineteenth century, the context in which Irish 'physical force' nationalism was debated was being redefined by international concerns about violence and warfare. A look at diverse publications of the time reveals that the *Irish World* article keyed into larger discourses on science, technology and warfare that fascinated several layers of society. Journalists, army officials, novelists and revolutionaries all participated, to varying degrees, in discussions about the consequences that new technologies held for society, and the Fenians were no different.

Revolutionary violence appeared to take an extremist turn in the late nineteenth century when Fenians, nihilists and anarchists all engaged in dynamite 'outrage' with chronological symmetry. Certainly, it would be helpful to examine the Fenians' dynamite campaign in the transnational context of revolutionary action during what has been termed the era of *attentats*. [4] However, measuring the scale of political violence by the activities of revolutionary movements can distract our attention away from exogenous contexts and factors, leading to blinkered understandings of the mechanisms that brought transformations and escalations in strategy. The Fenians, like other revolutionary movements, should be considered in the light of the worlds in which they lived, worked and conspired, in order for us to see what factors shaped their volatile tactics.

This chapter, then, investigates the extent to which a culture of scientific and technological innovation in the late nineteenth century influenced the Fenians' repertoire of action. Instead of a factual reconstruction of the events and intrigues of the dynamite campaign, attention here will focus on how the Fenians participated in a moment of collective inebriation, when faith in the transformative power of technology and science led to predictions of radical change in all aspects of society. I consider how different groups imagined science would reshape their worlds and assess the judgement of one Brooklyn Fenian that dynamite was as 'cheap as soap and common as sugar'. [5]

II

One of John Devoy's main criticisms of Patrick Ford's editorial style was that he frequently reproduced half-digested material from whatever book or magazine he happened to be reading, making him a 'mere student instructing the world'.[6] While Devoy's views were undoubtedly coloured by personal antagonisms, the *Irish World* was certainly hastily written and Ford's writings often reflected what he was reading in the New York press at the time. Hence, his article on dropping bombs from balloons was relatively unremarkable in the context of similar pieces in the mainstream press, where dramatic pieces on scientific innovations were regularly featured. Léon Gambetta's escape from Paris in 1870 in a hot-air balloon left an enduring image that sustained official and unofficial interest in new techniques of warfare. The *New York Times* regularly printed articles with titles such as 'Balloons for Military Purposes' and 'The Use of Balloons in Warfare', while the *Brooklyn Eagle* spoke of nihilist 'balloon plots' in Russia and earnestly reported on a local New York inventor who claimed 'one of my airships can hover over any one of your great cities and destroy it in an hour and you can do nothing to prevent the destruction'. The inventor's workshop was on Chambers Street, Manhattan, a few metres away from O'Donovan Rossa's office.[7]

Another of the Fenians' more ambitious proposals suggested the targeting of British commercial ships by privately manned boats, as the Confederacy had done with relative success during the American Civil War. Unlike the notion of aerial bombs, however, the opportunity to realise attacks on British vessels was actively pursued by the Fenians in 1876 when they hired an Irish inventor – John P. Holland – to develop a submarine. Over the next seven years, prototypes persistently failed and eventually, in 1883, patience ran out, funding was cut, and the submarine – what the *New York Sun* labelled the 'Fenian Ram' – was placed in a warehouse.[8] Although the plan had proposed a new 'secret' weapon, there was nothing secret about the submarine and the very public nature of the experiment led to heightened humiliation for Clan na Gael and did not help their reputation as serious revolutionaries. All of the New York dailies, along with weekly scientific periodicals and magazines, closely followed the machine's development. Interestingly, while the Fenian Ram was a conspicuous source of Anglo-American diplomatic friction, it drew more attention as an item of technological curiosity than as an unorthodox means of achieving Irish independence.[9]

O'Donovan Rossa was furious that the submarine had soaked up huge amounts of the 'Skirmishing Fund' which he had created to finance bomb attacks in Britain, and sneered that 'fifty fires like that would frighten England more than fifty rams lying dead in Jersey mud'.[10] The Skirmishing Fund had been established in New York in 1876 to finance explosive attacks against political and economic targets in British cities. 'Skirmishing' and scientific warfare were the preferred terms that were used to describe a strategy that would weaken the financial power of the British empire in ways that an insurrection in Ireland simply could not.[11] The Fenian Ram was initially imagined to be a model of revolutionary science, but its failure encouraged Clan na Gael to organise teams of 'missioners', as Rossa had done in 1881, to send across the Atlantic. In a dynamite campaign that peaked in the years 1883–5, skirmishers, with the help of several *agents provocateurs*, targeted parliament buildings, town halls, gasworks, railway and underground stations, bridges and press offices with infernal machines and nitro-glycerine.[12]

When O'Donovan Rossa had first begun to call for explosive attacks in the *Irish World*, the successful employment of dynamite and infernal machines was a realistic proposition, unlike submarines and aerial warfare. Logistically, at least, the techniques imagined by the contributors to the Skirmishing Fund had already passed through the laboratory stage. Contemporary newspapers, magazines and official sources all suggested that the use of dynamite or gunpowder was no novelty in postbellum America. In fact, across the United States combinations of explosive materials were regularly experimented with and mechanical bombs were frequently patented. Endless articles on technological advances, both fictional and factual, provided reliable copy for a print media industry that was constantly expanding. Periodical literature such as the *Scientific American*, *Van Nostrand's Eclectic Engineering Magazine* and *Prairie Farmer* reported regularly on advances in science, printing detailed instructions on how to handle dynamite and how to build sophisticated 'infernal machines' for use in both farming and industry. When the *Scientific American's* founder, the wealthy New England inventor Rufus Porter, died in 1885, O'Donovan Rossa paid tribute in a long obituary in the *United Irishman* that praised the life of Porter and the content of his journal.[13]

In the 1860s and 1870s it was not difficult to privately experiment with explosives at home, and many people did. As early as 1857, the *Chicago Tribune* reported that American inventors were gaining international reputations for breakthroughs in the design and manufacture of infernal machines. During the Crimean War, the Russian consul attempted to employ a Utah inventor who had 're-discovered ... the terrible Greek-fire of the ancients'. The inventor had established that

> old kegs, hollow trees, common boxes, anything in short which could be made contain a bottle of the burning fluid, a little powder, and a considerable amount of missiles, whether of balls, iron scraps, or pebbles and fragments of rock, could be converted into cheap and formidable batteries, whose discharge could be governed, at almost any distance, to a second of time ...[14]

The article was representative of an abundance of similar news stories describing scientific innovations that were often used for criminal as well as industrial or military purposes. In 1860 the 'Philadelphia infernal machine' was primed for use in the city by Confederate sympathisers, before police discovered the plot.[15] One year later, infernal machines were introduced on both sides in the American Civil War. During the conflict these devices were essentially torpedoes: metal cases filled with gunpowder and hammer mechanisms that were floated down river in the hope they would come in contact with enemy ships. Before long, however, infernal machines were developed from relatively crude and large devices to smaller, more sophisticated boxes which soon came to be used to settle feuds and vendettas across the country.[16]

In 1863 a courtroom battle over the patent rights to a type of railway brake turned nasty when a witness in the case received a parcel bomb in the mail, which was designed to explode once the lid was opened. Until the trial was concluded at the end of the year, the case caused considerable controversy and was widely reported in the national press.[17] In 1866 a Judge Fields of the Supreme Court received a small box full of gunpowder and missiles at his office in Washington, in return for a decision he had made in a dispute over property titles in California.[18] Throughout the following years, homemade explosive devices were found in a Jersey city opera house, the vestibule of a Cincinnati church, a California launderette, outside a newspaper office in Indiana, and in coal sheds, train carriages, liquor and grocery stores the length and breadth of the United States.

The infernal machine requiring the least effort to manufacture, the *Scientific American* contended, was that 'peculiar to the New York rascal, who occasionally dispatches it per express to politicians who have fallen from his good graces'.[19] In 1873 a parcel bomb was sent to Comptroller Green's office in City Hall, New York, an act that the press linked to his investigations into corruption at Tammany Hall. The parcel, which contained a six-by-four-inch box filled with gunpowder, did not explode on arrival due to the vigilance of postal staff.[20]

A few months later, similar investigations in Brooklyn led to a former district attorney, Judge Morris, being targeted by 'ballot box stuffers'. Morris's campaign against corruption in city politics and his proposed reforms had upset political interests in the 'Brooklyn Ring'. During one investigation into fraud an infernal machine was delivered to Morris's family home but failed to explode when opened. Attempts to find those responsible were rendered unworkable because the technique used left 'not the slightest clue' as to the identity of those involved.[21] Indeed, the parcel bomb could have been a hoax, staged in the hope that it would stir enough public outrage to secure the successful prosecution of the

Brooklyn Ring.[22] Either way, the political bargaining power of explosives had been realised by elements within the city administrations of Brooklyn and in Tammany Hall. Both of these episodes would not have gone unnoticed by Irish people who held considerable interests in city politics at the time. The New York Fenians did not need to look as far as European revolutionaries for models of action: gunpowder, dynamite and infernal machines were already being used locally for political advancement.

Access to explosive substances and a degree of mechanical competency were necessary requirements for the authors of these episodes. However, familiarity with bomb-making was not linked to employment in mining or building works, where explosives were tools of the trade. Instead, the chemical elements necessary to build an infernal machine were readily available through common stores, while periodicals regularly printed detailed instructions on the manufacture of explosives for practical use.

The Scientific American was established in 1845 with the ethos of publishing reader-friendly information on 'New Inventions, Scientific Principles, and Curious Work'.[23] Unsurprisingly, after Nobel's 1866 invention, articles on dynamite soon became a regular feature in the journal, with typical titles such as 'Novel Applications of Dynamite' and 'Experiments with Explosives'. These articles consistently argued that a basic knowledge of the manufacture and handling of explosives should not be restricted to professional chemists and scientists but available to anybody with a curiosity for experimentation. In addition, a *Scientific American Catalogue* was in circulation, from which readers could order articles on explosives, dynamite and infernal machines that were 'profusely illustrated' and accompanied by 'measures and scales'.[24] Manufacture of explosives was in no way confined to the military or to large commercial enterprises. Innovation in the field came from individual experiments that formed part of a culture of invention and entrepreneurship.

In the wake of the 1875 Bremerhaven tragedy in Germany, when an American-made bomb exploded on a German dock and killed eighty people, the *Scientific American* published a solemn article that accounted for the history of various types of explosives.[25] On this occasion, the journal refrained from printing detailed diagrams, citing fears that the instructions could easily fall into the wrong hands: 'We had prepared drawings of some of the ingenious machines which have been ascribed to diabolical uses, and contemplated publishing engravings of the same ... but on second thought, it seemed to us wiser not to do so ... the harm caused might vastly exceed the advantage of such knowledge as the pictures might impart.'[26]

When the Skirmishers' use of dynamite bombs became dramatically evident in the 1880s, the *Scientific American* noted that the problem did not lie in how the bombers could buy or lay their hands on industrial explosives, but in 'the ease with which the explosives can be made'.[27] In the late nineteenth century the pace of technological advances along with the growth of private scientific experimentation created an environment whereby the Fenians' political application of scientific warfare seemed more obvious than anomic. The manufacture of exploding devices in domestic homes was not uncommon, while instructions on how to assemble infernal machines were easy to find and materials were readily available to people regardless of geographic location or social class. During investigations into a series of explosions in Dublin in the early 1890s, it was suggested that the authors were miners or quarrymen. However, the Home Office's inspector of explosives remarked that this was not the case: instead, exploding devices were 'easily made by anyone possessing a slight knowledge of chemistry ... as to its use, the art of firing any of these explosives with a detonator fuse can be learned by anyone of ordinary capacity in a few moments'.[28]

III

The potential destructive power of these man-made devices was understandably a source of unease in many sectors. The criminal application of explosives threatened to catch civilians in the crossfire, and when used for political or military purposes infernal machines held the potential to transfer the landscape of violence from the battlefield to the city, hence engendering indiscriminate violence. These concerns were felt sharply among political groups of all stripes in Ireland. When Clan na Gael and O'Donovan Rossa's United Irishmen began to plan dynamite attacks they were vigorously opposed by the majority of Irish nationalists, who sought to avert the undertaking of 'active work' that would surely place civilian lives at risk.

Alexander Martin Sullivan, editor of the *Nation*, thought the new 'skirmishing' strategy was symptomatic of a general moral cowardice among Irish-American nationalists and believed Irish as well as English civilians would perish in 'fires which our chivalrous friends (safe and sound, 4,000 miles away) in New York are to start around us'.[29] The IRB was consistently hostile towards the employment of dynamite, and 'skirmishing' was 'viewed with jealousy and distrust by many who still consider themselves Fenians', according to informants' reports to the British consulate in New York.[30] The majority of 'physical- force' nationalists still advocated insurrection where the site of revolutionary action would be the battlefield, where volunteers met soldiers face-to-face. The skirmisher would work anonymously, in city streets and squares. John O'Leary publicly condemned the use of gunpowder and dynamite in the *Irishman* and, in a private letter, rebuked O'Donovan Rossa for 'desperate nonsense', advising him to remove himself from the plan as quickly as possible.[31] Like many Fenians, O'Leary believed skirmishing to be something illegitimate, beyond the limits of acceptable action, a tactic which would ultimately be politically counterprouctive.

Debates within Irish nationalism found striking parallels in a widespread discourse about violence and legitimate tactics that was taking place at the time. Central to this discourse was, firstly, the role of technology in warfare and, second, the question of where the landscape of violence or battlefield would be located in the future. Familiarity with technological advances was a prime concern for government and military officials, who kept one eye on the battlefield and the other on the workshop. By the end of the century, the commanding general of the US army recognised that 'great commanders' have been 'compelled to yield the first place in importance' to scientists.[32] However, divisions and anxieties over scientific warfare were as sharp in official circles as they were within the Fenian movement. Moral concerns regarding the use of new weapons jockeyed with advocates of swift and decisive battles made possible through technological innovation.

In 1879, at a military conference in West Point, New York, a Civil War veteran gave a paper entitled 'The Legitimate in Warfare'. Noting that aerial navigation would soon develop beyond the tentative stage into a fixed science, the veteran Clinton Sears asked his audience: 'Will we not be sending up balloons to rain upon the enemy from directly overhead every possible device for burning buildings, blowing up his magazines, and destroying his personnel? To fail to use such affairs when practicable would be, I think, a neglect of duty.'[33] During the Civil War, both the Union and Confederate sides used balloons for reconnaissance and throughout the following decades officials seriously considered the possibility of aerial warfare. The wars of the future 'will have to be conducted by scientists', wrote the *Brooklyn Eagle* when it reported on the inventions of a General Thayer of the US army. Thayer 'invented what he calls a dirigible balloon, which will not only rise into the clouds, but will go whithersoever its pilot chooses to direct it ... the particular purpose of such an airship is to sail over the enemy and drop dynamite bombs upon him'.[34]

At the West Point conference, Sears argued that the pace of scientific discovery blurred the 'rules of war'. The legitimacy of using tactics such as aerial bombing could only be measured on the principle that 'usage and precedent are the foundations of the laws of war'.[35] In answering the question of what was legitimate in 'civilised warfare', Sears responded that new technologies made all laws of war obsolete: all weapons were legitimate and the nation at war should not shirk from using all means available to it, less its enemies profit by them. Sears argued that if an invention were to appear that would 'demolish one thousand or even one hundred men at a blow', the army should immediately employ it. While 'the laws of humanity may condemn me, I will use it to the utmost with a satisfied conscience ... The laws of war will be quick to recognise its usefulness'.[36]

Sears' argument rested on the assumption that the decisive use of new inventions would dramatically shorten the lengthy campaigns that had characterised the American Civil War and the Crimean War. Scientific invention held the potential to speed up warfare, and hence, politics – 'an object for which we all, soldiers as well as civilians, should strive'. In turn, this would decrease the number of civilian casualties, as more precise targeting would be made possible by sophisticated infernal machines. Humane warfare was, however, secondary when Sears calculated the legitimacy of certain tactics. 'Are any of the deaths to which the greater number killed in war are put, strictly speaking, humane? What is the humanity of which so much is made?' Important advantages were frequently 'gained by that nation which sees the utility, overrides the objections, and boldly uses newly invented though terrible engines of war'. In short, when firing an arrow, why not poison the barb? If people desired warfare to be 'short, sharp, vigorous and decisive', then efficacy should dictate which tactics were legitimate.[37]

In 1884, when the Fenians' dynamite campaign was at its height, an essay entitled 'Dynamite and the Art of War' appeared in a US military journal. The author, an army captain named James Chester, favoured dynamite and other scientific inventions but for different reasons to Sears. Technological innovation was crucial to warfare as it brought equilibrium to conflicts that were previously one-sided; infernal machines could be made 'in any back kitchen ... every one can own and any one can use'. Consequently, the civilian population could be easily armed in times of crisis, to resist an enemy attack or repress an internal rebellion. Traditional weapons of war were expensive and meant that 'war can be waged only by the wealthy', but Chester envisaged dynamite to be the means of mobilising sections of society previously marginalised from political conflict: if the infernal machine 'may not fight for the king it will for the cobbler, and the cobbler takes to it kindly'.[38]

The idea that scientific warfare enfranchised actors previously marginalised from politics combined with an historical moment when distinctions were blurred between volunteers and professional soldiers. 'Dynamite and the Art of War' envisaged a new form of warfare that did not protect civilians from the hardships of conflict, but encouraged them to participate. Dynamite opened up immense possibilities for the arming of 'irregular partisan troops' when a more 'formal ... defence is impossible'.

'Raids' and surgical attacks, Chester predicted, would become the standard means of conflict:

> With dynamite or some kindred compound, in a safe, handy, manageable form, a body of raiders with no set task, no fixed objective, no lines of operation or retreat, free as birds of the air, able to fight or run away as it thinks best … would be a terrible weapon of war … It will not do, because we find the problem a hard one, to scout at its premises as barbarian war. War is by its very nature barbarous.[39]

In the late nineteenth century the US government, wary of a large standing army, emphasised the peacetime importance of the 'citizen soldier'. The American Civil War was characterised by both regular and irregular tactics and during the conflict distinctions between partisans and conventional soldiers were rendered hazier than in previous, more formal, inter-state wars. Civilians' exposure to violence during the conflict remodelled them as new actors with vested interests in the fighting.[40] True, this did not create a context for the legitimisation of urban guerrilla warfare during peacetime: however, the experience of irregular war contributed to a postbellum environment where 'irregulars' were imagined to be key elements of future conflicts. Technological transformations were perceived to be advantageous to the volunteer/irregular and would gradually diminish the importance of the professional army. Interestingly, contemporary discussions in most continental European states veered in the other direction, where the professionalisation of state armies was emphasised and civic militias were demobilised.

In 1884 an award-winning military essay predicted that future wars in the United States would be fought 'by armies composed principally of militia and volunteers: and the soldiers of the regular army will be simply a bit of leaven for a mass of inexperienced comrades'.[41] In 1870 the military analyst and Civil War veteran Emory Upton wrote *Tactics for non-Military Bodies, Adapted to the Instruction of Political Associations, Police Forces, Fire Organisations, Masonic, Old Fellows, and other Civic Societies*. The book emphasised the importance of the citizen-soldier and the role of skirmishers in preceding large battles.[42] Irish-American militia groups had appeared mid-century and although they faded in the early 1900s, they were considerably active in the 1870s and 1880s. In 1876 the Newark-based 'Hibernian Rifles (73 men)' sent $50 to the *Irish World* 'for the Skirmishing Fund and, if you want men to Skirmish, men to go'. *Irish World* journalist Thomas Mooney, who wrote under the pseudonym 'TransAtlantic', asserted that all supporters of the Skirmishing Fund should procure 'Upton's Manual' in order to learn the 'movements of a revolutionary force, opposed to regulars of high training'. It was by the 'total disregard of the old military tactics of the European kings and generals' that revolutionary forces were successful, and if the large number of Irish-Americans in 'civic and semi-military organisations would give the attention to this subject', they could make the dynamite campaign an effective strategy.[43]

The rhetoric that the *Irish World* and the *United Irishman* used to describe skirmishing and scientific warfare mirrored military thinking during the period. Neither 'The Legitimate in Warfare' nor 'Dynamite and the Art of War' drew a line between warfare and terrorism, the city and the battlefield, and Chester's vision of inconspicuous 'raiders' crossing borders echoed Ford's 'little band of heroes who will initiate and keep up without intermission a guerrilla warfare – men who will fly over land and sea like invisible beings – now striking the enemy in Ireland, now in India, now in England itself, as occasion may present'.[44]

When O'Donovan Rossa, John McCafferty and Patrick Crowe first proposed the skirmishing idea at Patrick Ford's house in the autumn of 1875, Augustine Ford was present and 'took the ground that Ireland and England were in a *state of war*. This fact had to be recognised at the starting point.'[45] Explaining the proposal in the vocabulary of warfare attempted to legitimise a repertoire of action that was otherwise viewed as out-of-hand and barbaric by many elements within the Fenian movement. McCafferty had fought as a Confederate guerrilla leader during the Civil War with Morgan's Raiders, a group that conducted operations behind Union lines, such as disrupting communication networks and railroad tracks, a strategy that was quite successful during 1863.[46] He also claimed to have engaged in kidnapping and hostage-taking with Confederate guerrillas and unsuccessfully advised the IRB to adopt the same strategy.[47]

When responding to criticisms of the legitimacy of the Skirmishing Fund, McCafferty contended that all means were legitimate as 'self-preservation is the first law of nature'.[48] Similar to Chester's pugilist who punched below the belt 'without any conscientious scruples' when fighting for his life and property, the skirmishers were not to be bound by rules dictated by the spectators.[49] Ford, however, was keen to demonstrate that it was not simply a proposal to 'blow up everything', as critics had remarked, and strove to show that there was a code of conduct for those involved. In 1878 'Maxims for Skirmishers' were printed alongside the appeal for donations that outlined the confines of the strategy to 'give intelligent men a clear idea of the whole intent and spirit'.[50]

The dynamite pamphlets sold through O'Donovan Rossa's *United Irishman* were a mix of the do-it-yourself style instruction of *The Scientific American* with military theories of future warfare. One pamphlet entitled *Dynamite Against Gladstone's Resources of Civilisation* declared that Irish independence could be won with merely one thousand volunteers, who were schooled in the 'arts of scientific warfare'.[51] The author – Professor

Mezzeroff – traded as a chemicals expert and Russian nihilist, who, aside from his association with Rossa, lectured to groups of Cuban nationalists and wrote occasionally in the German anarchist monthly *Die Freiheit*.[52] Mezzeroff's real identity was kept hidden, but he was almost certainly the more plainly named Richard Rogers, a New York-born child of emigrant parents.[53] However, his true identity was of secondary importance. His role was to bring credibility to Rossa's organisation of United Irishmen, who were regularly portrayed in the press as bunglers and swindlers of no real threat to anyone except the gullible Irish immigrants from whom they conned money. In comparison to the professional Russian revolutionary, depicted in the press as a master of secrecy, chemistry and conspiracy, the skirmishers fared badly. The *Washington Post* believed that while O'Donovan Rossa was 'a vapid, frothy character', Mezzeroff was 'to be more feared than a dozen Rossas'.[54]

In 1882 Mezzeroff took to the Fenian stage, employed by Rossa to instruct 'any man of average intelligence' in the manufacture of infernal machines, at a school based in Brooklyn.[55] In addition, he delivered numerous presentations of his bomb-making pamphlet at commemorative occasions and organised a weekly series of lectures entitled 'Scientific warfare or the Quickest Way to Liberate Ireland'.[56] Mezzeroff professed to be a soldier from the age of 16 and his experiences, notably in the Crimean War, had taught him that 'there is no such thing as honourable warfare ... any weapon is justifiable when it is used in defence of human life, liberty and property'.

Each speech produced the same argument: dynamite would imminently replace guns, cannons, and swords and become the sole method of warfare. Rather than providing a small revolutionary vanguard with the means necessary for dynamite attacks, Mezzeroff held that the ease with which internal machines could be manufactured meant that 'every trade society and workingman's club', indeed entire populations, could be armed for war. In Ireland, 'five millions of people armed with chemical science ... are invincible against any which the enemy can send against them'. Rossa agreed and urged that 'every Irishman and Irishwoman put a bit of dynamite in their pocket and become a walking revolution'.[57]

Insurrection required the patient training and arming of volunteer militias, but dynamite produced immediate results that some New York Fenians understood to be providential. In April 1883 Brooklyn Fenian Patrick McGahey asserted that dynamite was 'the poor man's weapon of warfare ... dynamite was an invention of Heaven, I believe, to help the poor man the world over to gain his freedom'. McGahey had recently attended a talk by Professor Mezzeroff in Hancock Hall, New York, on the 'Resources of Civilisation'.[58] In hindsight, the image of handfuls of volunteers armed with dynamite sticks and fighting national wars appears, to say the least, fanciful, especially when considering that civic militias had fallen into disfavour in Europe over thirty years previously.[59] Moreover, arming citizens with infernal machines and encouraging small-group operations in a battlefield with no frontiers was a proposition that would be indistinguishable, in today's vocabulary, from terrorism. None the less, in the context of the times, it was a realistic and serious consideration given the perceived pace of technological development. Given that military experts, newspapers and the scientific profession predicted that conventional warfare was a thing of the past, it was no surprise that elements of the Fenian movement did likewise, and began to rethink insurrection, the traditional vehicle of physical-force nationalism.

The influence of official thinking about legitimate war strategies on the Irish skirmishers was unmistakable in the 1870s and 1880s. At the root of their scientific warfare was the straightforward wish to furnish their organisations with the latest technology available to state armies. This was no more than the up-to-date expression of the desires of previous generations of Irish-American nationalists, the 'Irish Brigade' of 1848 and the Civil War veterans of the late 1860s, to apply the latest 'military science' to Ireland, which in their case had been firearms and drilling to 'complement the native pike'.[60]

Debates in the Fenian press over the merits of skirmishing corresponded to those in the organs of the state and military, and in the daily press. These discussions created contexts where the skirmishers, rather than being the protagonists of a new terrorism, borrowed ideas and technologies that were already in circulation. Dynamite should be considered, not in terms of its newness, but as something that was routine in the postbellum. The common criminal use of infernal machines along with official enthusiasm to accept new technologies into the arsenal provided the skirmishers with a framework in which they could collapse distinctions between civilised and uncivilised/regular and irregular tactics and claim they were merely acting in accordance with the most progressive ideas on warfare. Adherence to the 'rules of war' would have virtually outlawed many of the new technologies. Hence, both revolutionaries and government argued, with disquieting composure, that the rules should capitulate, not the weapons.

Distinctions that are frequently made between top-down and bottom-up terrorisms, the legal and illegal use of force, can be helpful when analysing the factors that generate transformations in political violence. However, they can also act as an analytical cage that causes the researcher to overlook the parallel paths taken by state and resistance. Both state and non-state violence demand our attention in order to construct a reasonable understanding of how escalations occur. This is not to deny the agency of the skirmishers, or other revolutionary groups of the period, and to imply that their behaviour was dictated by the 'great forces' of the times. Fenianism borrowed elements from multiple contexts, and this chapter has focused on merely one of them.

In 1885 the novel *A Modern Daedalus* described an Irish patriot who, 'in the last quarter of the nineteenth century, in the full blaze of scientific illumination, and in the very heyday of mechanical progress', invents mechanical wings and assembles a flying brigade to bomb Dublin Castle and attack the fleets in Dublin bay. Faced with such methods, the British agree to Irish independence. In 1886 Jules Verne's *The Clipper of the Clouds* warned that private inventions presented a new menace to national security. In the wrong hands, flying machines could cause untold destruction, giving anarchists the means of enacting their vision of a ruthless and bloody revolution. In the right hands, new technology could produce weapons so fearsome they would act as a deterrent to war, or at least reduce conflicts to short, incisive battles. Either way, these authors believed science was about to profoundly transform politics and warfare.[61]

It did not. And ultimately here was the place where the skirmishers' predictions belonged, the realms of science fiction. Whether they were uttered by the skirmisher or soldier, most of the ideas advanced during this period were illusory. The skirmishers participated in a moment of collective self-delusion in a society where speculations on future modes of warfare were found on several levels: government, military, media and revolutionaries were penetrated by deep anxieties over violence. These groups were alike in that they all misjudged the power of technological change to enact a complete transformation of politics and warfare. That in itself serves to underline the significance of their commentaries, since it emphasises the danger of interpreting the era of *attentats* in the light of subsequent events. The sober consideration of ideas, within the military and press, that technology would imminently render warfare unrecognisable to the common soldier, reflected generally held insecurities about changes brought about by the Civil War, how it redefined the boundaries of conventional warfare, and what the next step was. These debates were to recur in the 1920s when bombing, aerial warfare and civilian casualties again became a subject of much discussion.

Obsessions with science masked a real crisis among Fenians regarding what direction 'physical-force' action should take. Post-1848, the state's power and capacities grew in all directions, even in terms of urban planning, allowing the military to intervene effectively against street fighting and rendering traditional repertoires of revolutionary violence obsolete. By the 1880s Friedrich Engels had become convinced that an uprising in Ireland had 'not the slightest chance': violent challenges to the state's legitimacy were a thing of the past, he believed, and he ultimately advocated representation through parliament.[62] The state's gradual establishment of a monopoly on violence put the strategy of revolutionary action increasingly in question. Thus, the advocates of skirmishing tended to cling to notions of scientific advances as a way of vindicating their methods of struggle. This resulted in the quixotic exaggeration of the effectiveness of such methods, as in the belief that teams of three or four skirmishers could destroy whole cities. In the end, the majority of the bombs damaged some glass and timber, and little else.

NOTES

1. *Irish World*, 9 June 1877.
2. *New York Times*, 3 Mar. 1884; *Brooklyn Eagle*, 21, 24 June 1884. Stephens' comments should also be read as an act of self-publicity as he was a marginal figure in Irish republicanism by the 1880s.
3. *Irish World*, 16 Apr. 1881.
4. For an interesting introduction and primary source material on the 'era of *attentats*', see Ruth Kinna (ed.), *Early Writings On Terrorism*, vol. i (London: Routledge, 2006). David Rapoport has organised the history of terrorism in 'four waves': the anarchist *attentat* was the signature of the first wave, while the fourth wave has been characterised by the suicide bomb and al-Qaeda. However, his wave theory does not adapt well to the Fenian skirmishers. See Rapoport, *Terrorism*, 4 vols (London: Routledge, 2006).
5. *Brooklyn Eagle*, 21 Jan. 1884.
6. *Gaelic American*, 20 Oct. 1923.
7. *New York Times*, 17 June, 8 Aug. 1877; *Brooklyn Eagle*, 26 Nov. 1881, 5 June 1887.
8. *Gaelic American*, 23 June 1923; R. K. Morris, *John P. Holland: Inventor of the Modern Submarine*, 2nd edn (Columbia, SC: University of S. Carolina, 1998); K. R. M. Short, *The Dynamite War: Irish-American Bombers in Victorian Britain* (Dublin: Gill & Macmillan, 1979), pp. 37–44. The history and photographs of the 'Fenian Ram', now housed in the Paterson Museum, can be found at http://www.geocities.com/gwmccue/Submarines/Holland_2.html (accessed 16 Dec. 2008)
9. *New York Times*, 29 July 1881, 15 Oct. 1896.
10. *United Irishman*, 23 Dec. 1882.
11. *Irish World*, 18 Mar. 1876.
12. See Short, *Dynamite War*; C. Campbell, *Fenian Fire: The British Government Plot to Assassinate Queen Victoria* (London: Harper Collins, 2002); M. Ó Catháin, *Irish Republicanism in Scotland, 185–1916: Fenians in Exile* (Dublin: Irish Academic Press, 2007), pp. 126–38.
13. *United Irishman*, 10 Jan. 1885.
14. *Chicago Tribune*, 16 Nov. 1857.
15. *Philadelphia North American*, 16 May 1861.
16. *Chicago Tribune*, 3 Sept. 1861; *New York Times*, 1 May 1861; *Burlington Times*, 18 Jan. 1862; *Saturday Evening Post*, 22 Mar. 1862.
17. *Chicago Tribune*, 24 Feb., 1 Nov. 1863; *New York Times*, 1 Mar. 1863.
18. *Washington Star*, 17 Jan. 1866.
19. *Scientific American*, 29 Jan. 1876.
20. *New York Times*, 27 Nov., 5 Dec. 1873.
21. *New York Times*, 5, 6 Jan., 4 Feb. 1874; *Brooklyn Eagle*, 5, 7 Jan. 1874.
22. *Brooklyn Eagle*, 2, 3, 5 Feb. 1874.
23. *Scientific American*, 28 Aug. 1845.
24. Ibid., 13 Feb., 20 Nov. 1869; 9 Apr. 1870; 12 Oct 1878; 26 June 1880; 15 Apr, 5 July, 6 Dec. 1884.
25. On the Bremerhaven explosion see A. Larabee, *The Dynamite Fiend: The Chilling Tale of a Confederate Spy, Con Artist, and Mass Murderer* (New York: Palgrave, 2005).
26. *Scientific American*, 29 Jan. 1876.
27. Ibid., 14 Mar. 1885.
28. A. Ford, HM Inspector of Explosives, 28 Dec. 1892, The National Archives: Public Record Office, Home Office 144-247-A54529/2.
29. Letter sent to the *Irish American*, 24 Mar. 1883.

30. US Consul Archibald to Home Secretary, 20 Apr. 1876, TNA: PRO, Foreign Office 5 1556, 43.
31. John O'Leary to O'Donovan Rossa, 31 Jan. 1877, New York Public Library, Maloney Collection, Papers of Jeremiah O'Donovan Rossa, IHP 62; *Irishman*, 27 Mar. 1876.
32. John Schofield quoted in B. M. Linn, '"The American way of war" revisited', *Journal of Military History*, 66/2 (2002), pp. 501–33, at p. 515.
33. C. B. Sears, 'legitimate in warfare', *United Service: A Quarterly Review of Military and Naval Affairs*, 2/3 (Mar. 1880), pp. 350–66, at p. 363.
34. *Brooklyn Eagle*, 24 Jan. 1886.
35. Sears, 'Legitimate in Warfare', p. 350.
36. Ibid., p. 363.
37. Ibid., pp. 356, 364–6.
38. J. Chester, 'Dynamite, and the art of war', *United Service: A Quarterly Review of Military and Naval Affairs*, 10/4 (1884), pp. 3–12, at pp. 6–7.
39. Chester, 'Dynamite, and the art of war', p. 9.
40. S. N. Kalyvas, *The Logic of Violence in Civil War* (Cambridge: Cambridge University Press, 2006), pp. 55–8.
41. This essay was part of a larger debate on the role of the volunteer soldier. A. L. Wagner, 'The military necessities of the United States, and the best provisions for meeting them', *Journal of the Military Service Institution of the United States*, 5/24 (1884), pp. 237–71, at p. 249; Linn, '"The American way of war" revisited', pp. 501–33.
42. See D. J. Fitzpatrick, 'Emory Upton and the citizen soldier', *Journal of Military History*, 65/2 (2001), pp. 355–89.
43. *Irish World*, 22 Apr., 20 May 1876.
44. Ibid., 4 Dec. 1875.
45. Ibid., 16 Apr. 1881. Emphasis in original.
46. *Irish World*, 16 Apr. 1881. Some accounts have pointed to a lack of evidence to support McCafferty's activities during the Civil War in 1867. McCafferty helped to organise the IRB raid on an arsenal at Chester Castle and was allegedly involved in the Phoenix Park assassinations of 1882. W. O'Brien and D. Ryan, *Devoy's Post Bag, 1871–1928*, 2 vols (Dublin: Fallon, 1948), vol. i, p. 37; L. Ó Broin, *Fenian Fever: An Anglo-American Dilemma* (London: Chatto & Windus, 1971), pp. 126–8; P. Quinlivan and P. Rose, *The Fenians in England 1865–1872* (London: John Calder, 1982), pp. 26–8.
47. Owen McGee, *The IRB: The Irish Republican Brotherhood, from the Land League to Sinn Féin* (Dublin: Four Courts Press, 2005), p. 95; Ryan, *Devoy's Post Bag*, pp. 67–9.
48. *Irish World*, 20 May 1876.
49. Chester, 'Dynamite and the art of war', p. 8.
50. *Irishman*, 27 Mar. 1876; *Irish World*, 2 Mar. 1878.
51. 'Professor Mezzeroff', 'Dynamite Against Gladstone's Resources of Civilisation, or the Best Way to Make Ireland Free and Independent', Catholic University of America, O'Donovan Rossa Papers, 6, 1, undated (1883?).
52. *Die Freiheit* (New York), 12 June 1886.
53. *New York Times*, 30 Jan. 1884; *Brooklyn Eagle*, 15 Feb. 1885.
54. *Washington Post*, 5 Feb. 1885.
55. *United Irishman*, 30 Sept. 1882.
56. *Brooklyn Eagle*, 31 Oct., 21 Dec. 1883; *New York Times*, 4 Sept. 1883.
57. Mezzeroff, 'Dynamite Against Gladstone's Resources of Civilisation', pp. 19–22; *United Irishman*, 7 June 1884.
58. Quoted in the *Brooklyn Eagle*, 14 Apr. 1883.
59. Ralf Prove, 'Civic guards in the European revolutions of 1848', in H. G. Haupt and D. Dowe (eds), *Europe in 1848* (Oxford: Berghahn, 2001), pp. 683–93.
60. See John Belchem, 'Republican spirit and military science: "Irish Brigade" and Irish-American nationalism in 1848', *Irish Historical Studies*, 24/113 (1994), pp. 44–64, at p. 44; Ó Broin, *Fenian Fever*, pp. 6–7, 89–91.
61. Tom Greer, *A Modern Daedalus* (London: Griffith & Co., 1885), p. xiv; Jules Verne, *The Clipper of the Clouds* (London: Sampson Low & Co., 1887).
62. Engels to Eduard Bernstein, 26 June 1882, in Karl Marx and Friedrich Engels, *Ireland and the Irish Question: A Collection of Writings* (New York: International Publishers, 1972), pp. 334–5.

8

The Prince and the Fenians, Australasia 1868–9: Republican Conspiracy or Orange Opportunity?

Richard Davis

I

On 12 March 1868, at the Clontarf picnic grounds on Sydney harbour, Queen Victoria's second son, Prince Alfred, duke of Edinburgh, having embarked on the first-ever royal tour of Australasia, was shot in the back by Henry Joseph O'Farrell, a self-styled Fenian. The attack appalled the southern colonies which, until this incident, had been according the royal guest an almost hysterically positive welcome. A local newspaper expressed a common feeling of revulsion: 'At one moment all was good will, kindness, pleasure, and enjoyment; the next all was terror, confusion and raging passion.'[1] The incident marked a watershed in the development of Antipodean–Irish relations, highlighting the Catholic–Protestant divide, which had previously been reconciled, and introducing intense sectarianism.[2]

Australia by 1868 was already conversant with Irish nationalism. A number of the United Irishmen had been transported to New South Wales, while most of the Young Ireland leadership after 1848 was exiled to Tasmania. The Tasmanian premier in 1868, Sir Richard Dry, was the son of a United Irishman convict. A leading Young Irelander, Charles Gavan Duffy, already enjoying a ministerial pension, was soon to take office as premier of Victoria. In Queensland, Kevin Izod O'Doherty, transported to Tasmania as a Young Irelander, was now practising as a doctor and sat in the colony's Legislative Council.

The short-lived Dublin Fenian newspaper, the *Irish People*, had shown considerable awareness of the Antipodes in the early 1860s, frequently quoting from southern hemisphere newspapers. Strongly opposed to all Irish emigration, the editors, John O'Leary, Charles Kickham and T. C.

Luby, believed departure to Australia worse than to the United States 'inasmuch as it cuts Irishmen off completely from all effective work for Ireland. When the day of Ireland's destiny shall dawn, settlers in Australia will be too remote to be of any assistance in the strife.' The comparative ignorance of emigrants to Australia of Irish events and the distance between both countries made return to Ireland impracticable.[3] The newspaper was frequently in conflict with Archbishop (later Cardinal) Paul Cullen, a fervent opponent of non-denominational education and a believer in 'a special dispensation of God to disperse the Irish people over every country on the Globe', thereby disseminating the Catholic faith.[4] Although authorities like Seán Ó Lúing insist that Fenianism was established wherever Irishmen lived,[5] apart from the United States, its overseas contribution to the cause of Irish freedom appears to have been predominantly financial. What did impress T. C. Luby, who may have visited Australia in 1848,[6] was the heroic fight that the New Zealand Maori – 'one of the noblest savage races that ever trod upon God's spacious earth' – was currently waging against the British army. In several passionate editorials, Luby defended the Maori against the 'unconquerable propensity of the Anglo-Saxon to plunder the lands of other people – a propensity which manifests itself most strikingly alike in Ireland and New Zealand'. Aided by extensive quotes from Australian, New Zealand and British newspapers, Luby marvelled at the extraordinary fighting power of the Maori: 'When England's day of doom arrives – when the races she oppresses rise against her, many of them will be stronger than the Maories, but few can be braver.'[7]

II

Australasian newspapers, despite the inevitable delays in the transmission of news before cable communication was established in 1872, were equally informed about events in Ireland. The Sydney *Freeman's Journal*, founded by Tipperary-born Catholic Archdeacon John McEncroe in 1850, was particularly committed to Ireland. Branches of the Irish National League, a moderate body led by the former Young Ireland Tasmanian exile, John Martin, had a membership of over two hundred.[8] The *Irish People* ridiculed the National League, while Fenians disrupted its meetings. The latter strongly disliked Alexander Martin Sullivan, editor of the *Nation* and a firmly constitutional politician, who later sat at Westminster as a Home Rule MP. In 1866, however, Sullivan's younger brother, Richard, became editor of the Sydney *Freeman's Journal* and, ironically, won a local reputation as a Fenian supporter. In the months leading up to the Fenian revolt in Ireland in March 1867, Sullivan provided detailed information on Fenian activities throughout the world. He claimed that rebellion was inevitable and not unjustified in Ireland, but deplored it as certain to fail as an 'ill-timed, imprudent, and desperate action'.[9] He had scant respect for the movement's leaders, such as Fenian founders James Stephens, whom he considered 'miserably incompetent', and John O'Mahony, who he described as an 'infidel and imbecile'. This may have been related to the fact that Stephens had waged a vendetta against Alexander Sullivan. Both the *Sydney Morning Herald*, edited by the Revd John West, a Congregational minister and leading radical in the earlier anti-transportation movement, and the Melbourne *Age*, the influential liberal newspaper edited by David Syme, ignored such subtleties. When the *Herald* attacked a *Freeman* article on Stephens,[10] suggesting that it merited action by the attorney-general, Sullivan retorted that he was simply stating the facts: 'We merely deny that which it is not, and we fully admit that which it is.' Contrary to 'the stupid malignity' of the *Herald*, 'we have never in so much as a single sentence encouraged Fenianism, or applauded it, or endorsed it'. He had merely opined that the Fenians were not ruffians interested only in plunder.

West and Syme opposed the major preoccupation of Richard Sullivan's Sydney *Freeman's Journal* and Edmund Yates' Melbourne *Advocate*: their determination to safeguard Catholic schools against the threat of secular education legislation denying aid to denominational institutions throughout all Australasian colonies.[11] Here Sullivan's chief antagonist was Henry Parkes, colonial secretary in the New South Wales government. Cardinal Cullen, long the *bête noir* of the Fenian movement, was quoted not only on the necessity for Catholic education but also in condemnation of Fenianism.[12] Both Yates and Sullivan insisted that they had never supported Fenianism.[13] When pressed, Sullivan accepted the orthodox Catholic position that the movement's secrecy made it unacceptable.[14] Patrick O'Farrell has claimed that, abetted by Sullivan, the New South Wales Irish community was 'tearing itself apart'.[15] But even before the actual Fenian outbreak, and the assault on the prince, Sullivan and Yates grappled with a dilemma which confronted the Australasian Catholic Church for many generations. How could Irish immigrants be kept loyal to the perennial struggle for educational state aid without invoking their Irish patriotism, and how could Irish grievances be emphasised without alienating the general community and increasing its hostility to Catholic schools? Although recent analysts are sceptical of the assumption that nineteenth-century Irish emigrants were invariably passionate nationalists, more concerned with their homeland than with integration in their adopted country,[16] Irish patriotism was an obvious means of maintaining the cohesiveness of the Catholic community. In Ireland, Cardinal Cullen had tried to solve the dilemma by sponsoring an Irish National Association, which sought Catholic education and condemned Fenianism, but it had failed dismally.

As the first major Catholic newspaper in Australasia, the Sydney *Freeman's Journal* welcomed the new *Tasmanian Catholic Standard* as an ally in the education fight on its appearance in July 1867.[17] The long-anticipated Fenian uprising in Ireland had failed in March, and the trials of participants dragged on. In October, sixty-two prisoners were finally transported to Western Australia, a colony still receiving convicts. The *Freeman* rejected the Rising as an 'insane attempt', believing that the real rebellion was yet to come.[18] In its first issue, the *Tasmanian Catholic Standard* carried a pastoral from Cardinal Cullen concerning the restoration of penitent Fenians to full communion.[19] Like the *Freeman*, the *Tasmanian Catholic Standard* reported the latest news on the movement. Its editor, schoolteacher J. F. Roper, was more circumspect than Sullivan, making clearer the Church's objection. The daily press carried British and Irish reports on the revolt, initially confident that it had been 'a miserable and ignominious fiasco'.[20] Although the organisation appeared to have been shattered, and a number of commuted death sentences were announced, subsequent press reports revealed that Fenianism was still active in both Ireland and England. Australasia, however, was more concerned with planning its first royal visit from Queen Victoria's second son, Prince Alfred, duke of Edinburgh.[21] None the less, coverage of a daring rescue of two Fenian leaders in Manchester, in which a policeman had been killed, did cause initial concern.

When the prince arrived at Adelaide in December 1867 – intending to visit South Australia, Victoria, Tasmania, New South Wales and Queensland before proceeding to New Zealand – his appearance inspired an orgy of loyalty. Only critics like Sullivan quibbled at the inordinate expense.[22] Although the Revd John West's *Sydney Morning Herald* refused to apologise for the ardour of the participants in fêtes and demonstrations,[23] David Syme's Melbourne *Age* – no friend to Fenianism – later conceded that the prince's visit 'brought out an amazing display of flunkeyism'.[24] The visit, however, soon revealed tensions within the Australian community. In Melbourne, Orangemen displayed outside their Protestant Hall a transparency depicting William III triumphant at the Battle of the Boyne.[25] A Catholic crowd, incensed by the hated symbol, attacked it. After a shot fired from the hall killed a young Catholic, several Orangemen were put on trial but none were convicted. After the prince had left, a contentious election was fought in Victoria between January and March 1868. As in New South Wales and Tasmania, Catholics campaigned vigorously on their educational claims. The new *Advocate* opposed the *Age* in Melbourne.[26] Syme's *Age* accused the clergy of blatant intimidation, even to the extent of insisting that correct voting was a confessional issue.[27] To make matters worse, it was alleged that Fenians had been cheered at a private Catholic meeting on education addressed by

Duffy.[28] In Hobart, ministers of various Protestant bodies – possibly annoyed at the Catholic official presence – decided to take no official part in the procession or levée for the prince.[29] In Queensland, a party of Catholic schoolchildren was debarred from the procession because their banners were deemed unsuitable.[30]

III

While the prince was enjoying the adulation of Tasmania, news came through of the execution of three members of the rescue party in Manchester. Public opinion in England and Ireland was diametrically opposed on the incident. Most English people, affronted by the impudence of the rescue and the death of Sergeant Brett, rejoiced that the murderers had received their due. In Ireland, as Richard Sullivan's brother Alexander wrote: 'For the first time during years, the distinction between Fenian and non-Fenian Nationalists seemed to disappear.'[31] Irishmen, even constitutionalists like Sullivan and John Martin, insisted that the executions were judicial murder. There was no proof that any of the three, now publicised as the Manchester Martyrs, had fired the fatal shot. Their bearing in the dock and final cry of 'God Save Ireland' further ensured hero status. Richard Sullivan's second brother, Timothy D., penned a famous song bearing the same title. In London, Dublin, Cork and other Irish towns and cities, supporters organised processions with empty coffins. John Martin gave the oration in Dublin and was duly charged with sedition. He was found not guilty, but Alexander Sullivan was imprisoned for seditious publication. Colonial opinion was similarly divided. News of the Fenian attempt to blast a leader out of Clerkenwell prison, London, resulting in the death of five bystanders and the wounding of many more, fuelled local anti-Fenian 'loyalty fever'.[32] In contrast, the *Sydney Morning Herald* – accepting that all, especially the Anglican establishment, was not right with the British rule in Ireland – found murder by nitro-glycerine too hard to stomach. It accepted, however, that the opposition of the Catholic clergy to Fenianism was both sincere and self-interested.[33] The arrival of the *Hougoumont* with sixty-two Fenian convicts in Western Australia on 9 January did nothing to calm fears.[34] An irritant was the demand by the Secretary of State for the Colonies, the duke of Buckingham, that the colonies incorporate the British Treason Felony Act, first used against the Young Irelanders in 1848, into local legislation.

Many colonial Irish hoped to honour the 'Manchester Martyrs' with demonstrations similar to those which had occurred in Ireland and England. The initiative came not from Sydney or Melbourne but from Hokitika, centre of a gold-mining boom on the west coast of New

Zealand's South Island. The leaders, however, had Australian experience.
John Manning, a journalist who, with Peter Lalor, had taken part in the
Eureka Stockade affray of 1854, and a former teacher in Catholic schools,
combined with Fr James Larkin from Queensland to set up the *New
Zealand Celt* and organise, on 8 March, an Irish-style empty coffin
procession to the Catholic cemetery to erect a wooden Celtic cross for
the Manchester three. Other smaller demonstrations occurred nearby.
The *Age* reported placards advertising a similar funeral in Melbourne for
St Patrick's Day that were sure to arouse local fears of Fenian action. As
Duffy wrote: 'Police, infantry, and artillery, heavily armed, were distrib-
uted through the city at strategic points to suppress the procession.'[35]
The *Age* believed that this vigilance had prevented any demonstration.[36]
The *Advocate* dismissed the reports of a Fenian funeral as lies, intended
to win favourable treatment for the Orangemen accused of murdering the
Catholic boy in November.[37] Hokitika remained the only Australasian
town to demonstrate in support of the Manchester Martyrs.

When the prince duly arrived in Sydney in late January 1868,
Sullivan's *Freeman's Journal* rejoiced that there was no Orange participation
in the welcome: 'Hitherto we have lived in peace and quietness and we
believe that the good sense of the majority of the people will insist that this
shall continue as one of those blessings to be obtained by taking up a residence in New South Wales.'[38] A year earlier, in answer to the *Sydney Morning
Herald*'s claim that the *Freeman* was stirring up strife, Sullivan had replied:
'Here, at least we all occupy some sort of neutral territory, here we can forget old feuds, sink old differences and enjoy the blessings of free institutions in common.'[39] In Victoria, the *Saturday Review* complimented local
Irish inhabitants on keeping any personal sympathies for Fenianism to
themselves.[40] In the past Catholic and Protestant immigrants sometimes
shared the celebration of St Patrick's Day.[41] But could colonial society agree
to differ on serious issues that were not locally relevant?

IV

Such aspirations proved too optimistic for 1868. Significant divisions
were brewing in all Australasian colonies on the question of Catholic education. The community was polarised on Fenianism, and Orangemen had
drawn blood in Melbourne. It required only a spark to set alight a confla-
gration. This was duly provided by Henry J. O'Farrell when he shot Prince
Alfred on 12 March. While O'Farrell was – with difficulty – saved from
immediate lynching, the prince was only slightly wounded and able to
resume his duties before the end of the month with nothing worse than
a scar.[42] The *Launceston Examiner* considered hanging too good for the likes
of O'Farrell, who, it felt, should be torn limb from limb by wild animals.[43]

The would-be assassin exacerbated matters by declaring that – as a member of a Fenian circle – he had drawn the fatal lot to shoot the prince in retaliation for the execution of the Manchester Martyrs. Colonial Secretary Henry Parkes – who claimed that the New South Wales government had prior knowledge of local Fenian plotting – asserted the existence of further evidence of a widespread conspiracy. The *Sydney Morning Herald* was somewhat sceptical of O'Farrell's initial confession, but other newspapers encouraged a general panic.[44] Indignation meetings erupted throughout Australasia, although some held the motives of Catholics who attended to be insincere.[45] The *Advocate* provided considerable coverage of expressions of loyalty and abhorrence, but drew the line at a purely Irish meeting, which, it feared, would become a vehicle for renouncing Ireland's right to self-government.[46] The government of Parkes and James Martin, a former Catholic, rushed the British Treason Felony Act through the New South Wales parliament with absurd additions, such as the criminalisation of a refusal to drink the queen's health and lengthy terms of imprisonment for daring to suggest Ireland's separation from England. Sullivan – possibly confused with a John O'Sullivan – was accused of such an insult to the sovereign. There was also a demand that the *Freeman's Journal* be banned.[47] The government subsequently charged the *Freeman's Journal*, not with treason felony, but with a technical breach of the registration laws. However, Parkes and Martin lost office before the case came to court, and their successors dropped it.[48]

The treason felony legislation was so outrageous that the Colonial Office refused to submit it to the Queen, instead returning it for modification. Hysterical loyalty to the prince was transformed into sectarian paranoia. Alderman Pritchard of Sydney called for the Irish to be taxed like the Chinese.[49] Throughout various colonies, ludicrous arrests were made of drunks for claiming to be Fenians or speaking ill of the prince. At Tyagong, two men were seized for declaring that it would be no worse to shoot the prince than a black fellow.[50] Suspected Fenians were dismissed from the New South Wales police force. A group of railway workers also fell under suspicion. In Tasmania, a rumour circulated alleging that the Sydney police had dispersed a body of six hundred Fenians.[51] A Fenian warship was also reported to have arrived to free the Fenian convicts in Western Australia.

The Orange lodges – hitherto quiescent in New South Wales if not Victoria – now multiplied as a result of passionate anti-Fenian sentiment. In the Ballarat region, eight new lodges sprang up almost immediately after the O'Farrell incident.[52] A new Protestant Political Association appeared in New South Wales. In Tasmania an ultra-Protestant periodical, the *Leader*, was established to maintain a Protestant alliance and later a revived Orange lodge. The *Leader's* first issue alleged an amazing web of Fenian conspiracy in the centre of Hobart:

A head-centre enjoying the full confidence of the Government, for-
warding correspondence and remittances to Fenian agents; soldiers
drinking the health of O'Farrell in public places; officers tampering
with their men; the police force in an unhealthy condition; the
Corporation servants ditto; messengers, &c., in the Civil Service ditto
ditto; and all through the Government ditto repeato; and we received
information yesterday of a Fenian lodge existing in our midst, where
the Fenian oath is administered! not 1,000 miles from Elizabeth
Street [centre of the city].[53]

The Hobart *Mercury* appeared to agree, insisting that it could lay hands on
Fenians in the city who could only deny membership at the risk of chok-
ing.[54] Later, when these reports were not substantiated, the *Leader* did
'most candidly confess, that had it not been for the revolt of Irish
Romanists known as Fenians, in the Old Country, and the base, cowardly,
and disgusting outrage on H. R. H. the Duke of Edinburgh in these
colonies, we might have continued to put up with the inroads and insults
too long borne by a community composed of four fifths Protestants to one
fifth Romanists, at any rate until some such occasion had arisen'.[55] The
Tasmanian Catholic Standard, however, cited the famous statement of
Bishop Moriarty of Kerry that hell was not hot enough nor eternity long
enough to punish the Fenians.[56] The Sydney *Freeman* agreed that without
O'Farrell, Orangemen would not have dared to go public.[57] In other words,
if O'Farrell had not existed, it would have been necessary to invent him.

Irish Catholics were naturally distraught by O'Farrell's attack, praying
when they first heard of the assault that it was not one of their own countrymen. Leading representatives of the community, such as Duffy and the
Advocate in Victoria and Richard Sullivan in New South Wales, insisted
from the start that O'Farrell was an unbalanced man, acting alone. Duffy
pointed out – as the *Irish People* had done previously – that Australia was
too far from Ireland to serve as a Fenian base, insisting that had Fenians
wanted to take vengeance for the Manchester executions, there would
have been plenty of targets at home. In Queensland, the former Young
Ireland exile, Dr Kevin O'Doherty, did what the *Advocate* feared and
presided at a meeting of Irishmen to repudiate O'Farrell. The former
rebel then participated at a general meeting which sent condolences to
the queen, calling on the Irish community to cast out Fenianism. Like
Sullivan, he considered that the movement had no place in a colony without political inequality.[58] Catholic bishops and priests, commiserating
with the prince, insisted that Fenianism was banned by their church.
Butler Aspinall, a Victorian lawyer who had been accused of obtaining his
seat in the local legislature through Catholic clerical direction,[59] defended
O'Farrell on the grounds of insanity.[60] Aspinall showed that Edward
Oxford, who had been found insane after attempting to assassinate the

queen, had also constructed a crazy scenario of conspiracy.[61] The court, however, decided that the would-be assassin – regardless of his history of drunkenness and instability – had been reasonably sane in recent months. Despite the personal intervention of the prince, O'Farrell was hanged at Darlinghurst gaol on 21 April 1868. In his final confession, O'Farrell reversed his earlier claims, insisting that he had acted alone.

This by no means damped down the furore. Some militant Protestants asserted that his confessor, in order to cover up the undoubted links between the Catholic Church and Fenianism, had imposed O'Farrell's final confession on him.[62] The Catholic chaplain at Darlinghurst was sacked for leaking the confession to an anti-Parkes MP, but denied the main charge. Critics pointed to Fr Larkin and other priests on the west coast of New Zealand, who had given church sanction to the pro-Fenian demonstration, as indeed had many clergy in Ireland. Fr Larkin nevertheless denied emphatically that he was a Fenian. Although Larkin had attended sympathy meetings for the prince, he was suspended by his bishop and sentenced to gaol for his part in the famous procession. He later served as priest in Tuapeka, proving an energetic supporter of Catholic schools.[63]

One public man kept his balance in this Australasian crisis. Richard Davies Ireland – formerly a member of the Irish Protestant Repeal Association in 1848 and (twenty years later) a Victorian queen's counsel – found himself professionally engaged on both sides of the dispute. Defending an Orangeman accused of murder in the Protestant Hall affair in Melbourne, Ireland argued that the display of King Billy's image was not necessarily provocative in Victoria.[64] Crossing the Tasman Sea to defend Fr Larkin in Hokitika, Ireland did much to defuse a threatening situation. Persuading the court to drop two of the ten charges and challenging several of the others, Ireland showed that no disaffection towards the New Zealand government or desire to cause strife had been intended. The 'defendants, believing that the three men who were executed at Manchester did not intend murder, but to rescue those from custody who wished to redress those wrongs, should wish to evince their sympathy with them – not as murderers, but as men who had fallen in their attempt to redress the wrongs of Ireland'. Finally, he begged the people to 'live together in this community in unanimity and harmony'.[65] Ireland persuaded the protestors to plead guilty. Given the inflamed state of public opinion at the time, the sentences of a month's gaol and fines of £20 each, quickly paid out of subscriptions raised by the considerable sum of over £1,000, were lenient (as even the *Freeman's Journal* accepted).[66] Ireland was not only awarded a special presentation by his clients, but was also accorded the hospitality of the local bar, attorney-general and judge.[67] The prince, despite the promise of loyal Maori to carry Fenians away to the mountains, abandoned his plans to visit New Zealand. In

1869 there was a scare that Fenian gold-miners in the Thames district of the North Island were in cahoots with rebel Hau Hau Maori, the latter perhaps having read the *Irish People*. The New Zealand premier, E. W. Stafford, an Anglo-Irishman, rejected such fears. He denied that there were any real Fenians in the Thames, arguing that there were, at best, vague sympathisers.[68]

V

The distinction between sworn Fenians and vague sympathisers was the nub of the colonial problem. It suited Orangemen – concerned mainly with local issues such as state education and jobs in the public service – and politicians like Henry Parkes to deny such distinctions. In August 1868, despite a total failure to produce accomplices of O'Farrell and to the amazement of West's *Sydney Morning Herald*,[69] Parkes continued to maintain that he had evidence of a serious conspiracy. A subsequent commission found against Parkes, but the latter was able to manoeuvre a parliamentary majority to reject the report.[70] Though nothing positive ever emerged from the controversy, Parkes lived down the embarrassment to become a prominent premier, while New South Wales – like the other Australasian colonies – voted in favour of public schools with no aid for denominational institutions. A *Freeman* correspondent, W. M'Curtayne, suggested that Parkes had used Fenianism to turn the tables on the Catholics, who were giving him trouble over education.[71]

Syme's Melbourne *Age*, insistent that the *Advocate* and *Freeman's Journal* were Fenian papers, adopted a more sophisticated approach to the distinction. Accepting that there were few, if any, real Fenians in Australia, he maintained that newspapers patronised by eminent men indirectly influenced thousands. This was an attack on Duffy, who was believed to be the sponsor of the *Advocate*. In a letter, published in the Hobart *Mercury*, Duffy denied that he was the editor and supported the *Advocate*'s claim to provide hitherto neglected information on Ireland. He himself had never written a line on Fenianism.[72] Nevertheless, the *Age* insisted that 'indirect' Fenians were worse than active members of the movement. Believing that there were few, if any, of the latter in the country, it professed a preference for dealing with them rather than their misguided amateur supporters. Properly organised Fenians would never have been so foolish as to mount an attack on the prince, but unstable men like O'Farrell could easily succumb to propaganda and become their own centres in the committal of atrocities.[73] Sullivan's *Freeman's Journal* sarcastically inquired if O'Farrell was a reader of the paper.[74] The Hobart *Mercury* also feared indirect Fenians: 'It is the sympathisers with Fenianism, whether in the public service or out of it, that we most have to dread.'[75] The Melbourne Catholic *Advocate* attempted to turn the issue of loyalty on its head by insisting that it was the Liberal secularists, led by the Irish Protestant George Higginbotham, who favoured separation from England. The *Advocate*, on the other hand, regarded the British link as 'in truth a great advantage to us. Only a fool would not be loyal in Victoria.'[76] It quoted the former Young Irelander, D'Arcy McGee, who had been murdered by a Fenian in 1868 when he became a monarchist Canadian statesman. McGee had insisted that the Canadian Irish, unlike many of their United States brethren, were loyal to the British connection in Canada because they were accorded full civil and religious rights, having left misgovernment behind them in Ireland.[77]

The Fenian furore, despite Parkes' best efforts, gradually died down in eastern Australia and New Zealand. In 1869 twenty-five real Fenians appeared, following the initial release of IRB prisoners in Western Australia. Sullivan became secretary of a fund to enable them to return to Ireland or move to the United States. After they were refused entry to Victoria, R. D. Ireland – back from Hokitika – supported the ban, and the Fenians moved to Sydney. Sullivan tried to arrange a picnic in their honour at Clontarf, where the prince had been injured. The government and the *Sydney Morning Herald* were outraged. Sullivan – breaking with his partners on the *Freeman's Journal* – publicly denounced the clergy for interference in politics when they forbade Catholic attendance. He did agree, however, to cancel the picnic in the interests of the other Fenians who were still incarcerated. The *Herald*, attacking clerical influence on the perennial education issue in the ongoing New South Wales election, gave Sullivan, who soon left for the United States, no credit for his stand.[78] About a quarter of the sixty-two men transported to Western Australia remained in the country. Famous escapes such as that of John Boyle O'Reilly in 1869, and the rescue of the 'Catalpan six' in 1876, raised flagging Fenian morale. The former convict Michael Cody, settling as a businessman in Sydney, maintained a vestigial Fenian organisation in Australasia which collected considerable sums of money for the cause, especially from Irish goldminers. However, Australasian Fenians did not send representatives to the international Fenian congresses in the United States, suggesting that the *Irish People* was correct in its assumption that the Antipodes were too distant for direct influence.[79]

There were a number of lasting results from this episode. In most colonies, Orangeism received a rare boost and it went on to develop strongly, if fitfully, especially in New South Wales and Victoria. The Catholic Church continued to seek an organisation which would help to co-ordinate their Irish flock without alienating the general community, defying church law, or hindering the long campaign for educational state aid. The *Advocate* rejoiced that, unlike the United States where

'Fenianism has become synonymous with Irishism' (thus excluding the Catholic Church), there was no such division in Australia.[80] The Hibernian Australasian Catholic Benefit Society, under church control, had limited success, but the arrival of the constitutional home rule movement in the 1870s was a double blessing: it avoided the secrecy and violence so much disliked by the church and presented the Irish case in a manner acceptable to general colonial opinion. Ireland demanded only the same self-government within the empire which Australasia had already achieved. This consensus disappeared for a time when Sinn Féin displaced the Irish home rulers in the early twentieth century. After the 1921 Anglo-Irish treaty, the Irish issue began to fade from colonial recollection. Patrick O'Farrell has argued that Irish-Australians were assimilationist, but also that they provided the basis of subsequent Australian nationalism by offering a challenge to the Anglo-centred nineteenth-century majority. As West's *Sydney Morning Herald* put it, local Irishmen 'say and do many things which cold-minded Englishmen can hardly comprehend – certainly with which Englishmen have no sympathy whatsoever'.[81] The strife over Fenianism in 1867–8 was a first step towards multiculturalism and perhaps future republics in Australia and New Zealand. Could a good mid-nineteenth-century citizen in Australasia hold views on England's administration in Ireland diametrically opposed to those of the majority? Sullivan pessimistically complained that, after the assassination attempt, it was no longer true that 'all nationalities are on a footing of equality here, and that all which is required from any one is to be a good and loyal inhabitant of Australia'. While his brother Alexander was gaoled in Ireland for supporting the Manchester Three, it was still necessary in Australia to be an 'adorer of the British Government and a fiendish hater of any one endeavouring or wishing to ameliorate that Government as it exists in Ireland'.[82] Ironically, when, a hundred years later, multiculturalism became general Australasian policy, with state aid granted to Catholic and other religious schools, the descendants of Irish immigrants appeared part of an Anglo-Celtic establishment, looking askance at more recent arrivals from Southern Europe, China and Muslim lands.

NOTES

1. Robert Travers, *The Phantom Fenians of New South Wales* (Kenthurst: Kangaroo Press, 1886), p. 19.
2. See Brian McKinlay, *The First Royal Tour, 1867–1868* (Adelaide: Rigby, 1970); Keith Amos, *The Fenians in Australia, 1865–1880* (Kensington: University of New South Wales Press, 1988); Patrick O'Farrell, *The Irish in Australia* (Kensington: University of New South Wales Press, 1988).
3. *Irish People*, 6 Aug. 1864.
4. *Irish People*, 19 Nov. 1864.
5. Seán Ó Lúing, *Fremantle Mission* (Tralee: Anvil, 1965), p. 6.
6. John Devoy, *Recollections of an Irish Rebel* (Dublin: Shannon, 1969; 1st edn, 1929), p. 293.
7. *Irish People*, 23 July, 17 Dec. 1864; John O'Leary, *Recollections of Fenians and Fenianism*, 2 vols (London: Irish Universities Press, 1968, 1st Edn, 1896), vol. ii, pp. 186–9.

8. O'Farrell, *Irish in Australia*, p. 208.
9. *Freeman's Journal*, Sydney, 9 Feb. 1867.
10. *Sydney Morning Herald*, 13 Mar. 1867.
11. C. E. Sayers, *David Syme: A Life* (Melbourne: Cheshire, 1965), p. 108.
12. *Freeman's Journal*, 9 (education) and 23 (Fenianism) Feb. 1867. Cullen linked Fenianism with anti-Catholics such as Garibaldi and Mazzini, whom the Fenians regarded as heroes.
13. *Advocate*, 28 Mar. 1868. 'There never has been one line written in the *Advocate* relating to Fenianism, except to reprobate it for its sins and excesses.'
14. *Freeman's Journal*, 28 Mar. 1868.
15. O'Farrell, *Irish in Australia*, p. 212.
16. See Alan O'Day, 'Imagined Irish communities: networks of social communication of the Irish diaspora in the United States and Britain in the late nineteenth and early twentieth centuries', in Enda Delany and Donald M. MacRaild (eds), *Irish Migration, Networks and Ethnic Identities Since 1750* (London: Routledge, 2007), pp. 250–75.
17. *Freeman's Journal*, 7 Sept. 1867; *Tasmanian Catholic Standard*, 20 July 1867.
18. *Freeman's Journal*, 18 May 1867.
19. *Tasmanian Catholic Standard*, 20 July 1867: 'Exhort all who have been led astray, and who have incurred the censure of the Church by joining a secret organisation, to retrace their steps, to seek for absolution for their transgressions, and to determine to shun for the future all those societies which are so wisely condemned by the Church.'
20. *Mercury* (Hobart), 7 June 1867.
21. J. Milner and O. W. Brierly, *The Cruise of HMS* Galatea *in 1867–1868* (London: W. H. Allen, 1869); McKinlay, *First Royal Tour, passim*. The duke arrived at South Australia, 29 Oct.; Victoria, 22 Nov.; Tasmania, 6 Jan.; NSW, 21 Jan.
22. *Freeman's Journal*, 10 Aug. 1867.
23. *Sydney Morning Herald*, 21 Jan. 1868.
24. *Age*, 11 Apr. 1868.
25. McKinlay, *Royal Tour*, pp. 69–71.
26. *Advocate*, 1 Feb. 1868. The first editorial, entitled 'What interest have we in the pending elections', declared: 'They the Irish Catholics desire to rear their children in the faith of their fathers; not only because it is theirs by love and conviction, but because they are persuaded it is not possible to make good men and good citizens by any other method than systematically religious education.'
27. *Age*, 29 Feb. 1868.
28. *Age*, 25 Feb. 1868.
29. *Tasmanian Times*, 6 Jan. 1868.
30. *Freeman's Journal*, 14 Mar. 1868.
31. Quoted in E. R. Norman, *The Catholic Church and Ireland in the Age of Rebellion, 1859–1873* (London: Longman, 1965), p. 123.
32. *Advocate*, n.d., quoted in *Mercury*, 23 Mar. 1868.
33. *Sydney Morning Herald*, 22 Feb. 1868.
34. *Sydney Morning Herald*, 15 Feb. 1868. The same issue carried a leader dealing with Clerkenwell and information on the arrival of Fenian prisoners.
35. Quoted in *Advocate*, 18 Apr. 1868.
36. *Age*, 18 Mar. 1868. It suggested that Louis Ducrow, the organiser, had been an associate of O'Farrell at Ballarat.
37. *Advocate*, 21 Mar. 1868: 'There never was any intention of holding such a procession; the subject was never even mooted.' Sir Charles Gavan Duffy (*My Life in Two Hemispheres*, 2 vols (London: Fisher Unwin, 1898), vol. ii, pp. 298–9), in a passing reference to the affair, claimed that Ducrow had been a servant of squatters who were then attacking him.
38. *Freeman's Journal*, 25 Jan. 1868. The Protestant Alliance Friendly Society, generally allied to the Orange Institution, did participate in the welcome.
39. *Freeman's Journal*, 16 Mar. 1867.
40. Quoted by *Sydney Morning Herald*, 20 Feb. 1868.
41. A St Patrick's Friendly Society existed in Victoria, Tasmania and probably other colonies. It was non-denominational in theory, but it is not clear whether many, if any, Protestants were members.
42. *Sydney Morning Herald*, 25 Mar. 1868.
43. *Launceston Examiner*, 19 Mar. 1868.
44. *Sydney Morning Herald*, 19 Mar. 1868.

45. According to the *Tasmanian Catholic Standard*, April 1868, the newspapers were 'vile' against the Catholics, rejecting their professions of loyalty. See the editorial in the *Mercury*, 21 Mar. 1868.
46. *Advocate*, 4 Apr. 1868. The *Argus* had published a letter from a 'Loyal Irishman' in this vein.
47. *Sydney Morning Herald*, 12, 14 Mar. 1868 (Robert Wisdom's speech).
48. *Freeman's Journal*, 6 Mar. 1869.
49. *Age*, 25 Mar. 1868.
50. *Age*, 4 Apr. 1868.
51. *Tasmanian Times*, 21 Mar. 1868, quoted by *Freeman's Journal*, 4 Apr. 1868.
52. *Ballarat Courier*, quoted by *Advocate*, 21 Mar. 1868.
53. Quoted in *Launceston Examiner*, 4 Apr. 1868.
54. *Mercury*, 30 Mar. 1868.
55. *Leader*, 4 July 1868.
56. Cited by a correspondent in the *Tasmanian Catholic Standard*, March 1868. As the complaints showed, the issue was complex. When Moriarty objected to his brethren countenancing Fenianism through the mock funerals, a commentator suggested that both he and the Fenians were wrong. As the Manchester three had died reconciled to their Church, it was appropriate for Catholic clergy to officiate at remembrance services. On the other hand, the 'martyrs' could only have gained absolution by renouncing their Fenian oaths. But, as the Fenian leaders John Devoy and O'Donovan Rossa noted, some bishops and clergy were prepared to give absolution ignoring the oath. *Universe* (London), n.d., quoted in *Freeman's Journal* (Sydney), 28 Mar. 1868; Devoy, *Recollections of an Irish Rebel*, p. 316; O'Donovan Rossa, *My Years in English Jails* (Tralee: Anvil, 1967; 1st edn, 1874), pp. 28–9.
57. *Freeman's Journal*, 18 Apr. 1868.
58. Keith Amos, *The Fenians in Australia* (Kensington: University of New South Wales Press, 1988), p. 67; Ross and Heather Patrick, *Exiles Undaunted: The Irish Rebels Kevin and Eva O'Doherty* (St Lucia: University of Queensland Press, 1989), p. 164.
59. *Age*, 27 Feb. 1868.
60. *Advocate*, 11 Apr. 1868.
61. The Revd J. D. Lang, Presbyterian minister and New South Wales politician, was one of these. A. W. Martin (*Henry Parkes: A Biography* (Melbourne: Melbourne University Press, 1980), p. 242) declared that the second confession 'smacks strongly of the sacristy and not at all of the condemned cell'.
62. *New Zealand Times*, 13 Sept. 1879.
63. *Age*, 20 Mar. 1868.
64. *Launceston Examiner*, 4 June 1868.
65. *Age*, 2 July 1868: £1141.10.2d.
66. *Freeman's Journal*, 6 June 1868.
67. *Age*, 29 June 1868.
68. Richard P. Davis, *Irish Issues in New Zealand Politics, 1868–1920* (Dunedin: University of Otago Press, 1974), p. 21.
69. *Sydney Morning Herald*, 28 Aug. 1868.
70. Martin, *Henry Parkes*, p. 248.
71. *Freeman's Journal*, 28 Mar. 1868.
72. *Mercury*, 4 Apr. 1868.
73. *Age*, 21 Mar., 27 Apr. 1868.
74. *Freeman's Journal*, 25 Apr. 1868.
75. *Mercury*, 23 Mar. 1868.
76. *Advocate*, 6 June 1868 ('Allegiance to Church and State'), 18 July 1868.
77. *Advocate*, 11 July 1868.
78. Amos, *Fenians in Australia*, pp. 179–86; see *Freeman's Journal*, 20 Nov. 1869 for the dispute between Sullivan and other proprietors; *Sydney Morning Herald*, 23 Oct. 1869 and 23 Nov. 1869 (for criticism of clergy in politics).
79. See Amos, *Fenians in Australia, passim*, for this period in particular.
80. *Advocate*, 14 Mar. 1868.
81. *Sydney Morning Herald*, 28 Aug. 1868.
82. *Freeman's Journal*, 2 May 1868.

9

'The Black Hand of Irish Republicanism'? Transcontinental Fenianism and Theories of Global Terror

Máirtín Ó Catháin

I

Among the more fantastical claims of Fenian depredation, their supposed complicity in the nefarious activities of Jack the Ripper and the sinking of the *Titanic* are probably among the most outlandish. The association of the Fenians with such infamous events places them in a category far beyond that normally reserved for nationalist revolutionaries, or even perhaps for 'terrorists'. The erstwhile Irish-American suspect 'discovered' in Special Branch files in the mid-1980s by a dedicated 'Ripperologist' did have a connection with Clan na Gael, who despite the bloody murder of Dr Cronin by the Triangle faction a year after the Ripper murders, did not number London prostitutes among their list of possible targets. Equally, despite recent evidence of the possibly faulty state of Belfast riveting and sectarian animosities in the yard on the eve of *Titanic*'s launch, and notwithstanding memories both of O'Donovan Rossa's 'claim' that Fenians blew up HMS *Doterel* and the Skirmishing Fund's Fenian submarine endeavours, there could be little point in sinking a transatlantic liner with over a hundred Irish passengers on board.[1] The credulity of contemporary and later audiences may give strength to the aphorism that 'the world wants to be deceived', but still tell us something important about Fenianism. As the late J. M. Roberts observed of secret societies, 'the widespread belief in the rubbish talked about them is their most important as well as most interesting feature'.[2] A considerable amount of rubbish has been written and continues to be written about the Fenians and the Irish Revolutionary, or Republican, Brotherhood, but the cultural 'place' and cachet of 'the Organisation' even in contemporary Irish society – evidenced at least in part by the title of this present collection – is a strong one, still laden with myth and political import. The purpose of this chapter will be to explore aspects of this mythology, setting it against the historical record of judicious scholarship, and framing it mainly in the light of the 'terrorism studies' which extrapolate theories of the first international terror network out of the scatterings, actions and supposed originality of the Fenian movement.

II

Foremost among 'terrorism experts' to identify the Fenians as the progenitors of a strategical and tactical commitment to 'terrorism' is Lindsay Clutterbuck. The former London Metropolitan Police analyst surveyed the range and character of Fenian actions during the so-called 'dynamite war' of the 1880s and found that in symbolic target selection, cumulative attack strategy and the use of improvised explosive devices, as well as their nonchalance about possible civilian casualties, the Fenians were 'innovative and unique', unleashing 'terrorism in a form that was to become increasingly familiar across the globe in the twentieth century'.[3] Clutterbuck's work also identifies the issues of 'transference' (the adoption of Fenian 'terrorist' techniques in other parts of the world) and the 'movement of terrorists, material and finances across international borders' as being key to the Fenians' significance as progenitors of modern terrorism.[4]

M. L. R. Smith's study of republican strategy supports some of these contentions, though he uses the contemporary term *skirmishing* rather than *terrorism*. However, Smith regards the Fenians as less innovative than Clutterbuck and suggests that the idea of attacking targets outside of Ireland arose as a result of Fenian campaigns in Britain and developed from this time. Moreover, in relation to the dynamite campaign, he posits the notion of a 'protracted war scenario' where 'the thought of military action within an extended time frame' more or less supplanted the idea of a single rebellion consuming all resources.[5] A number of historians, most notably Jenkins, Gantt and Townshend, support these theories to varying degrees and locate Fenianism in the vanguard of the development of international terrorism.[6]

Aside from the ahistorical nature of some of these theoretical approaches, such contemporary studies are also disadvantaged by the requirement to analyse a movement still under development. One is reminded here of Leonardo Blake's 1939 publication entitled *Hitler's Last Year of Power*. Only H. B. C. Pollard's 1922 account, *The Secret Societies of Ireland: Their Rise and Progress*, could reasonably be seen as written at the near apogee of the IRB. Captain Hugh Bertie Campbell Pollard was an MI6 officer attached to Dublin Castle as an advisor to police between 1920 and 1922 and (like nineteenth-century secret service chief Robert Anderson) was thus able to draw upon secret government papers to write his examination of the secret societies. Unlike Anderson, however, his account adopted neither a temperate tone nor a measured assessment within its slightly crackpot pages. It did, nevertheless, have a wider audience and proved to be a more popular work on the Irish secret societies than any hitherto produced.[7] The Fenians emerge (as do, in fairness, every subsequent conspiratorial group and several political parties) as agents of world revolution in league with Marxists, anarchists, social revolutionaries, continental Freemasonry, Jewish Bolsheviks and mystic cults. Pollard was heavily influenced by the writings of Nesta Webster, an early member of the British Fascisti group and a proponent of *The Protocols of the Elders of Zion*, although Pollard conceded that the latter had not yet been 'wholly established to a point capable of definite proof'.[8] This position changed subsequently in later years when Pollard moved further to the right, recent evidence revealing his crucial role in helping General Franco to launch his coup against the Spanish republican government and his support for Nazism, which, despite his secret service position, almost saw him arrested in 1940. But for Pollard, the Jews had as little impact on Ireland as they did on 'the cannibal islands' as the country had 'neither that element of prosperity nor development of commerce which attracts the chosen, but discriminating, race', though he feared that this might change in the Ireland of the 1920s and 1930s.[9]

None the less, no Irish secret society in Pollard's account was left uncontaminated by dark forces bent on the destruction of civilisation and several, indeed, were initiated by them. Thus the seventeenth-century Gaelic leader Rory O'More (who, ironically, Pollard refers to as 'Roger Moore') is described as an 'instrument' in the hands of French and Spanish Jesuits preaching the secret doctrine of the Garduña society, marrying 'Catholicism with brigandage' to 'wild Irishry'. This is followed by the United Irishmen as merely the emissaries of the Illuminati, itself the product of Orleanist and Prussian Freemasonry (with some Jewish influence), as were in some senses both the Ribbonmen and Orangemen, whereas the Fenians were more obviously the Irish Carbonari and eventually a wing of the International Working Men's Association. The scheme, of course, was world revolution and its success was fully predicated on targeting Ireland as the 'weak spot in the solid armour of Britain'.[10] Ultimately, Pollard's conclusions centre on race. He identifies a general psycho-genetic predisposition to criminal conspiracy among the Irish based on their belief, one shared by the Zulus and Prussians, in racial superiority.[11]

Pollard is an under-studied individual and although his conspiracy theory on Fenianism is probably less enlightening than *A Busy Time in Mexico: an unconventional record of Mexican incident* (1913), it was none the less an important and enduring book produced by a senior government official. Pollard's position would have made it a sought-after item (he added 'late of the Staff of the Chief of Police, Ireland' after his name), lending it credibility as a guide not only to the Fenians but also to a vast range of other 'secret societies'. With the civil servant's characteristic talent for understatement, Leon Ó Broin cautioned discrimination in reading Pollard's book, but he is one of very few historians to comment upon the work, while many others who have employed it in studies of Fenianism have failed to consider its overall analysis or impact.[12]

III

Fenian accounts of their own organisation are scarcely more reliable than Pollard's and, as O'Leary himself was at pains to point out, his two-volume study published in 1876 was intended not as a history but merely as an account of his own recollections. He nevertheless reinforced the myth of a global Fenian threat, picked up a quarter of a century later by the egregious Pollard, when he wrote that Irish emigration effectively meant that 'England has the Irish enemy facing her in every quarter of the globe'.[13] Although Devoy and Rossa made similar claims, most Fenian accounts are highly personalised narratives that exude defensiveness over the movement's strategy and tactics and stress the apostolic succession subsequently endorsed with relatively little criticism or analysis by writers as diverse as Desmond Ryan, T. W. Moody and Leon Ó Broin.[14]

In contrast, Sir Robert Anderson, that great foil of the Fenians, has left us a biographical account from 1906 that has the benefit not only of hindsight but also of drawing upon his early study of Fenianism, published in 1872. In common though with O'Leary, with whom in some ways he bears comparison, Anderson is insistent that his book 'makes no pretensions to be "history". My aim ... is merely to make some slight additions to the stock of materials upon which historians may draw.'[15] Be that as it may, as with his 1872 publication and no doubt as a result of his original role in compiling a précis for the chief secretary, Anderson often tends towards summary and taut conclusions on the Fenian movement, of which he is by no means entirely critical. His views on the 1860s 'Fenian panic', moreover, provide a balanced corrective to some earlier writings and he expressed with frankness his amusement at the sense of terror engendered at the time by incidents as unconnected as the Clerkenwell explosion and the attempt to assassinate the duke of Edinburgh in Australia. For Anderson, the sight of pistol-packing civil servants in Whitehall was simply ridiculous; he added that their lives were more imperilled 'by London fogs than by Fenian plots'.[16] But an important and neglected observation of Anderson was that government responses to the more violent aspects of Fenianism, whether in the aftermath of the London bombings or the stabbings in the Phoenix Park, very often served to encourage the Fenians to pursue such methods. Writing from the removed perspective of his quiet Bayswater home in the opening years of the twentieth century, his depiction of the authorities' hysteria is obviously coloured by his preoccupation with demonstrating his 'cool head' all those years before. However, his assessment that the government's attitude 'always alternated between panic and indifference' is in marked contrast to the hyperbole of successors such as Pollard and the earlier works produced during the 1870s and 1880s.[17]

During the 1880s – a decade in which the battle for home rule raged, bombs exploded in London and the drama of the Parnell Commission unfolded – two works by anonymous authors appeared on Fenianism that promised to enlighten the world about the workings of the nefarious conspiracy. Public appetites had been whetted by salacious and graphic reports of the Phoenix Park slayings, the dynamite outrages and convictions and stories of Parnellite complicity with the 'Moonlighters' and 'Hillside Men'. *Incipient Irish Revolution* (1889) provided its readers with a map outlining the various centres of Fenianism, which it then proceeded to survey, contextualising its strengths and weaknesses with the assured tone of an unidentifiable author. It devoted particular attention to the notion of the Irish in Britain as fifth columnists, alleging a transatlantic conspiracy encompassing the single tax champion Henry George, the Knights of Labour trade union, assorted communistic influences and the Fenians.[18]

This conjunction of actors committed to ostensibly varying ends (which appears also in the work of Pollard) is a feature of the 1883 work *The Mysteries of Ireland*, which paid particular attention to the Phoenix Park affair and, in common with the speculation of the press, attributed responsibility for the event to a Fenian–Land League–Home Rule conspiracy. The book, however, is overwhelmingly composed of press clippings on a range of 'outrages' so well publicised as to make the claim of 'Mysteries' in the title quite redundant. Despite this, and the outlandish attribution to Fenian desperadoes of such incidents as the attaching of mines to the warship HMS *Lord Warden* while anchored in the Firth of Forth on Scotland's east coast in 1881, the book proved successful, apparently going into more than one edition, and being cited then and afterwards with little circumspection.[19]

Its theme of the confluence of agrarian outrage, dynamite and assassination with a latter-day malevolent compact between Fenians, parliamentarians and continental regicides also forms a key plank in the complicit memoirs of Anderson and Thomas Beach (whose testimony to *The Times*-Parnell Commission, under his alias as super-spy Henri Le Caron, proved so sensational). Exempting the dastardly Russians, Anderson none the less continued to insist that a Fenian–Land League–Home Rule embrace personified by Parnell and Davitt was responsible for driving the knives of the Invincibles into the bodies of Cavendish and Burke.[20] His agent, Thomas Beach, proves less reticent, however, about both Russian and communist influence, 'and a hundred and one wild schemes in which Dhuleep Singh, General Carroll Thevis [*sic*], Aylward and other soldiers of fortune or discontent all figured'. This traversing of three continents and possibly more by the Fenian conspirators under the direction of 'atheistic' Irish-American leaders spouting hatred with 'whiskey-laden breath' provides compelling and dramatic testimony, notwithstanding the demise of the commission, absolution of Parnell and the unmasking of Le Caron.[21] It was also an interpretation of considerable appeal in the *fin de siècle* world of bohemianism, anarchist 'propaganda of the deed', plots, scams, sensationalist murders, espionage and fifth columnists.

Le Caron's book appeared in 1892, the same year as the Walsall anarchist bomb trial; it was followed in 1894 by the Greenwich Park explosion, the assassination of Carnot, and the Dreyfus trial in France. Talk of bombs, spies and *agents provocateurs* found as ready and gullible an audience in supposedly non-fictional work as in the plethora of 'terrorist literature' novels and short stories that abounded in these years.[22] Conspiracy theories, some of elaborate depth and construction, replaced normative and empirical explanations for many people, perhaps forming part of a wider belief-versus-reason dialectic that grew out of the ontological controversy surrounding Darwinism, industrial growth, urbanisation, class conflict and migration. Fenianism was but one element in this over-hyphenated chain of Byzantine conspiracy, appealing to those who were convinced that the world was closing in around them.[23]

IV

The two-volume study by John Shedding Rutherford (1829–1889), *The Secret History of the Fenian Conspiracy* (published in 1877), is in some respects an unusual precursor to the fanciful accounts of the 1880s and 1890s. Generally seen as one of the better histories of the movement during a period when most accounts of Fenianism were aimed at the more sensational end of the market – titles such as *Fenianism, Irish Land Leagueism, and Communism* (1881) and *How to Kill Fenianism and Ribbonism* (1871) vied with *The Rottenness of Fenianism* (1865) and *The Irish Invincibles, Their Brotherhood of Blood* (1883) – it was fairly well received. Naturally, this did not extend to the Fenians themselves, O'Leary labelling it libellous and Denis Dowling Mulcahy complaining that it contained ten lies in every twenty lines.[24] More recent studies have treated Rutherford's book with caution and many of its 'inaccuracies' have been long since ironed out, but, like Pollard's work, it has nevertheless failed to receive extensive attention.[25] This is an important oversight as it was the first serious attempt at an historical analysis of the Fenian movement – though Foreign Office diplomat, Charles Abbott (3rd

Baron Tenterden, 1834–82), had produced a useful account of the Fenian Brotherhood in 1871 – and as such it undoubtedly proved an essential and influential read for other writers on Fenianism, Pollard included. Moreover, Rutherford set the template for Fenianism as a global threat with enough credibility for contemporaries to absorb its general analytical thrust while challenging some of its chronological or narrative deficiencies.[26]

Rutherford begins his study by flagging up some novel difficulties in producing such a work. The difficulty of writing an account of a secret society without access to the records of that society is, somewhat unusually, not admitted. Instead, Rutherford states that the power of Fenians through their wealth, willingness to kill, and exceptionally good journalism are the key difficulties facing the historian. Indeed even Rossa, he writes, 'that eminently truculent, vulgar, and illiterate demagogue wrote largely, handling the pen as with the rough paw of an unlicked bear, but always with coarse vigour and effect'.[27] These lines give us some idea of Rutherford's opinion of the Fenians, although at a later stage he asserts that while they lacked 'the gentleman-like element', they were 'not always and necessarily in the wrong' and showed a talent for organisation, having the 'schoolmaster type' do the organisation's administration, encouraging the commercial traveller class to disseminate revolutionary opinions and act as couriers, while relying on the adventurous spirits of 'riotous and rollicking' medical students for the fight.[28] There are some good and measured insights, subsequently well developed by Comerford in *The Fenians in Context* regarding the fact that some Fenians courted 'continental revolutionists and continental despots' equally, and he writes engagingly and perceptively of Stephens and O'Mahony respectively as the chiefs of Fenianism in the old world and the new.[29]

Despite this, there are also themes, re-emergent many years later in Pollard, of assorted arcana, racial explanation, co-ordinated transcontinental terror and, ultimately, world revolution. He describes the 'Celtic race' as being 'habituated to conspiracy for centuries'; devotes considerable attention to the impact of the 'Prophecies of St Columkill' on waves of Irish secret societies, the Fenians most recently; describes O'Mahony seeking the counsel of mediums; and makes some play of Masonic-like ritual.[30] Stephens features in the book, intriguing in Spain, Germany, Italy and London under the auspices of the 'Central Committee of Universal Revolution'; with the duc de Morny, French ambassador to Russia 'and men of like stamp' at Louis Napoleon's court; and successfully infiltrating the British army to such an extent that 'nearly all desertions' in Ireland during the Crimean War could be attributed to his efforts.[31] The image of the quiet residential street housing a bomb factory so beloved of later narratives appears in Rutherford, but his most important contribution may be his internationalisation of the Fenian threat, a threat, he insists, that remains in place in 1877 'recast and renamed ... secret everywhere', working in close connection with European revolutionists and English democrats, while hiding in the shadow of Irish nationalism.[32] Both the killing of D'Arcy McGee and O'Farrell's attempt to assassinate the duke of Edinburgh form a calculated part of Fenianism's 'reign of terror', implemented along the way and 'all over the empire' by a host of people paid to impersonate Stephens, Kelly, Deasy and McCafferty among other Fenian notables.

Assassination, Rutherford insists, provides the main plank of Fenian strategy, to be committed in the most spectacular manner by men willing to be caught and martyred 'to show that no rank, however exalted, and no distance, however vast, could interfere with the vengeance of the IRB – that it could strike down a prince as easily in Australia as a policeman in Dublin'.[33] Much of this, of course, was grist to the mill for some Fenians, especially Rossa and the 'dynamite journalists' Patrick Ford and 'Transatlantic' Mooney who – whatever their feelings on the impugnable thoughts of John Rutherford – were not entirely discomfited by his back-handed compliments as to the dangerous and extensive nature of their movement. Moreover, Rutherford was writing his book against the background of the furore raised by the Skirmishing Fund, with its bombastic promises to wreak all manner of havoc on Britain and the empire. As such, his depiction of Celtic fanaticists with a global presence 'always ready to court a struggle', employing any means, and lacking a racial ability to 'reason as the Teuton' marries well with contemporary anxieties and some nascent Fenian propaganda.[34]

At least some of this sensationalism may be attributable to the newspaper reports and caricatures of the period that compared the Fenians with extra-European groups such as the Indian 'thugee' cult or the Muslim agents of atrocity in the Balkans. Many of these shrill press reports, which associated Fenianism with contemporary conspiracies, also focused on the danger of Irish immigrant populations among the law-abiding and loyal majority – a transferable theme, presumably, given the growth of Irish migration after mid-century into British dominion territories in particular. Here we have the notion almost of a 'counter-empire' – an unquantifiable, unpredictable and seditious element *organised* wherever the Irish (and as a corollary, the British) find themselves in the world. The ragged contours of an at times thoroughly ironic critique of empire have only started to be drawn out by scholars and much remains to be done on what might be interpreted as a critique, both compartmentalised by Fenian activists in different dominion territories and forming part of the wider international propaganda of the movement.[35]

V

Peering out of his prison cell window in Mountjoy across a snowy and bitterly cold March evening in 1867, John Devoy contrasted the concert hall and bar-room *braggadocio* of stirring Fenian war lyrics with the fore-knowledge of the pitiful and pathetic 'counsel of despair' the rising was to be.[36] This gulf between image and reality was a constant for many Fenians, if at times startlingly less evident for many onlookers. While the manipulation of a supposed threat – the cultivation of Cohen's folk devils and moral panics – for political ends, be they related to immigration control, international extradition, security co-operation or simple scapegoating is not disavowed here, it is not central to this chapter: what was said and what was believed about Fenianism are.[37]

A striking feature of government papers relating to Fenianism is the high proportion of newspaper clippings they contain. These appear to lay down a basic skeleton of events upon which to hang intelligence reports. Sir Thomas Larcom's papers abound with assorted clippings, as do the papers of Sir Robert Anderson's brother Samuel, who worked out of Dublin Castle, and they even appear as supporting evidence among memoranda in both the Crime Branch Special files and Colonial Office papers.[38] Some of these press reports relate to events beyond the shores of Britain and Ireland and thus the reach, at times, of the authorities, but their frequent and important appearance, often without balanced annotation, demonstrates a remarkable level of reliance on journalists to fill in the gaps. This undoubtedly allowed the fanciful, the ephemeral and the downright ridiculous to find its way into government analyses and strategies from time to time, contributing to a tendency to both underestimate and exaggerate the Fenian threat. It seems probable that it also contributed to the tone and nature of some of the works that appeared on Fenianism during the movement's long existence.

The British government's decision to dispatch James Carey, the informer in the Phoenix park case, to far-flung South Africa in 1883 is but one of a surprising array of security measures demanded and taken to frustrate Fenian attacks globally. Paradoxically, Britain was as slow and hesitant as the United States at a later date in agreeing to anti-terror legislation and co-operation.[39] This poses a few challenges to the terrorism theorist, as to the historian looking for Dostoevsky's *Devils* in the scattered possessions of the British empire as well as at home. The terrorist hydra appeared to meet bombastic fringe half way in transcontinental policy formulation, Home Secretary Harcourt seemed to waver, Lloyd George laughed, and yet the Martin-Parkes administration in New South Wales, Macdonald's government in Ottawa, and the mayor of Port Elizabeth in the Cape Colony, Henry Pearson, responded with various degrees of hysteria.[40]

Moreover, while the 'Revolutionary Directory' formed to co-ordinate Fenian activity and contacts in Britain, Ireland, North America and Australasia may appear the type of world revolutionary conspiracy envisaged by Pollard and Rutherford, it was in fact most often a New

York–Dublin forum for debate, and as often, for dissension, the heterogeneity of the Irish nationalist movement being more striking than its perceived homogeneity. Here Rutherford actually lets in a chink of light, counselling that 'all conspirators are essentially nationalist, but all nationalists are not conspirators'.[41] Anderson, apparently, was as dismissive of the racial explanations so favoured by Rutherford and Pollard and laid down in the works of Cesare Lombroso (1836–1909) – popular among many secret policemen – though favourable to the less extreme anthropometrics of Alphonse Bertillon (1853–1914).[42] As to the specific contention of terrorist innovation proposed by some modern theorists, there is some evidence (despite Clutterbuck and Niall Whelehan's insistence that the Fenians did not self-designate as terrorists) that this was the idea; the term was employed occasionally by Rossa and Ford as propagandists as well as, more significantly, by William Mackey Lomasney as an activist.[43] Derek Offord's important research, however, indicates the problems of awarding the pioneering terrorist badge to either Russian Populists or the Fenians when the wider 'propaganda of the deed' and the earlier insurrectionary traditions with which it conformed were the province of Italian revolutionaries and agrarian Ribbonmen. Furthermore, contemporary research into the roots of what is termed 'modern political terrorism' increasingly highlights the importance of the anarchist 'propaganda of the deed' actions of the 1890s.[44]

Conspiracy theories work by telescoping explanations in an ahistorical tunnel, and both Fenianism's supporters and detractors have been brought together on more than one occasion in building the same kaleidoscope. While Fenianism undoubtedly sought expression far from Ireland, this was in many instances the result of local conditions and circumstances and was not directed from a central source or directly attributable to actual Fenian organisations. Three of the most notorious incidents of 'global Fenianism' – the shootings of D'Arcy McGee, the duke of Edinburgh and James Carey – were the work of lone individuals who were not members of Fenian organisations. Beyond this, most of Fenianism's most dramatic actions – the Canadian raids, the Manchester rescue, the Clerkenwell explosion and the bombing campaign – all took place outside of Ireland. Perhaps this alone explains the perception of Fenianism as a transcontinental network, and certainly this international dimension of the Fenian movement is an area that needs far more study. Replacing that with yet more theory – terroristic or otherwise – will continue to prove insufficient and lend itself to the creation of more of the myths cultivated for over a century.

NOTES

1. Stewart P. Evans and Paul Gainey, *The Lodger: The Arrest and Escape of Jack the Ripper* (London: Century, 1995) revealed the identity of the Irish-American suspect, Dr Francis Tumblety. His activities with the Fenians, and, possibly, the Phoenix Park killings added weight to his 'profile'. The claim is repeated in the general tome of Ripperology by Evans and Keith Skinner, *The*

Ultimate Jack the Ripper Sourcebook (London: Constable and Robinson, 2000). The idea of a Fenian link to the sinking of the Titanic is of older vintage and was mentioned most recently in Robin Gardiner and Dan Van Der Vat's controversial *The Riddle of the Titanic* (London: Orion, 1996).

2. J. M. Roberts, *The Mythology of the Secret Societies* (St Albans: Paladin, 1974), p. 23.

3. Lindsay Clutterbuck, 'The progenitors of terrorism: Russian revolutionaries or extreme Irish republicans?' *Terrorism and Political Violence*, 16/1 (Spring 2004), pp. 165–6.

4. Ibid., pp.172–3, 177.

5. M. L. R. Smith, *Fighting for Ireland? The Military Strategy of the Irish Republican Movement* (London: Routledge, 1995), pp. 8–9, 16–17.

6. Brian Jenkins, *The Fenian Problem: Insurgency and Terrorism in a Liberal State, 1858–1874* (Montreal: McGill-Queen's University Press, 2008); Charles Townshend, *Ireland: The 20th Century* (London: Edward Arnold, 1999), p. 26; Jonathan W. Gantt, 'Irish-American terrorism and Anglo-American relations, 1881–1885', *Journal of the Gilded Age and Progressive Era*, 5/4 (Oct. 2006), pp. 325–57.

7. H. B. C. Pollard, *The Secret Societies of Ireland: Their Rise and Progress* (Kilkenny: Irish Historical Press, 1998; 1st edn 1922, republished 1926). Robert Anderson, 'Fenianism: a narrative. By one who knows', in *Contemporary Review*, XIX (1872), pp. 301–16, 624–46.

8. Pollard, *Secret Societies*, pp. 40, 195; Roberts, *Mythology of the Secret Societies*, pp. 17, 364; Richard Griffiths, 'Webster, Nesta Helen (1875–1960)', in *Oxford Dictionary of National Biography* (Oxford: Oxford University Press, 2004) http://www.oxforddnb.com/view/article/71529, accessed 13 June 2008.

9. Pollard, *Secret Societies of Ireland*, p. 197; Graham D. Macklin, 'Major Hugh Pollard, MI6, and the Spanish Civil War', *Historical Journal*, 49/1 (2006), pp. 277–80. Brian P. Murphy discusses aspects of Pollard's career in his *The Origins and Organisation of British Propaganda in Ireland 1920* (Cork: Aubane Historical Society, 2006), *passim*.

10. Pollard, *Secret Societies of Ireland*, pp. 1–5, 11–15, 31, 34, 37, 48–9.

11. Ibid., pp. 79, 199.

12. Leon Ó Broin, *Revolutionary Underground* (Dublin: Gill & Macmillan, 1976), pp. 132, 176.

13. John O'Leary, *Recollections of Fenians and Fenianism*, 2 vols (London: Downey & Co., 1896), vol. ii, pp. 226, 239.

14. John Devoy, *Recollections of an Irish Rebel* (Shannon: Irish University Press, 1969; 1st edn 1929), pp. 449–57; Diarmuid O'Donovan Rossa, *Rossa's Recollections, 1838–1898* (Shannon: Irish University Press, 1972; 1st edn 1898), pp. 202–4, 262–4. I have not included P. J. P. Tynan's *The Irish National Invincibles and Their Times* (London, 1894), as this has been comprehensively explored by Charles Townshend, 'Terror in Ireland: Observations on Tynan's *The Irish National Invincibles and Their Times*', in Paul Wilkinson and A. M. Stewart (eds), *Contemporary Research on Terrorism* (Aberdeen: Aberdeen University Press, 1987), pp. 179–84.

15. Robert Anderson, *Sidelights on the Home Rule Movement* (London: J. Murray, 1906), p. 4.

16. Bernard Porter, 'Anderson, Sir Robert (1841–1918)', in *Oxford Dictionary of National Biography* (Oxford: Oxford University Press, 2004) http://www.oxforddnb.com/view/article/41262, accessed 6 June 2008; Anderson, *Sidelights*, pp. 37, 52, 55, 77–9; Anderson, 'Fenianism', pp. 301–16, 624–66.

17. Anderson, *Sidelights*, pp. 80–1, 91, 105–10.

18. 'Irish Revolution', *Incipient Irish Revolution, an expose of Fenianism of to-day in the United Kingdom and America, with the secret code of laws in force in London, etc.* (London: Eglington & Co., 1889); Michael de Nie, *The Eternal Paddy: Irish Identity and the Irish Press, 1798–1882* (Madison, WI: University of Wisconsin Press, 2004), pp. 166–7.

19. Anonymous, *The Mysteries of Ireland: Irish Secret Societies and Their Plots from … 1798 to … 1883* (London: Milner, 1883; 2nd edn 1884), pp. 132–45.

20. Anderson, *Sidelights*, p. 110.

21. Thomas Miller Beach, *Twenty-Five Years in the Secret Service: The Recollections of a Spy* (London: W. Heinemann, 5th edn 1892), pp. 109, 139–40, 142, 279.

22. Adrian Wisnicki, *Conspiracy, Revolution and Terrorism from Victorian Fiction to the Modern Novel* (London: Routledge, 2007).

23. Roberts, *Mythology of the Secret Societies*, pp. 362–76; Stephen Arata, *Fictions of Loss in the Victorian Fin de Siècle* (Cambridge: Cambridge University Press, 1996), pp. 1–10, 156–8.

24. Native of Prince Edward Island, *Fenianism, Irish Land Leagueism, and Communism* (1881); Francis Fuller, *How to Kill Fenianism and Ribbonism: A Practical Proposition for the Solution of the Irish Difficulty* (London: Alfred Boot, 1871); Milo McCaskey, *The Rottenness of Fenianism* (1865); Patrick J. Quinlivan, 'Hunting the Fenians: Problems in the historiography of a secret organisation', in

Patrick O'Sullivan (ed.), *The Creative Migrant* (Leicester: Leicester University Press, 1994), p. 137.

25. Quinlivan, 'Hunting the Fenians', pp. 31–2, note 31; Oliver P. Rafferty, *The Church, the State and the Fenian Threat, 1861–75* (London: Palgrave Macmillan, 1999), p.10. Marta Ramón's recent biography of James Stephens, for example, does not appear to employ Rutherford in spite of his visceral discussion of Stephens (John Rutherford, *The Secret History of the Fenian Conspiracy, its Origins, Objects and Ramifications*, 2 vols (London: C. Kegan Paul & Co., 1877), vol. i, pp. 49–50). Kelly and McGee similarly do not discuss Rutherford, though this may reflect the later period of their studies.

26. Charles Stuart Aubrey Abbott, *The Fenian Brotherhood: An Account of the Irish-American Revolutionary Societies in the United States from 1848 to 1870* (London: T. Harrison, 1871); R. A. Jones, 'Abbott, Charles Stuart Aubrey, third Baron Tenterden (1834–1882)', *Oxford Dictionary of National Biography* (Oxford: Oxford University Press, 2004) http://www.oxforddnb.com/view/article/13, accessed 12 June 2008.

27. Rutherford, *Secret History*, vol. i, pp. 2–6. Rossa, by way of riposte, was convinced that Rutherford was none other than the notorious Fenian informer, John Joseph Corydon (see William O'Brien and Desmond Ryan (eds), *Devoy's Post Bag* (Dublin: C. J. Fallon, 1948), vol. i, p. 301).

28. Rutherford, *Secret History*, vol. i, pp. 20, 56, 60.

29. Ibid., pp. 54, 49; R. V. Comerford, *The Fenians in Context: Irish Politics and Society, 1848–82* (Dublin: Wolfhound Press, 1998), pp. 39–40, 58–64.

30. Rutherford, *Secret History*, vol. i, pp. 8, 16–18, 50, 65.

31. Ibid., pp. 51–2, 71.

32. Rutherford, *Secret History*, vol. ii, pp. 156, 314–15.

33. Ibid., pp. 165, 307–9.

34. Niall Whelehan, 'Skirmishing, the *Irish World*, and Empire, 1876–86', in *Éire-Ireland*, 42/1–2 (Spring/Summer 2007), pp. 190–3; O'Brien and Ryan, *Devoy's Post Bag*, vol. i, pp. 141–4; Rutherford, *Secret History*, vol. i, p. 45.

35. De Nie, *Eternal Paddy*, pp. 166–7, 217, 236, 213–14; Stephen Howe, *Ireland and Empire: Colonial Legacies in Irish History and Culture* (Oxford: Oxford University Press, 2000), pp. 55–6, 43–9, 56–64.

36. Devoy, *Recollections*, pp. 186, 193.

37. Stanley Cohen, *Folk Devils and Moral Panics* (London: MacGibbon & Kee, 1972).

38. Sir Thomas Larcom Papers, National Library of Ireland, MS 7722; Samuel Lee Anderson Papers, NLI, MS 5970, MS 5965–69; National Archives of Ireland, Crime Branch Special files 7875/S, 6995/S, 3391/S (as random samples); Colonial Office Record Series vol. 1, Sinn Féin and Republican Suspects, 1899–1921, Dublin Castle Special Branch files (Dublin: Eneclann, 2006), file on Thomas St John Gaffney, Clan na Gael activist, CO 904/202/154.

39. Gantt, 'Irish-American terrorism', p. 328; Richard Bach Jensen, 'The International Anti-Anarchist Conference of 1898 and the origins of Interpol', *Journal of Contemporary History*, 16/2 (April 1981), p. 326; Richard Bach Jensen, 'The United States, international policing and the war against anarchist terrorism, 1900–1914', *Terrorism and Political Violence*, 13/1 (Spring 2001), pp. 15–46.

40. K. R. M. Short, *The Dynamite War: Irish-American Bombers in Victorian Britain* (Dublin: Gill & Macmillan, 1979), p. 92; Roberts, *Mythology of the Secret Societies*, p. 364; Keith Amos, *The Fenians in Australia, 1865–1880* (Kensington: New South Wales University Press, 1988), pp. 68–77; David A. Wilson, 'The Fenians in Montreal, 1862–68: invasion, intrigue and assassination', *Éire-Ireland*, 38/3–4 (Fall/Winter 2003); Dónal P. McCracken, 'The troublemakers part I: insurgents and adventurers, 1806–1899', in Dónal P. McCracken (ed.), *The Irish in Southern Africa 1795–1910* (Durban: South African-Irish Studies, 1992), p. 45.

41. O'Brien and Ryan, *Devoy's Post Bag*, vol. i, p. 130; Rutherford, *Secret Societies*, vol. ii, p. 315.

42. A. P. Moore-Anderson, *Sir Robert Anderson: Secret Service Theologian* (London: Marshall, Morgan & Scott, 1947) http://www.newble.co.uk/anderson/biography/biog4.html (4 of 11), 23/7/2004, accessed 8 June 2008.

43. Clutterbuck, 'Progenitors of Terrorism', p. 179, note 31; Whelehan, 'Skirmishing', p. 182.

44. Derek Offord, 'Political terrorism in Russia in the 1880s: the Fenian lesson', *Irish Slavonic Studies*, 5 (1984), pp. 27–31; Matt Carr, 'Cloaks, daggers and dynamite', *History Today*, 57/12 (Dec. 2007).

IV
PRINT CULTURE

10

Richard Pigott, the Fringe-Fenian Press and the Politics of Irish Nationalist Transition to Parnellism

Margaret O'Callaghan

I

On the last day of February 1889 – a Friday – the British ambassador to Spain, Sir Clare Ford, was informed by the Home Office that Richard Pigott, whose breakdown before the Special Commission was the talk of London, was staying at Hotel de los Ambajadores in Calle de la Vittoria in Madrid.[1] Since a warrant for his arrest on a charge of perjury was out, the ambassador was asked to instruct the Spanish police to detain Pigott, pending the arrival of a witness to identify him. Quite why Pigott chose Madrid after Paris to flee to is impossible to say.[2] He was indeed staying at that hotel under the name Rowland Ponsonby. One account suggests that he had been detected through a telegram that he sent the previous day to J. Shannon, a solicitor, at 58 Lincoln's Inn Fields, London. The telegram read: 'Please ask Mr S- to send what you promised.'[3] An interpreter and guide later came forward and admitted to having spent most of Thursday looking at the museums and churches of Madrid with Pigott. On the Friday the commissaire of police arrived at the hotel with an interpreter. Pigott, according to newspaper accounts, asked who the gentleman who wanted to see him was and on being told said 'All right'. However, it was claimed that, as the interpreter turned to the door to admit the commissaire, Pigott drew a revolver from his breast pocket and, instantly applying it to his mouth, blew his brains out with one discharge. He had a scapular on his body and carried a letter to Henry Labouchere, an address book with many Dublin addresses, and not much else.[4]

So who was Richard Pigott? Known to posterity almost exclusively through his notorious role as forger of letters purporting to be from Charles Stewart Parnell that represented Parnell as a supporter of murder and assassination, he appears on closer examination to have been a very considerable figure in nationalist politics from the early to mid-1860s.[5] However, James O'Connor, who wrote a brief memoir of Pigott after his

death, suggests that even in the years of his public political significance
he had other strings to his bow. 'Piles of old invoices from London houses
are extant, showing that thirty years ago i.e. about 1859 and after that
date he did a considerable trade in photographs, stereoscopic lenses, etc,
turning over many hundreds a year.' It is from this source and perhaps
general talk of the times, now vanished, that his reputation as a pornog-
rapher is derived. Parnell's biographer, R. Barry O'Brien, recalled that
'Almost everyone versed in Irish politics knew "Dick" Pigott, or knew of
him.'[6]

II

Richard Pigott was the son of George Pigott of Ratoath in Co. Meath and
his wife, a woman from Roscommon. George Pigott was initially
employed by Peter Purcell of Dublin, who held the contract for the transmission of the mails from Dublin to the provinces. After Purcell's death
George was employed at the Dublin office of the *Tablet*, the publication
run by Frederick Lucas, MP for Meath and English Quaker convert to
Catholicism and Irish nationalism. This connection exposed Richard, the
youngest and only surviving son, to the world of Dublin newspapers and
periodicals. Taken out of school at a young age to work in the early 1840s
as an office boy in the offices of the *Nation*, Richard Pigott was 'good at
figures'. Though there is little evidence of formal schooling beyond his
early teens, he subsequently presented himself as an educated man,
which he does indeed appear to have been. Leaving Dublin he got a job
as a bookkeeper on the *Ulsterman*, founded in 1857 in Belfast, in the
employ of Denis Holland, where he rapidly gained confidence and
advancement. James O'Connor wrote later that he had great powers of
organisation, excellent business faculties, calculating shrewdness and a
prescience that should have enabled him to reach great heights. He was
soon effectively running the *Ulsterman* and presided with Holland over its
renaming as the *Irishman* and its relocation to Dublin in 1859. However,
in *Personal Recollections of an Irish National Journalist* (1882), Pigott claimed
that an earlier version of the *Irishman* had been founded in 1849 at 4
D'Olier Street, and that it was there his career had begun. This original
Irishman was founded by Trinity men of the advanced party who were
increasingly critical of Charles Gavan Duffy's now restrained *Nation*, but
it collapsed on 25 May 1850. Pigott's own account is that he then went
to work with Frederick Lucas.

In November 1855 a new national journal, the *Tribune*, was published
by Pigott, with Thomas Clarke Luby as associate editor. Out of this,
according to Pigott, came the *Irishman* in July 1858. This suggests that
Pigott's time in Belfast may have been limited to a period of two or so

years, and that the founding of the *Irishman* may have been more complex than O'Connor allowed. It is during the early years of the *Irishman* that A. M. Sullivan notoriously 'got up a hue and cry' about the emerging Fenians, and in December 1858 the *Irishman* made much of this, implying that Sullivan's *Nation* was instrumental in the decision of the authorities to set up a special commission for the trial of prisoners in Cork and Kerry that led to the prosecutions of O'Donovan Rossa and others through the information of 'the approver', Daniel Sullivan of Goula. This laid the ground for a lifelong enmity between Pigott and the so-called 'Bantry gang'.

Pigott pursued a rhetoric of categorising Sullivan and his circle as Grattanite nationalists or West Britons, in alleged contrast to those earlier referred to as Mitchelites, revolutionists or simply nationalists (who were later designated Fenians). His valuable account of this period in *Personal Recollections* suggests a strong continuity between the politics of residual Young Ireland of the late 1840s and the emergent Fenian movement, though he does document the politics of accommodation of the late 1850s as well. According to Pigott's account in *Recollections*, both at the time and later the *Irishman* mocked the moderate nationalism of Sullivan, typified by the presentation of a sword to Marshal McMahon in 1860 by George Sigerson, Sullivan and others from the circle around the new *Nation*. In 1862 this persistent baiting culminated in Sullivan taking a libel action against the *Irishman* for the publication of a letter from O'Donovan Rossa in which Sullivan was denounced as an informer. Sullivan received six pence in damages, not the £1,000 he had sought, and Pigott continued to taunt him and others as 'felon-setters'.

In 1865, through a series of serendipitous occurrences, the *Irishman* newspaper effectively passed into Pigott's hands, and he henceforth described himself as a proprietor or publisher. In Holland's hands the newspaper had become the organ of the extreme and active section of the national party and published 'advanced' articles. Subsequently taken over by the maverick politician, P. J. Smyth, the *Irishman* rapidly began to lose its identity as a forum for advanced national views. The Fenians, sick of its unpredictability, had set up their own newspaper, the *Irish People*, in November 1863. This appeared to deal a fatal blow to Smyth and Pigott's *Irishman*. Smyth walked out on the operation in 1865 leaving Pigott in possession of 'plant, type, machinery, debts and all'. Number 33 Lower Abbey Street became Pigott's operational base for the next fifteen years until the plant became the new journalistic headquarters of Parnell's party through its new organ, *United Ireland*.

Pigott was lucky in his timing. In a welter of rumour and expectation Dublin Castle suppressed the *Irish People* in 1865 and Pigott's *Irishman* alone stood as the journalistic voice of advanced national opinion in

Ireland. From 1865 to 1869 the *Irishman* was crammed with Fenian news and its circulation went from a few thousand to fifty thousand in a week as it reported on the arrests of the staff of the *Irish People* and of hundreds of others all over the country in anticipation of a Fenian rising. The paper published vigorous and passionate leading articles and editorials in defence of the 'prisoners of the new movement'. As O'Connor stated, the high point of Pigott's popularity was when he was prosecuted and imprisoned for the publication of a remarkably able article entitled 'The Holocaust' – a hymn of praise to those later known as the 'Manchester Martyrs'.[7] Having served his short time he was greeted with a public banquet on his release.[8]

III

Throughout the 1870s, James O'Connor, the IRB supreme council's treasurer from 1869 to 1872 and former assistant manager of the *Irish People*, was assistant editor of the *Irishman*.[9] The paper's support for the Amnesty movement and publication of a lot of American Fenian material made it appear on the surface at least to be practically a Fenian paper.[10] This would have been a mistaken assumption, because for Pigott it was principally a commercial operation and his crypto-Fenianism was dependent on a market for it. He misappropriated IRB funds from the newspaper's safe and appears to have offered his services to Robert Anderson at Dublin Castle to provide information on the IRB in the middle of 1872. The IRB treasurer Patrick Egan initially tried to buy Pigott out in 1873. According to T. W. Moody, in 1875–6 members of the IRB (Joseph Biggar, John Barry, Patrick Egan and John Doran) in conjunction with Butt, Parnell and other home rulers had an even more frustrating encounter with Pigott.[11]

By this time the *Irishman* was no longer a single publication – alongside it and from the same premises Pigott published the *Shamrock* and the *Flag of Ireland*. Not since the Repeal reading rooms had there been such a demand for patriotic coverage, and Pigott sought to meet this demand. His own political beliefs can be deduced from the pages of his *Recollections*. He was at the very least steeped in the idiom, the personages and the public presentation of Fenianism and advanced nationalism in these years. A quasi-martyr for his half-year in prison, he was released to a stunning public banquet in his honour. It appears that even at this time he had back-channels to Dublin Castle and a social circle around the Kingstown Yacht Club that would have been anathema to many nationalists.

The series of Dublin addresses that we have for Pigott during his lifetime suggest that he lived close to the coast of Dublin Bay in an area that included Sandycove, Kingstown and Monkstown. He was of average height, with neat features, a tendency to plumpness and a receding hairline. He was described as a man of considerable, if apparently controlled, appetites. He swam almost daily in Dublin Bay and amazed observers by the length of time he could spend in the water and the distances out to which he swam. He kept a virtually open house from the early 1860s and was hospitable and convivial. He was disciplined and regular in his daily habits, but loved fine foods, champagne and good wines, which he consumed in copious quantities in the evenings, with no apparent ill effects. There are anecdotes of his generosity and ostentatious spending. He lived at considerable pace and style, a manageable proposition at particular periods when his publishing career often brought him an income of over £2,000 a year. This became less maintainable in the late 1870s when his income was less that a tenth of that sum. He was said to have the constitution of an ox.

Socially Pigott did not associate with politicians, journalists or 'serious men'. At the Kingstown Model Yacht Club his associates by the 1880s were usually both Protestant in religion and unionist in politics. He himself seems to have remained a reasonably devout Catholic, if the scapulars and holy medals found later on his body are reliable indicators. His public disagreement with A. M. Sullivan was to throw a shadow over his career. Sullivan, a key figure in what retrospectively became the Bantry Gang, was a formidable opponent and their disagreements ended up in the courts, with Sullivan prosecuting Pigott for libel. Their rows were shaded by that topic that never again went away for Pigott – national party funds and their appropriation. Sullivan seems to have accused Pigott of misappropriation of Amnesty funds, a claim which stuck, probably justly. Funds were subscribed in small and large sums for the support of Fenian prisoners' families and much of the money passed through the offices of Pigott's papers. Pigott levelled counter-accusations fairly widely to deflect attention from his own somewhat cavalier attitude to the handling of finances, the recording of funds and their accounting being the Achilles heel of all late nineteenth-century Irish political campaigns. Certainly his own public reputation was tainted in this regard early on in his career. The assumption in informed circles appears to have been that he had become accustomed to extravagance and simply could not shake it off.

IV

Politics became cooler in the early and mid-1870s, though Pigott managed another spell in prison on political grounds, thus retaining his credibility in advanced circles. But the circulation of his papers dropped very considerably in quieter times and his income plummeted. Twice in these years he carried private arrangements with his creditors to deal with his debts through half-negotiated sales, but the problems increased and he seems to have resorted to a highly complex system of cheque manoeuvrings that barely enabled him to stay one step ahead of his creditors. His sons were, however, sent to Clongowes, his sisters were kept in some style, and the champagne continued to flow at his maritime addresses. He seems to have been an affectionate and indulgent father, a loving brother and an amiable friend. According to his nationalist enemies, in later years he was guilty of the 'appropriation of trust funds' and according to O'Connor 'recent discoveries ... show that he had been trading upon forged bills of exchange and promissory notes.'[12] This may be a somewhat harsh reading of his manoeuvres, which seem to have had a Micawber-like assumption of better things to come at their core.

In a bid to boost circulation, his papers took a more divided editorial line as the 1870s progressed and he published both pro and anti pieces on the emerging home government movement, particularly after the convention of 1873. He entered into negotiations with Isaac Butt, with whom he was reasonably acquainted, and later on with the Land League Treasurer Patrick Egan, with a view to the new movement buying out his press interests. There is a suggestion that certain sums had been advanced to Pigott, but that the sale had none the less collapsed. Certainly retrospectively there were whispers of impropriety on Dick Pigott's part. Thus, from the late 1870s he was involved in public disputation with the leaders of the new movement.[13]

While Michael Davitt was still in prison, in January 1877, he sent Pigott a poem in five parts entitled 'Christmas Musings in Prison', with a note to say that a few pounds were needed 'for a particular purpose'.[14] As T. W. Moody comments, the poems were not published and Davitt received no money. On Davitt's release from prison in December of 1877 Pigott was however still an apparently mainstream member of a kind of Irish political establishment. Dublin put on a huge reception for Davitt and three former Fenian British soldiers who had been released at the same time.[15] Pigott accompanied the four released prisoners on the train from Kingstown to Westland Row with the élite of what was to become the emerging new movement – Parnell, Patrick Egan, John Ferguson, John O'Connor Power and Major Purcell O'Gorman, MP. Pigott was also present at a breakfast for the four at Morrison's hotel the following morning, during which one of them, Charles Heapy McCarthy, collapsed and died.[16]

In fact, Pigott was resolutely opposed to the New Departure from the outset, partly because its architects plainly displayed their contempt for him and their intention of replacing his newspaper with one of their own if they could not buy him out. In a letter to the *Freeman's Journal*, dated New

York, 11 December 1878, John Devoy announced that the new politics would not allow the misrepresentation of their position by figures like Pigott: 'men who live by scribbling cheap treason'. Michael Davitt, replying on 28 January 1879 to an attack by Pigott on John Devoy, stated that 'Nationalists have selected not to look any longer upon the *Irishman*, that is Mr Pigott – as their mentor in Irish politics, or continue to consider him *sans peur et sans reproche* in times of trial or trust.' In September 1880 Davitt wrote to Devoy about his irritation at the *Irishman*'s constant critique of the new movement, and at Pigott's attempt to pass himself off to new MPs as a figure of immense influence with the Fenians.[17] None the less, Pigott continued to be mentioned prominently in newspaper reports of significant nationalist gatherings, like the Thomas Moore Centenary Committee, but his marginalisation was underlined by the death of the already marginalised Isaac Butt in May 1879. His closeness to Butt was emphasised by his presence among the small private party of the Butt and Swanzy families and close friends who set off from Amiens Street station to bring Butt's body for burial at Stranorlar in Donegal. Some days later Pigott appeared yet again among the group who met at the Mansion House to start a fund for Butt's family. In late 1879 a public row broke out in the columns of the *Freeman's Journal* about alleged misappropriation of monies from the 'Donegal Fair Trial Fund', set up to assist in the defence of those accused of the murder of Lord Leitrim. It was practice at this time for monies 'in the national interest' to be contributed to a series of designated individuals, of whom Pigott was usually one. In a publicly printed letter T. D. Sullivan, the brother of Pigott's old adversary, blatantly demanded that the funds listed as having been received by the *Irishman* should be handed over.

Finally, in August 1881, Pigott lost his editorial platform after he made a deal with Parnell, Patrick Egan and others of the Parnellite party to sell all of his titles for a sum of £3,500, most of which went to meet his debts.[18] The Parnellites now had their own newspaper, *United Ireland*, though they initially continued the *Irishman* and the *Shamrock* while incorporating the *Flag of Ireland*.

V

In the early 1880s Pigott seems to have edged from dubious bookkeeping and messy financial imbroglios to blackmail, forgery and chicanery on a real scale. Dick Pigott, deprived of his former position, a *persona non grata* among the new Parnellite establishment who cast him aside, was reduced to sending begging letters to the proprietor of a bicycle shop near Kingsbridge, where he was attempting to have the bicycle of one of his sons reconstituted as a Christmas present. He offered his services, for money, to everyone and anyone. This was made clear by Patrick Egan's decision, in exasperation at Pigott's bad-mouthing of the Land League, to make public a sequence of private communications between himself and Pigott that effectively held Pigott, formerly a figure of considerable substance, up to public ridicule and opprobrium. In these communications Pigott offered to aid the Parnellites by assisting them in deflecting accusations made against them, principally by himself; it was a form of blackmail.[19]

The publication of Pigott's memoir, *Recollections of an Irish National Journalist*, on 17 April 1882 was a declaration of war on the new movement through the medium of a history of national movements, particularly Fenianism, over the preceding decades. It can be seen as a coded advertisement for the range of his nationalist knowledge and a laying down of an analysis of the new movement as a force for 'the demoralisation of what is called public opinion in Ireland'. He made a case against the corruption and brutality of the Land League in contrast to the high chivalry of Fenianism. He criticised the uses to which American money was put, the appropriation of funds for the relief of evicted tenants and the financing of the parliamentary movement, the social background of Parnellite MPs and their role in initiating a doomed social revolution through incitements to violence.[20]

Pushed to the margins, Pigott lived by his pen and thereby came to the attention of the newly founded Irish Loyal and Patriotic Union (ILPU) and its secretary Edward Caulfield Houston in mid-1885. According to Tim Healy, Pigott was close to Sir Rowland Blennerhassett, ex-Liberal MP for Kerry, and other Liberals who later became Liberal Unionists. His contacts seem to have been not so much Tory as Liberal Unionist, as Sir Richard Grosvenor, the former Liberal Whip, may have been the medium of his first contact with Houston.[21]

Pigott claimed that he had evidence linking John Devoy with the Invincibles, and that he had further information that could substantiate a story of wider connections between the Parnellite party and crime. Initially he wrote the piece 'Parnellism Unmasked' which was published by the ILPU as part of an ongoing series that sought to discredit the home rule case. Houston, a stringer for *The Times* in Dublin, also doing 'Special work', retained Pigott at the not inconsiderable rate of a guinea a day plus expenses and the promise of considerably more, in order to secure documents substantiating his stories about what he called 'Parnellism and Crime'. Pigott travelled to Lausanne, Paris and the US on his quest for material which would blacken the parliamentary party. The letters that he ultimately provided appear to have been paid for by George Buckle and MacDonald of *The Times* through the medium of Dr Thomas Maguire, rather than the ILPU.

Pigott's alleged sources were a motley collection of demi-mondaine Paris Fenians and he claimed that his chief source was Eugene Davis.[22]

Piggot himself had a series of letters from Parnell and Patrick Egan, dating back to the newspaper sales some five years earlier in his possession which proved viable for cutting and pasting. In May 1886, Pigott returned from New York with a sealed letter which he claimed to have received from J. J. Breslin instructing certain people in Paris to hand over eleven letters that apparently implicated Parnell and Egan directly in inciting and ordering murders. Houston and Maguire went to Paris in July 1886 and were given the letters, which they passed on to MacDonald of *The Times*. It was intimated that other, even more damning, letters would be forthcoming in due course. It appears to have been as late as 1888 that a key letter, in which Parnell apparently condoned the murder of Thomas Henry Burke, was provided. It had allegedly been found by Pigott in his own papers. Other letters also materialised in February or March 1888 and July 1888, through the same sources.

Pigott supplied precisely those materials incriminating the Irish Party and Parnell himself that confirmed the worst propaganda statements and fears of active Irish unionists and their London allies in these years. The publication of the series of articles known as 'Parnellism and Crime' in early March 1887 coincided with Arthur Balfour's first significant intervention as Irish chief secretary – the passage of his Crimes Bill that sought to recast the Irish agitation of the previous eight years and underline the now fixed Tory position against home rule. These articles, subsequently revealed to have been partially written by the Dublin civil servant and secret service employee Robert Anderson, interspersed with Pigott's forgeries, effectively presented the Irish nationalist project as a sustained criminal conspiracy from the late 1870s. This was of course what Pigott had been proclaiming publicly for some years, and what most of unionist Dublin believed to be the case.

Tim Healy and others, in association with Henry Labouchere, seem to have suspected Pigott's role in the affair from the moment of publication. Michael Davitt directed the forensic investigation that revealed Pigott so pitilessly before the Special Commission. Archbishop Walsh, one to whom Pigott had repeatedly turned in the past, revealed the nature of his representations and strange lies. Details of his offers of the early 1880s to Forster to assist Dublin Castle filtered out. His earlier battles with Patrick Egan were re-run in the public consciousness. Henry Harrison, the young Irish Party MP, remained convinced that Captain O'Shea had been involved in the politics of the Special Commission that built upon *The Times'* earlier publications. Harrison devoted his life to exposing the role of the Liberal Unionist Joseph Chamberlain, through the medium of O'Shea, in effecting Parnell's downfall. He saw the Special Commission and the later divorce case as of a piece. It is perhaps worthy of comment that Pigott met his death, apparently by suicide, in Madrid, a city in which O'Shea had a network of connections and Pigott himself had apparently none. Archbishop Walsh appears to have financially assisted Pigott's sons, one of whom was in Clongowes at the same time as James Joyce; they are said to have changed their name.[23]

VI

Richard Pigott is a lens through which the transitions in Irish nationalism in the late 1870s and early 1880s can be better understood. Tracking Pigott leads into the complex divisions within nationalism in these years, years during which he was a considerable political player in public circles. The scale of the 'Parnellism and Crime' debacle made it desirable for nationalists subsequently to diminish Pigott's former role. He protested against his marginalisation by the new movement and their authoritarianism in suppressing nationalist dissent. While they may well have known of his chicanery and double dealings, it was also evident that he well understood nationalist politics in their rich complexity before the 'New Departure' presented a new narrative of united nationalism and the myth of an inactive 1870s – a trope of the non-achievement of a previous generation that was to dog the Parnellites in their turn.

Pigott not merely shows a way in to the complexity of nationalist politics in the 1870s, but his career also provides access into the vicious propaganda wars that marked the emergence of mass-democratisation in the 1880s. His appeal to the unionist opponents of home rule used precisely the knowledge he had so painfully gleaned through decades in the shadowland Dublin of press and Fenians. Through spies, informers, old contacts and resources, Pigott's assistance to the unionist case placed Fenian methods and Fenian violence – much of it initiated by spies and *agents provocateurs* – back on the front pages of newspapers, and undermined the Parnellite attempt to achieve home rule through control and distancing the Fenian and agrarian threats. He may have muddied the waters and confused the issue, but he achieved his revenge on a new movement that thought to dispense with his services and ignore his complicated knowledge and lore.

NOTES

1.   Special Commission Act, 1888; reprints of the shorthand notes of the speeches. Proceedings and evidence taken before the commissioners appointed under the above-named Act HMSO, 1890, and Report of the Special Commission (c 5891), Parliamentary Papers, 1890, xxvii, 447–640. (Referred to hereafter as Parnellism and Crime enquiry.)

2.   William O'Shea, husband of Parnell's mistress and later wife Katharine O'Shea, had strong Madrid connections. See Myles Dungan, *The Captain and the King* (Dublin: New Island Books, 2009). He was in fact in Madrid at this time. An alternative to the story of detecting Pigott through his own telegram is provided, also in the *Irish Times* of Monday 4 March, in which it is stated that prior to Pigott's arrival in Madrid the police were informed and that he was 'shadowed' from the moment of his arrival.

3. *Irish Times*, 4 Mar. 1889.
4. He had left London on the previous Monday. He had gone to a firm of booksellers in the Strand to collect a cheque for £25 for a parcel of books that they had sold for him. He then went to a tradesman he knew to cash it. The money was paid chiefly in gold. He purchased with a portion of the money a bag and some linen and took the 6.25 cheap service from Victoria for Paris. Arriving in Paris after 11 the next morning he stayed at Hotel Des Deux Mondes. On Wednesday morning he left Paris by the Western of France railway and reached Madrid on Thursday morning. *Irish Times*, 4 Mar. 1889.
5. For the politics of the Special Commission see Margaret O'Callaghan, *British High Politics and a Nationalist Ireland: Criminality, Land and the Law under Forster and Balfour* (Cork: Cork University Press, 1994); Margaret O'Callaghan, 'Franchise reform, "first past the post" and the strange case of unionist Ireland', *Parliamentary History*, 16/1 (1997), pp. 85–106, and Margaret O'Callaghan, 'New ways of looking at the state apparatus and the state archive in nineteenth-century Ireland: "Curiosities from that phonetic museum" – Royal Irish Constabulary reports and their political uses, 1879–91', *Proceedings of the Royal Irish Academy*, 104C/2 (2004), pp. 37–56.
6. R. Barry O'Brien, *The Life of Charles Stewart Parnell* (London: Thomas Nelson and Sons, 1910), p. 440.
7. See 'The Prosecution of the *Irishman*', *Irish Times*, 24 Jan. 1868. See also 15 Feb. 1868.
8. 'Banquet to Mr Richard Pigott, of the *Irishman*', *Irish Times*, 21 Oct. 1868. Pigott could not attend owing to the death of his father.
9. Owen McGee, *The IRB: The Irish Republican Brotherhood from the Land League to Sinn Féin* (Dublin: Four Courts Press, 2005), p. 44. He gives the *Irishman*'s circulation figures as 10,000 a week.
10. McGee, *The IRB*, p. 45 and T. W. Moody, *Davitt and the Irish Revolution, 1846–1882* (Oxford: Oxford University Press, 1981), p. 51.
11. Moody, *Davitt*, p. 245.
12. James O'Connor, *Recollections of Richard Pigott* (Dublin: M.H. Gill & Son, 1889).
13. John Devoy, describing the crucial Paris meeting that consolidated the 'New Departure', wrote: 'At the time of the Paris meeting (December 1878) Pigott, while posing as an extreme and irreconcilable Nationalist and denouncing Davitt and Devoy as backsliders, had really mortgaged himself to the parliamentarians of the day. Isaac Butt had more than once raised money for Pigott and on the last occasion had raised funds from Mr William Shaw, Mitchell Henry, Sir Joseph Neale McKenna and others. I was informed at the meeting that the amount was £3,000 that Butt had taken a mortgage on the *Irishman* for that amount, as security and to enable him to keep a "Sword of Damocles" suspended over Pigott's head. I was further informed that Mr Butt had given power of attorney to Patrick Egan to act for him.' See Carla King and W. J. McCormack (eds), John Devoy, *Michael Davitt, From the Gaelic American* (Dublin: UCD Press, 2008), pp. 82–3.
14. Moody, *Davitt*, p. 174.
15. Ibid., pp. 188–9.
16. He lay in state at the Confraternity Room of the Carmelite Church in Clarendon Street. McCarthy was a Fenian and this was the only church in Dublin that would receive his body. Moody, *Davitt*, p. 190. The *Irishman* reported the funeral to Glasnevin as the largest since O'Connell's, though that of Terence Bellew MacManus may have been as big if not bigger.
17. Moody, *Davitt*, p. 406.
18. See Pigott's letter to the editor entitled 'Mr P. Egan, Mr R. Pigott and Mr John O'Leary' in *Freeman's Journal*, 14 and 19 Dec. 1881. For earlier ridiculing of Pigott see Michael Davitt's letter to the editor, 'A cry for mercy', *Freeman's Journal*, 28 Jan. 1879.
19. *Freeman's Journal*, 14 and 18 Dec. 1881.
20. Richard Pigott, *Personal Recollections of an Irish Nationalist Journalist* (Dublin: Hodges, Figgis and Co., 1882) pp. 376–447
21. On 2 August Pigott sold his titles to the Irish National Newspaper and Publishing Company Ltd, formed for that purpose by Parnell, Egan, Biggar, Justin McCarthy, Dr Kenny, Richard Lalor and William O'Brien. O'Brien was appointed editor of *United Ireland* from 13 August, when it replaced *Flag of Ireland*.
22. These bewildering circles are best explored in the pioneering work of Christy Campbell. See in particular his *The Maharajah's Box: An Imperial Story of Conspiracy, Love and a Guru's Prophecy* (London: Harper Collins, 2000) and *Fenian Fire: The British Government Plot to Assassinate Queen Victoria* (London: Harper Collins, 2003).
23. He had married Theresa McDermott of Blackrock, Co. Dublin, on 17 February 1874. She died in August 1886. Their children were therefore orphaned by his death. Michael Davitt managed to extract £10 from Mr Soames of *The Times*.

11

Narratives of Confinement: Fenians, Prisons and Writing, 1867–1916[1]

William Murphy

I

In 1889 a truly awful novel was published in London by the prominent publishers Chapman and Hall. It was written by J. D. Maginn who, for many and obvious reasons, did not go on to literary greatness. As is often the case with bad fiction it had an alliterative title, *Fitzgerald: The Fenian*. In the course of the novel the eponymous hero comes to believe that pride in Irish nationhood is compatible with friendly relations with England, a realisation symbolised by marriage to an Englishwoman. Before settling down, however, Dick Fitzgerald spends his youthful days in rebellion followed by imprisonment. On his release, Fitzgerald informs his father that he has not wasted his time while in gaol, but has written a memoir, *Meditations of a Prisoner*, in which a London publisher is already interested. Later, Fitzgerald impresses his wife-to-be, Miss Cuthbert, with the information that his *Meditations* has made it to a third edition, to which she replies: 'Oh, yes; I have heard your book spoken of with great praise. It is in every drawing room, and every one reads it.'[2]

By the second half of the nineteenth century, not only had imprisonment become a common experience for advanced Irish nationalists, but prison memoir had attained a prominent place in nationalist culture. Ireland was not alone in this. Across Europe, just as the prison became the primary means of punishing crime,[3] so too it became the most important weapon available to states attempting to control political dissent.[4] One of the side-effects of this was the emergence of the prison memoir as a significant genre and the political prisoner memoir as an important sub-genre.[5] The Italian nationalist, Silvio Pellico, achieved continent-wide fame when his *My Prisons* was published in 1832 and subsequently translated into at least a dozen languages, including English.[6] In 1861 the English liberal journalist John Alfred Langford wrote that, through his memoir, Pellico had 'made the House of Hapsburgh [*sic*] a thing of shame, and his narrow home of iron and stone a more glorious spot than the crime-stained court of Vienna'.[7]

The Fenians were not the first Irish rebels to be imprisoned or to write prison memoir. Among their predecessors was William Steel Dickson, a prominent United Irishman, who recounted his prison experiences in the aftermath of the 1798 rebellion in *A Narrative of the Confinement and Exile of William Steel Dickson, DD*. Perhaps the most widely read of the narratives of confinement written by an Irish rebel was the *Jail Journal* of the Young Irelander John Mitchel, which was published in 1854.[8] Captivity as experienced by the Fenians was different, however, and, consequently, their memoirs were different. Steel Dickson described a comfortable regime of military detention at Fort George, Scotland, and Mitchel, while typical of later prison memoirs in his less sanguine attitude towards his treatment, had been transported rather than imprisoned. Although sixty-two Fenians were transported in September 1867, a majority of Fenian convicts found themselves confined within a thoroughly modern English prison system,[9] a system characterised by 'uniformity' and 'severity'.[10] Fenian prison memoir then described a particular experience of imprisonment and took on a particular tenor which was to prove inordinately influential. This influence was ensured by the longevity of the Fenian tradition combined with the recurring importance of imprisonment within that tradition and because Fenian prison memoir appeared when the Irish national narrative was taking its modern shape in the context of a burgeoning nationalist print culture.

An exploration of writing by and about Fenian prisoners and their imprisonment in the years 1867 to 1916 suggests that this literature – both memoir and fiction – passed through several identifiable phases. In its first phase it was autobiographical, and the prisoners' primary concern was to influence the telling of their story. Casey A. Jarrin has described Tom Clarke's prison memoir as 'a textual refusal of carceral silence' and this is an equally apt description of earlier Fenian prison memoir.[11] It was produced in direct opposition to the state's presentation of Fenian imprisonment and the tone was propagandistic. Its aim was to alter the prison status and treatment of Fenian prisoners or to achieve their release. This first phase of Fenian prison writing implied a general critique of the English prison system, a critique that became more explicit with time. It is this shift in emphasis that is characteristic of the second phase, which includes Michael Davitt's later writing on prison. A third phase might be dated to the years 1909 to 1913, when a series of fictional treatments of the role of the former Fenian prisoner appeared at a time when the future of radical separatism seemed doubtful. This phase was quickly succeeded by yet another when a new generation of radical separatists, who looked to the Fenians as 'a source of emotional energy, as a storehouse of memory and example', were imprisoned.[12]

II

Writing on South African prison memoirs of the apartheid period (and with Michel Foucault in mind), Paul Gready has argued that 'to be a prisoner is to be variously written, to be contested through writing' and that 'autobiography chiefly served to restore elemental political ground to the prisoner, and can be seen as the most sophisticated articulation of the oppositional "power of writing"'.[13] During the late 1860s and the 1870s the treatment of Fenian prisoners was the subject of an intense battle of words which took place on platforms, in parliament, in newspapers, in hundreds of confidential minutes and memoranda, and in official reports. For the most part the prisoners' experience was represented by others. The state, in the form of bureaucrats and politicians in power, generally defended the Fenians' imprisonment and their treatment, while amnesty campaigners and sympathetic Irish nationalists – most often politicians and journalists – made the case that the Fenian prisoners should be released or afforded ameliorated treatment. Producing autobiographical accounts afforded Fenians the opportunity to act as witnesses on their own behalf and influence the interpretation of their prison treatment that would prevail in contemporary culture and for posterity.

In the first instance, the prisoners' story was presented through an amnesty campaign, which attracted widespread support in Ireland. This campaign pointed to the death in Woking prison of Patrick Lynch in June 1866 and employed images of Fenian prisoners who were 'starved, overworked, thrust into association with sodomists and syphilitics, driven mad and denied medical treatment'.[14] In May 1867, in response to this battery of allegations, the home secretary, Spencer H. Walpole, decided to commission an inquiry to be conducted by two officials, Alex A. Knox and George D. Pollock. On 16 March 1867, while the Home Office inquiry was still in train, the *Irishman*, a determinedly nationalist newspaper which gave much coverage to the prisoners' cause, published a letter that had been smuggled from Millbank prison, alleging maltreatment and persecution in vivid and evocative language.[15] From an early stage the prisoners' advocates were conscious of the value of first-hand accounts by prisoners. Accusations, true or otherwise, seemed more authentic when made by one of the alleged victims. The letter in the *Irishman*, which caused embarrassment to the authorities and outrage in Ireland, was the work of Jeremiah O'Donovan Rossa. O'Donovan Rossa was to become the most iconic of Fenian prisoners. He had been convicted in Dublin on 13 December 1865 and transferred to England later that month. There, in various prisons, a contest ensued between him and the prison authorities; a contest in which, in the words of Seán McConville, 'defiance and punishment continued unceasingly'.[16]

It was in this context that Knox and Pollock submitted their report to parliament in June 1867. It concluded by praising the staff and management of prisons in the highest terms, noting that the 'only true cause of complaint the treason-felony convicts have against them [the authorities] is that they can't get out'.[17] They took care to depict O'Donovan Rossa as a crank and an instigator of discontent: a portrait that was not without credibility. They derided his letter in the *Irishman* as 'a letter stuffed full of the most absurd and unfounded accusations against everybody … It contained the story of his wrongs and was to set the country ablaze'.[18] While in the most telling sentences in the entire report, the commissioners argued that 'the word of a convict is not taken against the word of a warder or other prison official. If this were so, of course there would be nothing for it but to throw open the gates of the prison, and to tell the convicts they were at liberty to depart."[19]

None the less, the reaction of the prisoners' advocates was, when possible, to meet the words of Knox and Pollock with more of the prisoners' words. They did this confident that many in Ireland would take the word of a Fenian convict against that of an English prison official. In 1869 the *Irishman* published a pamphlet entitled *Things Not Generally Known: England's Treatment of Political Prisoners*. It was an account by an unnamed Fenian prisoner and consisted of paragraph after paragraph of alleged brutalities. The author expressed revulsion at close association with non-Fenian convicts, men he characterised as 'the vilest criminals' and 'leprous outcasts', and insisted that many of them 'suffer from the most loathsome and infectious diseases, syphilis, &c'.[20] In contrast, the author was portrayed as 'a chivalrous young Irishman of superior education and spotless honour' in an introduction, probably the work of the editor of the *Irishman*, Richard Pigott.[21] This text was an explicit response to the official report of 1867 and is marked by an insistence that the prisoners were more reliable witnesses than their gaolers. In the introduction readers are told that the 'details within these pages have been corroborated by those prisoners who have been liberated. They cannot, therefore, be contradicted. By these the public may judge how deceptive was the report of the so-called "Commission"', while the prisoner concluded with the hope that his account would 'enable the public to form a more correct judgment on the report published by Commissioners Pollock and Knox'.[22]

In February 1869 fifteen of the thirty-nine Fenian prisoners then held in English prisons were given an amnesty.[23] In June of that year efforts to obtain an amnesty for the remaining men were redoubled under the auspices of the newly established Amnesty Association.[24] While in November O'Donovan Rossa won a by-election in Tipperary after a campaign which traded on his growing reputation as a prison rebel.[25] In 1868, when John Savage's *Fenian Heroes and Martyrs* was published in Boston, O'Donovan Rossa was introduced as 'an unbending and defiant patriot in his chains'. Savage wrote that 'the authorities have laboured, by putting him at the most loathsome duties, and by treatment of the harshest kind; by bodily chastisement, and the starvation system known as the "lightening process", to break him down; but he is indomitable, and will only succumb to death'.[26] In May 1870, in the face of continuing complaints the Home Office commissioned a further inquiry. On this occasion the appointed commissioners, chaired by Lord Devon, were more independent and their report reflected this.[27] Again, they did not find any grounds to believe that the Fenians had been systematically, or even regularly, subjected 'to any exceptionally severe treatment'. On the other hand, they did make several criticisms of the prison authorities' approach and found that there was substance to two of O'Donovan Rossa's litany of complaints. Further, they acknowledged that the Fenians found their association with criminals 'degrading' and suggested that they might be segregated from other prisoners.[28] In practice the Fenian prisoners had by then received a series of ameliorations and most of them, including O'Donovan Rossa, were released in December 1870.

With so many former prisoners free it was only a matter of time before one produced a full-scale prison memoir. In the spring and summer of 1870 amnesty campaigners, including Pigott, had again canvassed former prisoners for accounts of their prison life with the purpose of supporting 'the charges of harsh treatment denied by the Government'. Although it remains incomplete, and was not published until 2005, John Sarsfield Casey's account of his imprisonment in England and subsequent transportation seems to have had its genesis in these requests.[29] When a memoir did arrive it can hardly have been a surprise that the author was O'Donovan Rossa. He was resident in America when his memoir was published by the American News Company in New York in 1874. It was his attempt to have the last word on his prison experience and more than any other text *O'Donovan Rossa's Prison Life: Six Years in Six English Prisons* has fixed a particular image of political imprisonment in the mind of the Irish nationalist public. It is, appropriately, a jeremiad, infused with a profound sense of persecution, while aspiring to be a portrait of proud defiance. O'Donovan Rossa depicted his experience of imprisonment as the persistent imposition of humiliation and degradation 'among the garrotters and Sodomites of England'.[30] Contrary to the reports of 1867 and 1871, he maintained that the Fenian prisoners were not treated like all other prisoners: 'I would not grumble or wonder if, as political prisoners, it were exceptionally better, but no, it was exceptionally worse than the worst criminals of society.'[31]

In 1878, when Michael Davitt began to present his prison experiences for public consumption, it was in the context of a renewed amnesty campaign. Following seven and a half years in prison, Davitt was released in December 1877. Almost immediately he joined the efforts to secure the release of eight men who remained in prison; on 9 March 1878 he addressed an amnesty meeting in London and the speech formed the basis for a pamphlet which appeared in May of that year.[32] The pamphlet was entitled *The Prison Life of Michael Davitt by himself* and in it Davitt, like his predecessors, provided an account replete with the indignity of invasive strip-searches, the oppression of silence, and the severity of poor diet and heavy physical labour. Davitt depicted a prison system that sullied all those within its grip, describing men who had become 'animal-like' as a consequence of a hunger which drove them to 'eat old poultices found buried in heaps of rubbish I was assisting in carting away, and I have seen bits of candles pulled out of the prison cesspool and eaten, after the human soil was wiped off them!'[33] As in the case of O'Donovan Rossa, Davitt insisted that 'the fact of my being a political prisoner exposed me to, rather than saved me from, the most inconsiderate treatment at the hands of the prison officials'.[34] Davitt has rightly acquired a reputation as the Fenian prisoner who was most concerned at the treatment of ordinary convicts, but in 1878 his pressing concern was the release of his fellow Fenians and he wrote disparagingly of those they shared prison with, decrying 'the degradation of being placed on a footing, or rather below, the vilest offscum of crime and infamy'.[35]

In this first wave of Fenian prison writings a narrative was established which successor prisoner-memoirists and fiction writers tended to mimic. Imprisonment was not only brutal, but it was especially cruel for Irish political prisoners because they were peculiarly persecuted by the authorities and forced to associate with men who were morally and socially inferior to them. The role of the Fenian political prisoner became one of individual perseverance or resistance in the face of this fate. Both O'Donovan Rossa and Davitt mentioned their Fenian colleagues – and were motivated to write their accounts, at least in part, to assist those colleagues they left behind – but in essence the Fenian prisoner, as exemplified by these authors, was forced to stand alone against the system. That is not to deny that they, and many of their Irish readers, viewed the prison struggles as integral to a 'national' struggle. O'Donovan Rossa stated as much when he wrote of his abandonment of an early intention to approach prison with stoicism: 'My whole nature arose in arms, and I felt that even against prison government I could be a rebel too.'[36] Indeed, in these memoirs the prisoners' personal subjection and resistance became a metaphor for the nation.

III

Later editions of these memoirs reflected the changing concerns of the authors and, perhaps, the audience. *O'Donovan Rossa's Prison Life* appeared again in 1882 and 1889, but by then it carried the title by which it remains famous, *Irish Rebels in English Prisons*. It included a new preface which had little to do with O'Donovan Rossa's prison life, but constituted a significant addition to the text. Based on an article published in the *United Irishman* in January 1882, the preface offered a defence of the dynamite campaign.[37] New editions of *The Prison Life of Michael Davitt* appeared in 1882 and 1886. Both included Davitt's evidence before the Royal Commission on Penal Servitude of 1878, signalling a shift in emphasis in his public pronouncements on imprisonment; the concern to inform the public as to the status and treatment of Irish political prisoners remained, but greater stress was now afforded to his broader critique of the prison system.

Michael Davitt's second major work to draw on his prison experiences, *Leaves from a Prison Diary*, was published in 1885. It was not a memoir, but was dominated by an analysis of the population and management of the prison system. As Carla King has explained, these reflections first took shape under the title 'Traits of Criminal Life and Character' which Davitt wrote in late 1881 during his second term in prison.[38] Davitt's chief concern in *Leaves* was to delineate a taxonomy of convicts and, on the basis of this, to argue for the separation of the troublesome or hardened from those he regarded as more amenable to reform. The rhetoric used to describe non-political prisoners is markedly different from Rossa's and that in his own earlier pamphlet; he wrote: 'Pity, however, is the predominant feeling which so much moral deformity excites in the breast of an ordinary mortal who is doomed to behold the ruin which it has made of so many fellow-creatures.'[39] In later chapters Davitt outlined his views on various social ills and the governance of Ireland, but it was the prison sections that drew most attention and praise. In general the British press was impressed, preferring the more detached, almost anthropological, tone of this element of the book.[40] For instance, a review in the *Scotsman* stated that Davitt had proved himself an exception among Irish politicians because the volume did not contain 'one word of querulous complaint, one indication of a sense of personal injury'.[41] By September 1885 two editions had sold out and plans for a third, cheap, edition were in hand.[42]

Davitt's general assault upon the prison system was mirrored in *Moondyne Joe: A Story from the Underworld*, a novel by another former Fenian prisoner, John Boyle O'Reilly. It received a mixed critical reception, but was a considerable popular success for several decades. Beginning in November 1878, it was published in serialised form in the important Boston-based, Irish-American newspaper, the *Pilot*, which O'Reilly edited.[43] In the following year the Pilot Publishing Company of Boston published it in novel form and it was soon picked up by publishing houses in New York, Australia and Britain. In 1913 a film based on O'Reilly's novel, *Moondyne*, was made in Australia, while the novel was translated into Irish as *An Múindín* and published by the Government Publication Office of the Irish Free State in 1931.[44] Although it drew on O'Reilly's experience as a political prisoner and transportee and took its title from the nickname of a real western Australian bushranger, Joseph Bolitho Johns, *Moondyne Joe* was neither a fictionalised account of O'Reilly's life nor that of the actual Moondyne Joe. Instead, it was an attack on, what O'Reilly believed to be, the inhumanity and cruelty of both the English convict system and transportation.

O'Reilly described the English prison system as a brutal 'convict-mill' and portrayed the 'Board of Directors' of England's prisons as bureaucrats whose bounded vision had cruel consequences. The prisoners were captives of the system, but O'Reilly's prison directors were captive to the ideal of the systematic. One of the novel's heroes, Will Sheridan, meets the directors and is struck by

> the stupendous conceit and incompetence of these men. They talked glibly about the weight of a prisoner's loaf, and the hours to light the cells in the morning; they had statistics at their finger-ends to show them how much a convict could perform on a given number of ounces of meat, but they knew nothing whatever of the large philosophy of penal government.[45]

Even less sympathetic was his depiction of Sir Joshua Hobb, a thinly disguised portrait of Sir Edmund du Cane, a director of convict prisons from 1863 and chairman of the Directorate of Convict Prisons from 1869 to 1895.[46] O'Reilly emphasised his character's preoccupation with unvarying order: 'Confound the man ... he would take a hundred men, with as many diseases, and treat them all for cholera.'[47] When Hobb appears before a parliamentary committee to dismiss proposals for a humane and graduated penal system in Australia, he cites the mild treatment of a Chartist convict and the alleged subsequent crimes of that man to illustrate his argument against any leniency. Inevitably, Hobb's allegations prove false and instead the maligned Chartist convict emerges as the hero of the novel, once Moondyne Joe but now the respectable, yet mysterious, advocate of penal reform, Mr Wyville. Although it is not the central concern of his novel, it is evident that O'Reilly – in common with all Fenian authors – assumes the moral superiority of the political prisoner.

Despite the campaigns and the memoirs, political prisoners were not afforded a discrete category. The Prisons Act of 1877, which applied in England,[48] and the Prisons in Ireland Act of the same year, which established the General Prisons Board of Ireland, did provide that those convicted of sedition, seditious libel or contempt of court should be held under the least punitive of penal regimes, that of first-class misdemeanant. Very few political prisoners, however, were to be convicted of these offences. Although the efforts of the Fenian memoirists (and books which were influenced by them such as George Sigerson's *Political Imprisonment at Home and Abroad* published in 1890) did much to convince the general public that political prisoners were 'special men' who deserved special treatment, the state continued to withhold acknowledgement in law that political prisoners were different.[49] The Fenian critique did contribute, however, to what Martin Wiener has characterised as a 'disillusion with the prison' or at least an erosion of certainty among administrators, politicians and the public that all prisoners should be treated uniformly and with severity. Consequently, the Fenian campaigns and memoirs (along with several other critical perspectives) eased the eventual introduction of more flexibility into the English prison system through the Prisons Act of 1898, which reformed penal servitude and separated first-time offenders from recidivists.[50]

IV

Writing by, and about, Fenian prisoners entered a new phase in the years immediately prior to the Irish revolution. In a period when revolutionary nationalism seemed moribund, the uncertain legacy of the Fenian prisoners attracted the attention of a series of writers. In May 1909 the first play staged by the newly established Cork Dramatic Society was a work by that society's leading light, the writer and critic Daniel Corkery. The ethos of the Cork Dramatic Society reflected Corkery's commitment to cultural nationalism.[51] In 1909, however, he was not a radical separatist and Patrick Maume has described the play as a 'Moranite satire on Irish politics, constitutionalist and physical force'. The central character of the play was a former Fenian prisoner who Corkery named John Whitelaw O'Loughlin. At the beginning of the play O'Loughlin, who is in straitened conditions, is finagled a job as a workhouse master by the local Irish Party organisers. In this O'Loughlin is clearly based on O'Donovan Rossa, who returned to Ireland between 1904 and 1906 when he was offered the job of corresponding secretary to Cork County Council. While the party bosses of Corkery's play calculate that it is politic to acknowledge O'Loughlin's sacrifice and that it is worthwhile to be associated with him, they also believe his brand of idealism belongs in the past. Among the younger generation, however, O'Loughlin finds one convert to radical separatism, Lawrence Kiely, who turns his back on the party and a guaranteed parliamentary seat. In his turn, Kiely discovers that this is an unprofitable and often unpopular road, but he remains inspired by the prison sacrifice of

O'Loughlin and too finds an acolyte among the succeeding generation, young Daly, who is willing to flaunt convention and embrace separatism.[52]

While Corkery acknowledged that in the Ireland of 1909 a Fenian prisoner retained a powerful, if limited, capacity to inspire using his story of sacrifice, others doubted whether this was the case. Lennox Robinson was among these. Though more famous for his relationship with the Abbey Theatre, Robinson began his career as a playwright with the Cork Dramatic Society.[53] He was familiar with *The Embers* and took up the theme of the returned Fenian prisoner in his own play, *Patriots*, which was first staged at the Abbey in April 1912.[54] Robinson wrote the play while on tour in America with the Abbey in the autumn of 1911,[55] and Chris Morash has written that 'it captures the mood of the years in which Yeats wrote "September 1913" with its well-known refrain "Romantic Ireland's dead and gone / It's with O'Leary in the grave"'.[56] *Patriots* tells the story of the return of James Nugent to his family and home town after eighteen years in prison for 'political murder' (shooting an informer). News of Nugent's release reaches home before he does, prompting his former colleagues to reveal their expectations of a former political prisoner: 'He'll be greatly changed', 'his health ruined', and 'his spirit broken too'. His daughter is told: 'Ah, you'll never have seen the real James Nugent, Rose. You'll only see an old broken man creeping home to die.' Before he dies, however, they would be delighted if he would attend a demonstration, maybe with a band and some bonfires, and if he would give a lecture. A lecture called 'Behind Lock and Key' or 'Prison Bars' would be 'the very thing. Why he'll have any amount to tell us, all about the prison and how he was treated – most interesting – most interesting.'[57]

What they do not want, and what they get, is an unrepentant rebel intent on carrying on where he left off prior to prison. He is not content to become a revered symbol in a nationalism of nostalgia: 'Good God, you seem to think my life is an anecdote – a thing to be told stories about ... I've been dead for eighteen years. I've come back from the grave.'[58] He dismisses constitutionalism as 'that old Parliamentary game' and derides any reform as 'sops, sops'.[59] When Nugent organises a meeting to relaunch radical separatism under his leadership, however, he is confronted by disinterest, antipathy and disillusion. He discovers a town, family and old friends who are motivated by money and notions of respectability. Most people prefer to attend other events, the parish mission or a moving picture being shown in the town hall. A colleague from the old days tells him that 'they don't want to hear you speak ... They are tired even of laughing at you.'[60] For a time Nugent seems intent on fighting on, but in the face of desertion by his old friends, bitter denunciation from his wife who tells him of the pain he has caused, and his failure to rouse support from the youth Nugent ends the play addressing the ghosts of the republican dead who used to visit him in his prison cell: 'I have tried – tried as you tried – and been broken.'[61] Although Robinson's conclusion suggests that he foresaw little future for the physical-force movement, contemporary reviewers of the play, both admiring and critical, indicate that the character of Nugent evoked approval and sympathy from sections of the Abbey's audience. J. P. M. of the *Evening Telegraph* disapprovingly noted that Nugent was the best-drawn character and that his speeches received 'loud applause', while Jacques of the *Irish Independent* reported 'loud applause from the deeply impressed pit'.[62]

Similar issues are addressed in the final work of the most popular Irish novelist of this period, Canon P. A. Sheehan. *The Graves at Kilmorna: A Story of '67* was written around the same time (1910–11), although it was not published until 1915 when it became an immediate best-seller.[63] It tells the story of Myles Cogan from idealistic participation in the Fenian Rising, through prison, and on to his life after release. Sheehan had first-hand experience of the Fenians in Dartmoor. While a curate in Exeter in 1876 he had on occasion filled in for the prison chaplain at Dartmoor,[64] and *The Graves at Kilmorna* features just such a priest.[65] Cogan's prison experiences mirror those of O'Donovan Rossa,[66] and like O'Donovan Rossa he is in no doubt that he is of a different – superior – moral order to the prisoners around him:

> To have to look into the face of a reprieved murderer or burglar; to have to listen, as they moved around, arm in arm, to a Cockney voice narrating, with gusto, the story of an abominable crime, or to have to hear ribald talk, and sometimes blasphemous comments on the sacred mysteries of the faith that was so dear to him – this was the cruellest punishment of all this brave young fellow had to bear.[67]

Like O'Loughlin and Nugent, Cogan finds that the Ireland he returns to appears indifferent or apathetic toward his ideals and sufferings: 'The insignificance of his release, and the unimportance of the whole affair, hurt him deeply.'[68] In an Ireland where going to gaol had 'gone out of fashion',[69] Cogan stands 'aloof ... in silence'.[70] The novel ends when, after many years, Cogan is tempted to break his silence to speak at an election rally in favour of a young independent nationalist candidate, the son of a woman who had loved him before prison, and is killed by a stone thrown at the platform by one of the unprincipled mob. In Sheehan's pessimistic vision, the Fenian prisoner is once more an heroic figure, but once again he is isolated and his fate is tragic.

Between them, these three Cork writers offered little hope to radical separatists; however, in hindsight it is evident that the IRB was on the brink of reinvigoration, as older elements within the organisation were challenged by younger men such Patrick McCartan, Seán McDermott and

Bulmer Hobson. In late 1911 these groups disputed control of the IRB's monthly paper, *Irish Freedom*, and by the beginning of 1912 the younger faction had gained control of the paper and the organisation.[71] A significant factor in their success was the support of Tom Clarke, who was revered as a former prisoner. Perhaps because the split had precipitated a dearth of contributors, but perhaps more importantly because the younger clique needed to assert their ownership of the Fenian heritage, they began to fill the pages of *Irish Freedom* with lengthy autobiographical accounts of the Fenian activities of John Daly and the prison experiences of Tom Clarke. Beginning in January 1912, Clarke began a series called 'Glimpses of an Irish Felon's Prison Life'. In all, thirteen instalments were published, the final appearing in July 1913. Clarke's account is very much in the tone and style of O'Donovan Rossa and Davitt's first memoir. This is once more a tale of 'English brutality'[72] and Fenian resistance: 'Never one moment,' wrote Clarke, 'did I forget I was an Irish Political Prisoner.'[73] It gained a wider audience when published posthumously as a book under the same title in 1922, but in 1912 and 1913 it had an important impact upon the small cohort of IRB activists and sympathisers who would be among the first to go to prison during the revolutionary period. Among young radical separatists, the former Fenian prisoner remained a potent symbol.

V

In 1915 the authorities in Ireland began to imprison a new generation of advanced nationalists. Prior to the Easter Rising of 1916, most of the small number of Irish Volunteers jailed were prosecuted under the Defence of the Realm Act (DORA) as a consequence of anti-recruitment activities. It is evident that this new generation had a keen familiarity with the Fenian literature of imprisonment and was influenced by it in several ways which had important consequences. Firstly, the Irish Volunteer prisoners' knowledge of Fenian prisoners shaped their expectations of imprisonment. Secondly, it influenced their experience of imprisonment. And, thirdly, it impacted upon their representation of their own prison experience.

During Ernest Blythe's first night in Belfast prison in July 1915 he imagined the horrors that awaited him.[74] He later explained that not many Sinn Féin people had been imprisoned before him, but that he was aware of the treatment meted out in an earlier generation to Tom Clarke and John Daly.[75] The extent to which the prisoners, and the advanced nationalist public, had come to take for granted a Fenian-conceived image of imprisonment is illustrated by the case of Herbert Moore Pim. Pim was jailed, along with Blythe, in the summer of 1915. On 7 August *Nationality* printed a poem entitled 'To Ireland' by A. N. (frequent readers of the advanced nationalist press would have recognised this as Pim). The poem purported to be a despatch from prison: 'I tread the ground that felons tread / And sleep within a house of thieves / High is the window, hard my bed / Yet whoso loves thee never grieves / Thus felony and honour blend / The weeds are garnered with the sheaves / Hell upon earth shall have an end / So whoso loves thee never grieves.'[76] Pim had not written the poem in prison but had composed it while awaiting arrest, drawing on the tropes of Fenian prison writing. He then entrusted it to his amanuensis, who was instructed to send it to the newspapers after a few weeks.[77] The readers of *Nationality* received it as an authentic despatch from a new prison martyr and Blythe remembered that for some time Pim had a high reputation with Sinn Féin devotees, largely based on these verses.[78]

In reality, the treatment meted out to early Irish Volunteer prisoners was nothing like that imposed upon O'Donovan Rossa, Davitt or Clarke. Penal servitude as described by the Fenians had ceased to exist and, in any case, these men were not sentenced to penal servitude. They were jailed in Ireland and their imprisonment was managed by a Dublin Castle regime that was sensitive to the possibility that repression could feed disorder rather than prevent it. Therefore, although the Irish Volunteer prisoners were not accorded a separate 'political' status, they were treated as exceptions and their prison regime was a privileged one. By 1915, in part as a consequence of suffragette prison campaigns,[79] the Irish authorities had broad scope for granting privileges and it is clear that the DORA prisoners as a body could have achieved a whole raft of further privileges if they had simply sought them in a concerted manner.[80] That they did not do so is an indication of the extent to which their image of political imprisonment, rooted as it was in Fenian experience, circumscribed their ability to recognise that prison had changed and that a different approach was appropriate. Anna Bryson has correctly noted that prison memoirs function 'to educate and inspire future generations of political activists',[81] but in this case Fenian memoirs provided the Irish Volunteer prisoners with a misleading model. They remained so in the thrall of the rhetoric of individualised martyrdom that they were slow to realise that their prisons were not the Fenians' prisons. As a consequence they had no strategy for the attainment of political status prior to their imprisonment and did not develop such a strategy during their imprisonment. As Blythe asserted: 'Ní raibh aon duine tar éis smaoineamh fós ar staideas agus cóireáil ar leith do phríosúnaigh pholaitíochta a éileamh, mar níor thuigeamar go raibh na Sasanaigh tar éis dul i mboige ó aimsir na bhFíníní.' In other words, they had not yet given thought to claiming the status and treatment of political prisoners because they did not understand that the English had 'gone soft' since the time of the Fenians.[82]

In contemporary propagandistic memoir these men wrote themselves into the Fenian tradition and in the nationalist press they were portrayed as joining the martyr élite. They were the new O'Donovan Rossas, the latest Clarkes. As with their influential predecessors, the memoirs produced by the early Irish Volunteer prisoners were firmly propagandistic in intent. In *Memories of Mountjoy*, which was serialised in the *Hibernian* in late 1915 and published as a book in 1917, Seán Milroy's aim was to expose, as he affected to see it, the felonising of Irish political prisoners. He wrote that his experience in Mountjoy was 'not an isolated incident' but 'just one link in the chain of criminal degradation with which England has sought to shackle and overpower the Irish Nation'.[83] Hebert Moore Pim also wrote a prison memoir, *What It Feels Like*. It was serialised in *Nationality* in late 1915 and published as a pamphlet before that year was out. In it Pim also dwelt on the failure to grant the men political status, insisting: 'We are, of course, political prisoners. But England treats her political prisoners as felons.'[84]

The funeral of Jeremiah O'Donovan Rossa in August 1915 encouraged the prisoners and propagandists to link the Irish Volunteer prisoners with the Fenians. Seán Milroy was one of those in Mountjoy on the day of the funeral. He recalled the occasion in his memoir, writing that he felt transformed somehow as he circled the exercise yard. He looked at his companions, Seán McDermott and Liam Mellows, and remembered O'Donovan Rossa and other patriots:

> Yes, the path I am treading is no longer the ring of Mountjoy merely. It is the pathway of Irish history, and we three – Mellows, McDermott and I, felons of 1915 – are marching with the men who suffered for the same cause and stood against the same power as that which has deprived us of our liberty, and which holds us in its tenacious grip. Round and round goest the marching tramp, and with the trend of these steps I hear the chains which Rossa drags after him; and my ears seem to catch, as from afar off, the sobs and sighing that echoed along the track of history which my companions of this hour have made so sacred with their sufferings.[85]

In his famous funeral oration Patrick Pearse suggested that not only were the mourners in spiritual communion with O'Donovan Rossa and with 'those who suffered with him in English prisons', but with 'our own dear comrades who suffer in English prisons to-day'.[86] This theme was reprised in Eily McCarthy's poem, 'The Funeral of O'Donovan Rossa', which appeared in the *Hibernian*: 'Now they pass near the prison wherein / To-day are men as noble and true / Who follow with joy the thorny way / That was trodden so long by you.' The poem concludes with the promise that on the day of revolution 'We will snatch from the gloom of their prison den / The dauntless souls who there / Are keeping the faith of the Fenian men / Through sorrow and torturing care.[87]

If Irish nationality of the late nineteenth and early twentieth centuries was published or imagined into existence,[88] then Fenian prison memoir was a significant element in that process. These widely read and influential memoirs provided stories of martyrdom for the nation. They provided stories of resistance. The memoirists succeeded in shaping public opinion and sometimes prison policy. By the 1910s the Fenian prison memoir and the Fenian prisoner as a symbol of principled separatism were familiar to most nationalists. Within the culture of advanced nationalism the Fenian prisoners and their writings carried particular weight, helping to fashion in subtle, and obvious, ways the prison lives of another generation of radical nationalists. The memoirs of Fenian prisoners provided future prisoners with models which guided their actions and a written tradition which they sought to emulate. In Reading jail in July 1916, Terence MacSwiney found that his experience was immediately being read in this way by his friends outside. On 12 July Con O'Leary wrote to MacSwiney, citing *The Embers*, to suggest that the tradition of the Fenian prisoner was animated, that 'John O'Loughlin, Laurence Kiely and young Daly are in good health and very well',[89] while, three days later, his sister Nan predicted: 'We'll have a lot of interesting literature in the near future from "Irish Rebels in English Prisons".'[90]

NOTES

1. I would like to acknowledge the assistance of the IRCHSS.
2. J. D. Maginn, *Fitzgerald: The Fenian*, 2 vols (London: Chapman and Hall, 1889), vol. i, p. 240, vol. ii, pp. 70–1.
3. Michel Foucault, *Discipline and Punish: The Birth of the Prison* (London: Penguin, 1991); Dario Melossi and Massimo Pavarini, *The Prison and the Factory: Origins of the Penitentiary System* (London: Macmillan, 1977); Michael Ignatieff, *A Just Measure of Pain: The Penitentiary in the Industrial Revolution 1750–1850* (New York: Pantheon, 1978).
4. Barton L. Ingraham, *Political Crime in Europe: A Comparative Study of France, Germany and England* (Berkeley: University of California Press, 1979); Robert J. Goldstein, *Political Repression in Nineteenth-Century Europe* (Kent: Croom Helm, 1983).
5. Philip Priestley, *Victorian Prison Lives* (London: Methuen, 1985).
6. Silvio Pellico, *My Prisons* (Oxford: Oxford University Press, 1963); W. B. Carnochan, 'The literature of confinement' in Norval Morris and David J. Rothman (eds), *The Oxford History of the Prison: Practice of Punishment in Western Society* (Oxford: Oxford University Press, 1995), p. 398.
7. John Alfred Langford, *Prison Books and their Authors* (London: William Tegg, 1861), p. 4.
8. William Steel Dickson, *A Narrative of the Confinement and Exile of William Steel Dickson, DD* (Dublin: J. Stockdale, 1812); John Mitchel, *Jail Journal* (Dublin: M. H. Gill, 1913).
9. For the most scholarly account of the treatment of Fenians in prison, see Seán McConville, *Irish Political Prisoners, 1848–1922: Theatres of War* (London: Routledge, 2003), pp. 140–213, 276–325, 361–404.
10. Martin J. Wiener, *Reconstructing the Criminal: Culture, Law and Policy in England, 1830–1914* (Cambridge: Cambridge University Press, 1990), p. 309.
11. Casey A. Jarrin, 'You have the right to refuse silence: Oscar Wilde's prison letters and Tom Clarke's *Glimpses of an Irish Felon's Prison Life*', *Éire-Ireland*, 43/3–4 (2008), p. 101.
12. M. J. Kelly, *The Fenian Ideal and Irish Nationalism 1882–1916* (Woodbridge: Boydell & Brewer, 2006), p. 239.

13. Paul Gready, 'Autobiography and the "power of writing": Political prison writing in the apartheid era', *Journal of Southern African Studies*, 19/3 (1993), p. 493.
14. McConville, *Irish Political Prisoners*, pp. 175–82.
15. Leon Radinowicz and Roger Hood, 'The status of political prisoner in England: the struggle for recognition', *Virginia Law Review*, 65 (1979), pp. 1440–1; Owen Dudley Edwards, 'Jeremiah O'Donovan Rossa', in *Oxford Dictionary of National Biography* (Oxford: Oxford University Press, 2004), vol. 47, p. 858.
16. McConville, *Irish Political Prisoners*, p. 173.
17. *Report of the Commissioners on the Treatment of the Treason-Felony Convicts in the English Convict Prisons* in British Parliamentary Papers (1867), xxxv, p. 24.
18. Ibid., p. 23.
19. Ibid., p. 11.
20. *Things Not Generally Known: England's Treatment of Political Prisoners* (Dublin: The Irishman, 1869), p. 9.
21. Ibid., p. 4.
22. Ibid., pp. 4, 27.
23. McConville, *Irish Political Prisoners*, p. 227.
24. Ibid., pp. 219–20.
25. R. V. Comerford, *The Fenians in Context: Irish Politics and Society 1848–82* (Dublin: Wolfhound Press, 1998), pp. 178–9.
26. John Savage, *Fenian Heroes and Martyrs* (Boston: P. Donahoe, 1868), pp. 344, 354.
27. For an assessment of the composition of the Devon Commission, see McConville, *Irish Political Prisoners*, pp. 196–7.
28. *Report of the Commissioners appointed to inquire into the Treatment of Treason-Felony Convicts in English Prisons* in British Parliamentary Papers (1871), xxxii, pp. 27–8.
29. See the introduction to Mairead Maume, Patrick Maume and Mary Casey (eds), *John Sarsfield Casey, The Galtee Boy* (Dublin: UCD Press, 2005), p. 6.
30. Jeremiah O'Donovan Rossa, *Irish Rebels in English Prisons* (New York: P. J. Kennedy, 1882), pp. 139–40.
31. Ibid., p. 73.
32. T. W. Moody, *Davitt and the Irish Revolution* (Oxford: Oxford University Press, 1981), p. 147; McConville, *Irish Political Prisoners*, pp. 310–11.
33. Michael Davitt, *The Prison Life of Michael Davitt* (Dublin: Lalor, 1886, 3rd edn), p. 18.
34. Ibid., p. 29.
35. Ibid., p. 32.
36. O'Donovan Rossa, *Irish Rebels in English Prisons*, pp. 139–40.
37. Ibid., pp. i–xiv.
38. Carla King (ed.), *Michael Davitt: Jottings in Solitary* (Dublin: UCD Press, 2003), pp. ix–xxx.
39. Michael Davitt, *Leaves from a Prison Diary or, Lectures to a 'Solitary' Audience* (London: Chapman and Hall, 1885), p. 10.
40. See the volume of review clippings: Trinity College Dublin, Michael Davitt Papers, MS 9664.
41. *Scotsman*, 17 Feb. 1885.
42. *North Eastern Gazette*, 2 Sept. 1885 (in the volume of press cuttings in TCD, MDP, MS 9606).
43. A. G. Evans, *Fanatic Heart: A Life of John Boyle O'Reilly* (Nedlands: University of Western Australia Press, 1997), p. 210.
44. John Boyle O'Reilly, *An Múindín: Scéal ar Shaoghal Braighdeach san Astráil* (Dublin: An Gúm, 1931). The translation was by Conchubar Ó hArgáin.
45. John Boyle O'Reilly, *Moondyne Joe: A Story from the Underworld* (New York: P. J. Kennedy, 1879), p. 101.
46. McConville, *Irish Political Prisoners*, p. 361.
47. O'Reilly, *Moondyne Joe*, pp. 94–9.
48. Radinowicz and Hood, 'The status of political prisoner in England', p. 1480; McConville, *Irish Political Prisoners*, p. 3.
49. George Sigerson, *Political Prisoners at Home and Abroad* (London: K. Paul, Trench, 1890); G. Shaw Leferve, *Irish Members and English Gaolers* (London: K. Paul, Trench, 1889); E. Dwyer Gray (ed.), *The Treatment of Political Prisoners in Ireland* (Dublin: Freeman's Journal, 1889).
50. Wiener, *Reconstructing the Criminal*, pp. 308–36.
51. Christopher Morash, *A History of the Irish Theatre, 1601–2000* (Cambridge: Cambridge University Press, 2002), pp. 150–1.
52. This relies heavily on Patrick Maume's analysis of 'The Embers': see his *Life That Is Exile*:

Daniel Corkery and the Search for Irish Ireland (Belfast: Institute of Irish Studies, 1993), pp. 20–2. The play was subsequently published in a volume which is very difficult to obtain, Richard Burnham and Robert Hogan with Lloyd Worley (eds), *The Cork Dramatic Society: Lost Plays of the Irish Renaissance, Volume 3* (Newark: Proscenium Press, 1984).

53. Morash, *History of the Irish Theatre, 1601–2000*, pp. 150–1.
54. Lennox Robinson, *Patriots* (Dublin: Maunsel & Co., 1912).
55. Lennox Robinson, *Curtain Up: An Autobiography* (London: M. Joseph, 1942), p. 43.
56. Morash, *History of the Irish Theatre, 1601-2000*, p. 151.
57. Robinson, *Patriots*, pp. 14–17.
58. Ibid., pp. 34–5.
59. Ibid., p. 24.
60. Ibid., p. 41.
61. Ibid., p. 49.
62. Robert Hogan with Richard Burnham and Daniel P. Poteet, *The Abbey Theatre: The Rise of the Realists 1910–1915* (Dublin: Dolmen Press, 1979), pp. 184–6.
63. M. P. Linehan, *Canon Sheehan of Doneraile: Priest, Novelist, Man of Letters* (Dublin: Talbot Press, 1952), p. 112; Catherine Candy, *Priestly Fictions: Popular Irish Novelists of the Early 20th Century* (Dublin: Wolfhound Press, 1995), p. 135.
64. Linehan, *Canon Sheehan of Doneraile*, p. 34.
65. Canon P. A. Sheehan, *The Graves at Kilmorna: A Story of '67* (Dublin: Clonmore and Reynolds, 1950), p. 167.
66. Ibid., pp. 189–96.
67. Ibid., p. 168.
68. Ibid., p. 212.
69. Ibid., p. 322.
70. Ibid., p. 229.
71. Kelly, *Fenian Ideal*, pp. 193–4; Owen McGee, *The IRB: The Irish Republican Brotherhood from the Land League to Sinn Féin* (Dublin: Four Courts Press, 2005), pp. 351–4.
72. *Irish Freedom*, Jan. 1912.
73. Thomas J. Clarke, *Glimpses of an Irish Felon's Prison Life* (Dublin: Maunsel and Roberts, 1922), p. 62.
74. Earnan de Blaghad, *Slán le hUltaibh* (Dublin: Sáirséal & Dill, 1971), p. 175. His exact phrase was the wonderful 'Bhíos ag iomlasc sa bhrionglóidíocht ghruama.'
75. De Blaghad, *Slán le hUltaibh*, p. 175.
76. *Nationality*, 7 Aug. 1915.
77. A. Newman, *What It Feels Like* (Dublin: Whelan & Son, 1915), p. 14. Pim is unique among political prisoners from this period in boasting an amanuensis.
78. De Blaghad, *Slán le hUltaibh*, p. 182; Witness Statement of Ernest Blythe, National Archives of Ireland, Bureau of Military History, WS 939.
79. William Murphy, 'Suffragettes and the transformation of political imprisonment in Ireland', in Margaret Ward and Louise Ryan (eds), *Irish Women and the Vote: Becoming Citizens* (Dublin: Irish Academic Press, 2007), pp. 114–35.
80. See Chapter 3 of William Murphy, 'The Tower of Hunger: Political Imprisonment and the Irish, 1910–1921' (Ph.D. thesis, UCD, 2006).
81. See the introduction to Anna Bryson (ed.), *The Insider: The Belfast Prison Diaries of Éamonn Boyce 1956–1962* (Dublin: The Lilliput Press, 2007), p. 2.
82. See de Blaghad, *Slán le hUltaibh*, p. 182.
83. Seán Milroy, *Memories of Mountjoy* (Dublin: Maunsel & Co., 1917), p. 73.
84. Newman, *What It Feels Like*, p. 26.
85. Milroy, *Memories of Mountjoy*, p. 45.
86. Patrick Pearse, *Collected Works of Pádraic H. Pearse: Political Writings and Speeches* (Dublin: Maunsel & Roberts, 1922) pp. 133–7.
87. *Hibernian*, 21 Aug. 1915.
88. Benedict Anderson, *Imagined Communities* (London: Verso, 1991); Marie Louise Legg, *Newspapers and Nationalism: The Provincial Press, 1850–1892* (Dublin: Four Courts Press, 1998).
89. Maume, *Life That Is Exile*, p. 52.
90. Nan MacSwiney to Terence MacSwiney, 12 July 1916, in University College Dublin Archives, MacSwiney Papers, P48b/8.

V
CONTEXTS AND CONCEPTS

12

Fenianism: The Scope and Limitations of a Concept

R. V. Comerford

I

The significant event of one hundred and fifty years ago marked by this book was the foundation of an organisation. But it was to be many years later before James Stephens and the others would realise that on 17 March 1858 they had launched something called the Fenian movement. Its founder intended the new entity to be nameless, and simply known as 'the organisation' or by some other common noun. That was a characteristic conceit of Stephens': an idea inspired by something he had read about a continental conspiracy, that might have worked if the business were over and done with in an Apocalyptic wave, such as the new organisation was intended to prepare for. In the mundane circumstances that continued to prevail there was recourse to a name, and IRB (Irish Republican Brotherhood or Irish Revolutionary Brotherhood) came to be used, at least among the cadres. It was lack of awareness of a name among the rank-and-file and outside observers that led to the confusion of the new organisation, on its extension into the south-west later in 1858, with the pre-existing Phoenix Literary and Debating Society of Skibbereen. The advantages and disadvantages of anonymity were still factors in late 1861 when Stephens used his following to such good effect in taking control of the funeral of Terence Bellew MacManus. Several observers, including concerned churchmen, mistakenly identified the independently founded and non-oathbound National Brotherhood of St Patrick (admittedly infiltrated by Stephens) as the organisation behind the funeral.[1]

Anonymity had fewer advantages in America, where a succession of names utilised by Stephens' allies, most memorably the Emmet Monument Association, had given way by 1859 to that of the Fenian Brotherhood. In the course of 1863 there emerged widespread awareness, spread mainly by hostile commentators, that the Fenian Brotherhood had an apparently well-organised Irish-based counterpart. Now Fenians could be discerned on both sides of the Atlantic, and simultaneously flesh-and-blood Fenians were subsumed into a collective Fenianism. In a short time

IRB members adopted, and eventually gloried in, their new designation as Fenians. And in due course their orators and pen-bearers would join in the rhetorical discourse on 'Fenianism'.

Awareness of Fenianism in Britain and Ireland was initially promoted with the intention of inspiring fear and disgust. Indeed, one of the principal usages of the concept has been negative and propagandist. In the mid-nineteenth century and beyond, the masses of impoverished Irish flooding into British and North American cities created an inevitable sense of dread. Linked to its predominant Catholicism, this invasion readily lent itself to menacing characterisation. In this context Fenianism became the token of imponderable threat. This was given blood-curdling plausibility by the armed actions in Britain and Ireland associated with the attempted insurrection of March 1867. Further weight was added by the outrage at Clerkenwell on 13 December of the same year, when an explosion that was part of an attempted jailbreak killed and maimed numerous bystanders. Dynamite campaigns in the 1870s and 1880s freighted the term with further intimations of terror. Fenianism in this menacing sense provided the butt for some of *Punch*'s more vitriolic images. This Fenianism connotes the violent menace of the terrorising extreme of a destabilising ethnicity, a conspiracy against decent order, ruthless destructiveness, and connivance with foreign enemies.

Perhaps the most startling direction in Fenian scholarship in recent years is that represented by Christy Campbell's *Fenian Fire: The British Government Plot to Assassinate Queen Victoria*.[2] Evidence from police sources presented by Owen McGee supports the impression of quite bizarre goings-on in the realms of the *agent provocateur*.[3] While academic historiography has yet to come to terms fully with this murky business, its basis lies in the presumed efficaciousness with British public opinion of a terrorising concept of Fenianism. It is against this background of a malevolent Fenianism that the term *Fenian* continues to be in certain quarters a term of abuse.

Of course the 'ism-isation' of the Fenians can be hugely laudatory in intent. The brotherhood of the mid-1860s came quite quickly to accept their designation as Fenians, although when the organisation was revamped in the later 1860s it retained the title of Irish Republican Brotherhood. But their intervention in Irish life was henceforth hailed as Fenianism, which from this perspective represents national resurgence and self-assertion, the fight for freedom, self-reliance, republicanism and brotherhood.

The main concern of this chapter is with the implications for the writing of a history of Fenianism as a concept. Two usages are to be watched. *Fenianism* can be used as a collective term to cover Fenians, what they did, and what they said. In that sense it bears no more and no less risk than

other shorthand forms, although it can of course facilitate easy and unex-
amined generalisation. It would be difficult to engage in extensive historical discussion without the use of such collective terminology. This usage,
however, slips readily into another one, the more problematic invocation
of Fenianism in a reified sense to denote an immanent spirit.

That exceptionalism is the bane of national historiography is well
recognised. Historians of many countries, responding to the chauvinism
or prejudices of their national communities, have an understandable tendency to identify distinctive characteristics supposedly reflective of
national character or special circumstances. The issue has been most
closely debated with reference not to an originally positive but now negative formulation, the controverted German *Sonderweg*.[4] There is always
scope for debate about the distinction between what is merely unique
and what is quite exceptional in the case of a person or a community.
None the less one of the principal functions of scholarship is to probe
suspiciously at personal and national self-images. Popular versions of Irish
history are based on deeply exceptionalist presumptions. Scholarly historiography has not succeeded in changing this, and it is not to be presumed that all historians are endeavouring to change it. Fenianism as a
concept easily evokes a sense of Irish exceptionalism implying heroic
continuities and the triumph of indefatigable spirit against overwhelming
odds. Of course Fenianism will frequently be used in any historical
account to denote simply the activities of the IRB, its members and associates. A problem arises, as suggested above, when the term is used to
convey a package of supposed ideas, attitudes and policies. All too often,
implicitly and even explicitly, those who adopt the latter usage postulate
a Platonic-style Fenian ideal.

Idealist assumptions are a menace in discourse on political life past
and present. The default starting point for journalistic commentary on
current affairs is all too often the supposed philosophy (left, right or in
between) of a politician or a party, even though, at most, philosophy provides the typical politician with rhetoric rather than motivation. In the
academic sphere the uncritical approach to ideals is as outdated as the
silent movies. The idealist perspective has never been more succinctly
expressed than by P. S. O'Hegarty, who wrote in 1952: 'The Irish people
have never, in all their history, been moved by material motives of any
kind.'[5] This may have been intended as a riposte to Erich Strauss's *Irish
Nationalism and British Democracy* published the previous year. The latter's
sustained application of an uncomplicatedly Marxist interpretation to the
broad sweep of modern Irish history constituted an academic updating of
James Connolly's *Labour in Irish history* (1910). But Strauss remained an isolated figure and only in the 1970s, with the work of Paul Bew, was there a
systematic and successful attempt to introduce nuanced Marxist insights

to Irish historiography, focussing in particular on the Fenians and the Land War.[6] Since then Irish historiography has made considerable strides away from the simplicities of intentionalism, but idealism has not disappeared.

In his book *The IRB: The Irish Republican Brotherhood from the Land League to Sinn Féin*, Owen McGee avoids almost completely the word *Fenian* and its derivatives in favour of *Irish Republican Brotherhood.*[7] However, if Stephens, Kickham, Luby, O'Leary et al. were content to be designated as Fenians and to identify with 'Fenianism' it might seem contrived to write about them while avoiding these terms. This is comparable to writing the modern history of the neighbouring island without using the word *British* because of the inadequacy or the potentially distorting connotations of the term.

Even though he largely avoids invoking Fenianism, McGee certainly has not escaped from the hazards of idealism. At the core of this dense and poorly organised book (which has a wealth of detailed information – poorly digested – about the IRB in the period from 1878 to 1904) there lies a Platonic concept of the Irish Republican Brotherhood, which is other people's idealised *Fenianism* under another name. Circumscribed by such a limiting concept, it is more difficult to derive worthwhile new understandings even from a very large body of empirical evidence.

Matthew Kelly covers a somewhat longer period and does so in a more reflective fashion,[8] and on the basis of a more convincing grasp of late nineteenth-/early twentieth-century Irish history in general.[9] But as the title of the book signals, the author's main preoccupation in making sense of hard-won data is with identifying the fortunes of a Fenian ideal. Also at work here is a search for the heroic that chimes with the choice of Easter 1916 as the *terminus ad quem*. Unfortunately, 'the Fenian ideal' has but limited explanatory power in respect of the complicated political, social and cultural developments of turn-of-the-century Ireland, as Kelly's work illustrates. Fortunately, the interest and value of the book range more widely than its title suggests.

A reified and under-examined Fenianism stalks the pages of Oliver Rafferty's *The Church, the State, and the Fenian Threat, 1861–75.*[10] Perhaps the most striking recent example of the essentialising approach to Fenianism is to be found in Richard English's *Irish Freedom.*[11] Over more than ten pages (on the margins of which a tutor might inscribe several times 'Name your source here, please') English works to assemble a sketch of the Fenian archetype.[12] In this way his treatment becomes simply a bland restatement of received assumptions – giving the reader what he/she expects to hear – rather than constituting an attempt to advance understanding. And English takes out membership of the Vestal school of Fenian interpretation, in whose terminology Fenians keep a flame (or something) alive from one generation to another.[13]

To counteract the potentially distorting impact of the concept of Fenianism on understanding of the phenomenon, it is necessary to consider the extent to which activities and attitudes that are identified with Fenianism can be explained as normal nineteenth-century social activity without appeal to the mythic aura of the Fenian organisation. When Fenian fellowship promoted a sense of identification with a sovereign collectivity, it was serving the need for self-realisation through political identification that is one of the hallmarks of a modern society. O'Connell's campaigns in the 1820s and 1840s had served the same need. Associational culture flourished in nineteenth- and early twentieth-century Ireland as elsewhere in Europe of the time. In this context the IRB can be seen as a Freemasonry. Perhaps more to the point, it can be seen at different times and in different places as filling the functions of a variety of kinds of association: literary and debating society and sports club. Owen McGee reports the IRB's difficulty in retaining membership in country areas when the organisation was unable to supply cut-price guns and ammunition.[14] What use did local Fenians have for all this ammunition? Clearly for such people the IRB was an unregistered gun club dedicated to a popular rural pastime. Association for the purposes of mutual aid, more or less formally established, has been a vital economic lifeline for many across a wide spectrum of society and was one of the purposes served by Fenian fellowship.

Associational life was particularly important for the Irish in urban settings abroad. The Fenian movement was especially beholden to the associational culture of the Irish in New York and it was to thrive among the exiled Irish throughout the United States and Great Britain. It surely goes without saying that the Fenian movement was an opportunistic growth in these surroundings and that it was more beneficiary than cause of ethnic mobilisation.

For much of its existence the main role of the Fenian movement in Ireland may have been as an intellectual and strategic resource for those seeking refuge from a clerically dominated milieu. In any society where a clerical élite exercises significant social control there is almost certain to be a movement of reaction. Possessing the sense of self-value that enabled young and not-so-young men to throw off deference to priests, policemen, shopkeepers and landlords (if only behind closed doors, or abroad in open country) was probably the most significant way in which rank-and-file members of the IRB were republicans. Republicans in that sense are to be found in all modern societies.

The fact that an unknown number of Irish people involved themselves in the processes of modern life at least partially in some kind of connection with the Fenian organisation is a very large and important one. Historians have the task of elucidating the connections and influences

involved and finding plausible causations. The point is that the identification of a Fenian affiliation has to be seen as posing a question, not as
providing an explanation ready-wrapped in a mystical cloak. The task is
an unfinishable one, if only because the detailed evidence of Fenian
organisation at almost all stages is incomplete and fragmentary. Oath-
bound association was commonplace throughout late Victorian society,
but the subversive nature of the Fenian oath created an ethos in which
the recording of membership and organisational proceedings was felt to
be potentially hazardous.

Also, in dealing with the strategic and military postures identified
with the Fenian movement, care has to be taken to avoid exclusive
assumptions. The IRB may have nurtured the separatist perspective, but
separation either as prospect or ambition was more widely entertained.
At least as early as 1834 O'Connell had identified the case for separation
in the House of Commons (then to set it aside, but not to dismiss it for
all time).[15] Similarly, the invocation of foreign aid as a strategy of opposition to English power in Ireland has some centuries of history to it. None
the less it is important to appreciate the extent to which, from the 1850s
onwards, Fenians came to monopolise this particular strategy. It was precisely the prospect of an Anglo-French war that created the sense of
urgency lying behind the foundation of an organisation in Ireland in 1858.
The fear was that the opportunity would be lost for want of a military
organisation in Ireland to link up with potential French allies.
Forthcoming work by Dr Brian Sayers reveals the preoccupation of John
O'Mahony over several decades with engineering foreign aid. *De facto*, it
was within the context of the IRB that the strategic decision was taken
on the outbreak of the Great War that England's difficulty should be
indeed Ireland's opportunity.

II

On the basis that discussions like this quickly become pointless without
reference to primary sources, it is now proposed to consider two ballads
that have recently been brought to my attention by Dr Derek Barter.
Ballads have serious limitations as sources, but they do have a certain
authenticity. A ballad represents the judgement of an author and a print-
er – living and dying by the market – about what a public wants to hear.
When a ballad conveys news it does so with a slant that is calculated to
anticipate the emotions of the audience. No single ballad can of course
be treated as if it were a scientific survey of opinion, but any broadsheet
ballad with a clear political message deserves to be heeded as at least
a contribution to the recovery of widespread attitudes at the time of
its popularity.

The first of the two ballads, entitled 'O'Connell's dead!!', is attributed to P. McCabe of Carlow. While O'Connell died in 1847, the standpoint of the ballad – or at least of this version of the ballad – is the early to mid-1860s. The four opening stanzas might have been (and perhaps were) composed in the late 1840s. The fifth stanza, by contrast, with its reference to

> Maning the strangers battle guns
> in many a raging bloody fray

refers to the American Civil War (1861–5), so the present version is in all probability a reworking of an earlier. The final stanza, with its invocation of the prospective return of exiles to set Ireland free, is clearly a reference to the Fenians. This is supported by the mention of the sunburst, which was a distinctive feature of some Fenian Brotherhood insignia.

What is striking about this ballad for present purposes is the easy linkage between O'Connell and the Fenians. Perhaps even the Young Irelanders, 1848, and Ballingarry are alluded to in the mention of fighting

> On Tipperary's lofty hills.

Such a connection flies in the face of much Fenian self-representation and of the standard historiographical explanation of things Fenian derived from it. Of course, the implied continuity between O'Connell's campaign and the Fenian movement as vindicators of the populace amounts to a gross simplification, but it is salutary to be alerted to the possibility that, contrary to much repeated later assumptions, many contemporaries may not have drawn a distinction as to substance.

Although O'Connell repudiated the sword, the Fenian formula was anticipated in a letter from New York supporters read out at a Repeal Association meeting in Dublin in July 1843. It spoke of invading Canada and sending one hundred thousand stand of arms to Ireland, if 'England should persist in putting down Repeal by physical force'.[16] Fifteen years later the Fenian movement was formally launched in Ireland. And yet another fifteen years on, in 1873, the then Fenian leadership was falling into line with Isaac Butt's strategy as he launched the Home Rule League.[17]

There is no more firmly established trope in the received account of the Fenian movement than the execution of Allen, Larkin and O'Brien at Salford jail on 23 November 1867, leading to their subsequent apotheosis as the Manchester Martyrs, victims of British injustice who come to represent the emergence of Fenianism as the symbol of all Irish nationalist grievance and aspiration.[18] The defiant 'God save Ireland!' of the condemned men on the scaffold provided the refrain for a literary ballad composed a few weeks later by T. D. Sullivan that became the anthem of

mainstream Irish nationalism until 1916. Against this background
Gladstone came to power in 1868 promising concessions to Irish opinion
and particularly disestablishment of the state Church in Ireland. Some
historians suggest rather simplistically that the Gladstonian concessions
were wrung by Fenianism. Even those who take a more complex view of
the political context tend to assume that the public credited the Fenians
with Gladstone's conversion. In the light of these assumptions, what are
we to make of the second of the ballads below, 'The Downfall of Heresy'?

The Irish Church Act (32 & 33 Vict., c. 42) became law on 26 July
1869, and the ballad clearly dates from shortly thereafter. It was equally
clearly written for an audience deeply engaged with the subject. It has
several striking, perhaps even shocking, features. There is, for one thing,
the total absence of any reference to Fenians, or for that matter any other
Irish actor, as agents of change. 'Our gracious Queen' and 'the noble
Gladstone' are duly credited as benefactors. Most telling is the reference
to 'Mr Bright' and 'all the members ... combined'. This indicates a clear
sense of disestablishment as the outcome of a constitutional political
process. The promulgation of this line of interpretation by, say, an agent
of Cardinal Cullen would not be a surprise and might be seen as an
attempt to deny Fenian influence. But the ballad we are looking at is in
a genre that would be anathema to a reforming churchman (or indeed,
with its lack of orthographic and typographical perfection, to the editor
of a newspaper such as the *Nation*).

If the political line of this ballad is surprising, its sentiments might be
in other respects also startling. Disestablishment is welcomed simply as
a desirable turn in a contumacious, centuries-old contest for supremacy
('every man shall go to Mass'). There is no hint here of the spirit of religious toleration advocated by both Liberal and Fenian ideologues. It has
been suggested that disestablishment was never a popular political concern in nineteenth-century Ireland. It certainly was the main plank in the
platform on which sixty-six MPs were returned for Irish constituencies in
1868; and clearly at least one ballad-maker shortly thereafter considered
it to be highly marketable for a popular audience.

These two ballads are merely small scraps of evidence to be weighed
up alongside masses of other documentation. But because their witness
seems to run counter to our ensconced assumptions and accounts they
highlight that the importance of ongoing research – such as this volume
represents – lies not only in the accumulation of additional information,
but in the constant search for new perspectives and understanding.
Nothing is more inimical to this endeavour than the postulation of an
'essential' Fenianism.

O'Connell's Dead!![19]

O'Connell's dead, alas! for Erin,
    her sorrows and her wrongs,
That patriot soul no more shall yearn
    for the land of many rongs.
How are we changed, oh! land of woe,
    Since this great tribune died.
What countless evils to us flow
    In this unholy Saxon tide.
Ghastly famin's hedious form
    Stalks broadly through the land
Fierce hunger with its gnawing worm,
    walks most boldly hand in hand.
Extermination's iron rod,
    the peasant's cabin sweeps,
And where the poor man prayed to God
    now fatten flocks of sheep.
The best and bravest of her sons
    are exile's far away
Maning the strangers battle guns
    in many a raging bloody fray.
Spirit of a gallant race,
    Martyred in this worthless strife
Speak to your brethren words of peace
    Tell them to spare their brothers lives.
Or if in battle ye must fight
    then fight with fearless heart and will
For the cause of justice and of right
    on Tipperary's lofty hills.
And more across the broad Atlantic
    leaving friends and home behind,
Oh! The thought that drives them frantic
    is that their rulers are so unkind.
Let us pray that a day may yet come
    When our exile's returning shall float the
        green flag high,
And proudly bear it to their own home
    Where the sunburst shall wave to its God
        in sky.

A New Song on the Downfall of Heresy[20]

Good people all attention pay,

Unto those lines that I relate,
Concerning with Church has failed,
Tho Cromwell has proclaimed it,
The Parson now has cause to cry,
As Gladstone cut his loaf so tight
His greasy pot no more can boil,
With mutton, beef and bacon.

Chorus
The lofty wheel is moving round,
The side that's up is getting down,
A rotten creed cannot be sound,
When lust is its foundation.

Our gracious Queen we'll recognise,
Because she acted shrewd and wise,
The noble Gladstone to appoint
To be our Liberator.
The Lord that died upon the Cross,
Has built his Church upon a rock
And said no other Creed but that
Should ever gain salvation.
The prophecy has come to pass,
That every man should go to Mass,
There is but on earth one true flock
Protected by our Saviour,
There are many Pulpits made of late,
Where every common man could preach,
But the Lord a malediction laid
On every alteration.
The Parson now will lose his fat,
His rosey cocks are getting slack,
His coach and 4 and all his stock,
Is near exterminated.
His wife must sell her hat and vail,
To buy herself some India mail
And wean herself from bread and tea,
To buttermilk and potatoes.
The parson now must emigrate,
And leave his handsome dwelling place,
To preach the creed that Luther made,
He read his recantation,
He said alas what shall I do

To the glebe of Shannon view,
Where rents or rates I never knew,
Since Luther's reformation.
Says the Parson we'd have better times,
If Bess and Harry were alive,
For they'd roast the Papists in the fire,
Both Bishop, Priest and Deacon.
But Gladstone now and Mr Bright
And all the members are combined,
To take from us what William signed,
When Seamus was defeated.

NOTES

1. For Stephens see Marta Ramón, *A Provisional Dictator: James Stephens and the Fenian Movement* (Dublin: UCD Press, 2007).
2. Christy Campbell, *Fenian Fire: The British Government Plot to Assassinate Queen Victoria* (London: Harper Collins, 2002).
3. Owen McGee, *The IRB: The Irish Republican Brotherhood from the Land League to Sinn Féin* (Dublin: Four Courts Press, 2005).
4. See Jürgen Kocka, 'German history before Hitler: the debate about the German *Sonderweg*', *Journal of Contemporary History*, 23/1 (1988), pp. 3–16.
5. P. S. O'Hegarty, *A History of Ireland Under the Union, 1801–1922* (London: Methuen, 1952), p. 140. (O'Hegarty acknowledged receiving valuable suggestions from Dr George O'Brien, professor of political economy at University College Dublin.)
6. Paul Bew, *Land and the National Question in Ireland, 1858–1882* (Dublin: Gill & Macmillan, 1979).
7. McGee, *The IRB*.
8. M. J. Kelly, *The Fenian Ideal and Irish Nationalism, 1882–1916* (Woodbridge: Boydell & Brewer, 2006).
9. Although his summary of the Fenian movement prior to 1880 (pp. 1–3) suggests several misapprehensions.
10. Oliver Rafferty, *The Church, the State and the Fenian Threat, 1861–75* (London: Macmillan, 1999).
11. Richard English, *Irish Freedom: The History of Nationalism in Ireland* (London: Macmillan, 2006).
12. Ibid., pp. 179–93.
13. Ibid., p. 191.
14. McGee, *The IRB*.
15. Cited in M. F. Cusack (ed.), *The Speeches and Public Letters of the Liberator* (Dublin: McGlashan & Gill, 1875), vol. i, pp. 433–4.
16. *Freeman's Journal*, 13 July 1843. I am indebted to Dr Michael Keyes for this reference.
17. David Thornley, *Isaac Butt and Home Rule* (London: MacGibbon & Kee, 1964), pp. 138–75.
18. For example, R. V. Comerford, *The Fenians in Context: Irish Politics and Society, 1848–82* (Dublin: Wolfhound Press, 1985), pp. 148–50.
19. Copy supplied by Dr Derek Barter from Firth Collection, Bodleian Library, Oxford.
20. Copy supplied by Dr Derek Barter from the Gilbert Collection, Dublin City Library, Pearse St.

13

The Fenians and the International Revolutionary Tradition

Peter Hart

James Stephens' idea was the best ... Circles of ten so that a fellow couldn't round on more than his own ring. Sinn Fein. Back out you get the knife. Hidden hand. Stay in, the firing squad. Turnkey's daughter got him out of Richmond, off from Lusk. Putting up in the Buckingham Palace hotel under their very noses. Garibaldi.

Leopold Bloom[1]

I

Consider the two Fenian risings: 1867 and 1916. Anyone familiar with modern Irish history can place them in their immediate contexts – where they came from, how they happened, what their consequences were. If we widen our horizons to take in the rest of Europe, however, we can also see them as part of a wider revolutionary history. A year before the 1867 Rising there was a rebellion in Crete; in 1863–4, Polish guerrillas waged an eighteen-month campaign against the Russian government; in 1859–60, Garibaldi and other Italian nationalists were fighting to overthrow local governments and Hapsburg rule. Moving forward a few years, we come to the Paris Commune in 1871, and to the attempted Bulgarian uprising in 1876.

The Easter Rising's immediate predecessors include the 1911 republican revolution in China, the 1910 Portuguese revolution and the 1905 revolutions in Russia and Poland. And, needless to say, 1917 brought the Bolshevik seizure of power. We can play the same game with the Invincibles and the Dynamitards of the 1880s too. Their way was paved by Russian Populists in the late 1870s, and they were followed by Anarchists, in Spain (or Catalonia) in particular. Irish-American plans to invade Canada similarly echoed John Brown's Harper's Ferry scheme.

So how does the history of the Irish Republican Brotherhood fit in with this rich international tradition? What can other groups and rebellions tell us about Ireland? My exploration here of these questions will necessarily be partial, sweeping and schematic, but I hope it will serve to identify some connections, parallels and differences, and to raise some interesting issues worth pursuing. In order to narrow it down a bit, though, I am going to focus on organisations that took the same basic and distinctive form as the IRB: that is, revolutionary secret societies.

Secret societies in general can be found all over the world and in many periods – from medieval Asia to present-day Skull and Bones at Yale – and there is a significant body of sociological and anthropological writing about them.[2] In historiographical terms, they are particularly important in China and in the Chinese diaspora;[3] in Ireland as well, at least between 1750 and 1850.[4] Revolutionary societies were a small and historically bounded sub-set of this phenomenon: groups formed with the express purpose of overthrowing a government or a social order. By definition, these were organisations founded in secrecy, whose membership was supposed to be known only to fellow members. Joining meant taking an oath – of loyalty, obedience, silence, and dedication to the cause. Betrayal of that trust was usually declared to be a capital offence.

Mystery was required because of the illegality of the society and its aims, and because of the usually accurate presumption that the state was trying to find and expunge them. Thus, these organisations were designed to be invisible and impenetrable. To be found out was to be arrested, imprisoned, tortured, exiled or killed. Hence the necessity (and fun) of codes, invisible ink, secret couriers, disguises and all the rest of it. But also, of selectivity and trust. Prospective recruits were almost always supposed to already be known and accepted by existing members, to be vetted and – in some organisations – to be tested in rites of initiation. This fundamental element of risk was as defining a feature as the revolutionary aim.

Form follows function, so such secret societies were also typically organised in a characteristic way so as to keep governments at bay. This meant compartmentalisation and keeping secret knowledge on a need-to-know basis. Some groups went as far as mandating that a recruit only know his recruiter, and then only by a pseudonym. However, the usual arrangement was a cellular structure in which the rank-and-file belonged to a small 'circle', 'lodge' or 'cell' (also known by many other names) of a dozen or fewer people, completely separate from any other such unit and often, in theory, known to each other only by false names or even numbers. Only the recruiter or leader was supposed to know who or what was above them in the underground chain of command, and he or she might only know his or her leader, or the local committee, and so on up the organisational pyramid. The point, of course, was that if any given member was arrested, he or she could only tell the authorities about what he knew, thereby preserving everyone else from discovery.

The classic expression of this formula was Auguste Blanqui's Society of the Seasons in 1830s Paris. This was made up of cells called 'weeks', in which the members were known only as Monday, Tuesday, etc., with Sunday being their captain. Above 'weeks' were 'months', then 'seasons'.[5] Here lay the inspiration for G. K. Chesterton's novel, *The Man Who Was Thursday*. Secrecy and democracy do not mix, so it is not surprising that such conspiracies were almost always strictly hierarchical. In principle, if not always in practice, they were organised from the top down and run by a small group at the top – or even by a single man. James Stephens was not the only 'dictator', although it was Blanqui above all who epitomised this leader principle.

One of the functions of the membership was usually propaganda – distributing posters, leaflets or, classically, an underground newspaper, which often meant a secret printing press (a common focal point of revolutionary endeavours). This in turn required a smuggling and distribution system, and at least some societies were built up around such a system so that the newspaper created the organisation rather than vice-versa. Lenin famously stressed this point in *What Is To Be Done?*, his classic manifesto for an underground party.[6]

Nevertheless, the fundamental end of all revolutionary secret societies – at least in theory – was armed action: the insurrection. When that day arrived, members became soldiers, under orders to carry out whatever plans their leaders had devised. Indeed, most of their underground activities were supposed to have been devoted to this end, whether collecting arms and explosives or drilling in back-rooms, basements or off in the forest.

Put together, these characteristics define revolutionary secret societies as a specific organisational genre. Of course, as with all such definitions, it blurs at the edges. These groups could be placed on a continuum, with apolitical or non-revolutionary secret or semi-secret societies on one side – Freemasons, for example – and full-blown underground parties and paramilitary armies on the other: the African National Congress (ANC) and Umkhonto we Sizwe (MK). They share many features with other kinds of organisations, but it is still useful to think of them as categorically different.

These societies belong to particular national revolutionary traditions, and to a specific era in European (and world) history. Behind them all lies the Masonic order, which spread from Britain through Europe in the eighteenth century, but the real origin of the species lies in the French Revolution, with the Conspiracy of Equals led by Gracchus Babeuf in 1796. Babeuf, a journalist and Jacobin activist, wanted to complete the unfinished Robespierrean revolution. He pretty much invented the whole formula for underground revolutionary movements, from organising a compartmentalised conspiracy to the classic insurrectionary plan of action. He also revealed many of the key weaknesses of such schemes, including violating his own security rules and, as a result, was caught and killed.[7]

Nevertheless, one of his co-conspirators, Filipo Buonarroti (an Italian enthusiast of French republicanism) survived and went on to become the world's first professional revolutionary. After Napoleon was defeated, Buonarroti built up a succession of international networks of radicals, run – at least on paper – by his own secret societies, the Sublime Perfect Masters and Le Monde. He operated mostly from exile in Geneva and Brussels, while his followers were found mostly in France and northern Italy.[8]

Buonarroti never actually did very much in concrete terms. Much of his purportedly vast secret domain might well have been fantasy or bluff, although it was good enough to make him the great bogeyman of the Metternichian counter-revolutionary right. His one lasting achievement was to write *The History of the Conspiracy of Equals*, his tribute to Robespierre and Babeuf, which laid out the latter's plans in great detail. This was the first of many revolutionary self-help and how-to books – a key component of the international tradition – and would become a bible or textbook for rebels for the next hundred years.

Buonarroti's strategy was not to build from scratch, but to work from within existing groups: to create a conspiracy inside (or above) other conspiracies, allowing him – at least in his own imagination – to control it all from behind the scenes. His hosts were the myriad of societies spawned by the French Revolution and Napoleonic wars, known collectively as the Carbonari in Italy, Spain and Portugal, and under that name, or as the Charbonnerie, in France. These organisations, usually made up of Masonic-style lodges, were involved in the first post-war wave in western Europe of liberal revolutions in the 1810s and 1820s. Similar societies were created in Greece and Russia – the Society of Friends and the Union of Welfare (better known as the Decembrists) – to similar effect.[9]

Out of the Carbonari, and with Buonarroti acting as godfather, came a new generation of rebels in the 1830s, led by Giuseppe Mazzini and Young Italy in Italy,[10] Auguste Blanqui and his various Societies (of Families, and of Seasons) in France, and by Polish radical nationalists led by the Polish Democratic Society.[11] Notable efforts in this period include Mazzini's attempted coup in, and invasion of, Piedmont in 1833–4, Blanqui's 1839 Rising in Paris (putting the Seasons to the ultimate test), and the thwarted Polish revolt of 1846 – among dozens of other plots and adventures, all highly romantic, tragic and retrospectively glorious.

The great political tsunami of 1848 now intervened, neither planned nor caused by secret schemes of course, but sweeping their members along, often to positions of temporary power, as with Mazzini in the Roman Republic. In a few cases, societies were created where none had existed before, as in Bohemia and Ireland.

The last great roll of the dice by the French underground came in 1851, when democrats rose up in resistance to Louis Napoleon's *coup d'état*. Blanquists were back plotting in the late 1860s, and played a role in the Paris Commune of 1871.[12] Still, this was not *their* insurrection, properly speaking. In Italy, Mazzinians – now called the Party of Action – tried again in Milan in 1854, and had a hand in the unification struggles of 1859 and 1860. By this time, however, liberals and moderates were out-organising the old master on the ground.[13] He continued to plot to recover Rome and Venice in the 1860s, but these matters were closed after 1870. In Poland, nationalist struggle came spectacularly to an end in 1863, with the January Insurrection. This took the form of both urban and rural guerrilla warfare, run by a clandestine National Government fuelled by a National Loan.[14] It was a terrible failure but also a harbinger of rebellions to come, not least in Ireland.

After 1870 the golden age of secret societies was almost over in their old western European heartland, petering out with Michael Bakunin (one of the last great revolutionary warhorses) and his anarchist disciples in Italy and Spain. Only on the very edge of the continent, in Portugal, did the Carbonari survive to launch a successful republican revolution in 1910.[15] The model was successfully exported to eastern Europe, however: to Bulgaria in the 1870s and then on to Macedonia in the 1890s and Serbia and Bosnia thereafter, with well-known results. From here, and from Paris and London, it spread throughout the Ottoman empire (the Committee of Progress and Union – i.e. the Young Turks)[16] and to Egypt, India, and China and its diaspora.[17] Last in line was Latin America. Perhaps the final uprising along classic Blanquist lines was carried out by Acción Comunal in Panama in 1931, while the last revolutionary campaign mounted by a true secret society was that of the ABC against the Machado regime in 1930s Cuba.[18] Here we can see a fascinating circulation of ideas at work, moving outwards from western Europe towards various peripheries.

However, even in western Europe, the golden age was not quite entirely over, thanks to Ireland. The Irish Republican Brotherhood did not follow its counterparts in France, Italy and Poland into oblivion. It carried on and on, until the 1916 Rising fulfilled the great insurrectionary dream – and even after that, through the Irish revolution until 1922. So how do the Fenians fit into this overall picture, and how do they compare to their continental cousins?

II

The best place to begin comparisons is at the beginning. The first Fenians were veterans of the Irish Confederation and its offshoots: prod-ucts of failed rebellion, proscription and exile in France and the United States. The same could be said of Blanqui's societies, driven underground by repression, Mazzini's Young Italy and Party of Action, which grew out of failed rebellions in 1830, and the Polish Democratic Society, based in the 'Great Emigration' after the disaster of 1830–1.

It is notable, though, that nineteenth-century Irish radicals were very late adopters of the secret society model – a full one or two generations behind those in other European countries. Not that secret societies were absent from Irish history, of course. Leaving aside the many variants on Whiteboyism (which were not organised in the same way, nor politically radical), it could well be argued that the United Irishmen were at least co-inventors of the whole concept along with Babeuf's Equals, at least once they were forced into hiding and dedicated themselves to violent rebellion. Moving ahead into the early years of the subsequent century, we also have Robert Emmet's 1803 rising and the Ribbon societies – which were themselves descended from the Defenders of the 1790s. For the purposes of my argument here, however, the Ribbonmen were not really revolutionary or insurrectionist and Emmet seems not to have had a secret society as such.[19] The United Irishmen have indeed been erroneously neglected by historians of European revolution, but there was no organisational tradition connecting them to the Fenians – who do not appear to have modelled themselves in any way on their distant predecessors. If it had been Wolfe Tone or one of his colleagues, rather than Buonarroti, who had written the blueprint for republican insurgency, they would be far better known. But Irish rebels never produced any such text.

The reason for this absence of a revolutionary underground before the late 1850s can, I think, be found in the fact that Ireland's political environment was far more permissive than in most of the rest of Europe. Parties could organise openly, there was no Papal Inquisition or equivalent to Metternich's secret police, and the O'Connellite coalitions around Emancipation, Tithes and Repeal were able to peacefully pursue a liberal and nationalist agenda. In short, there were plenty of political opportunities available to would-be activists and no one was being forced underground. Why, then, did Fenianism emerge? The answer may again have to do with opportunity (or lack thereof), as artisans and lower middle-class men, radicalised in the Repeal and Confederate movements, were now largely left out of politics, and so were open to rival mobilisations.[20]

As for seizing the opportunity, that had a lot to do with the autonomous role of exiles and émigrés, who brought their own money, drives and projects into the equation and imposed themselves on the situation at home.[21] This was an enormously salient feature of IRB history. American funding and sponsorship created 'the Organisation' in the first place, Irish-American politics did much to determine its development, and when the rising finally took place in 1867, it was largely an American-run operation. The 'New

Departure' that brought parliamentarians and revolutionaries together was another transatlantic affair, as were the dynamite campaigns of the 1880s.

There was nothing unusual in this, though. Most revolutionary conspiracies were transnational – especially (albeit perhaps ironically) nationalist ones. Blanqui aside, most of the great revolutionary heroes of the nineteenth century were exiles or refugees at one point or another: Buonarroti, Mazzini, Garibaldi, Kossuth, Herzen, Bakunin, and on up to Pilsudski and Lenin. James Stephens, John O'Mahony and John Devoy were in distinguished company in this regard. If anything, exile was a prerequisite for building a revolutionary career, often poverty-stricken but also subsidised by émigré communities or foreign sympathisers – and even by government pensions in London, Paris or Milan.

With exiles came the always peculiar dynamics of exile politics, with their personality conflicts, abstract ideological disputes, faction fights, power struggles, scandals over missing or misspent money – a hardy perennial – and the inevitable splits. All very familiar to Fenians, of course, as was the recurring tension over the necessity and timing of action, with the away teams in Marseilles or Zurich or New York pressing for action and results while the men on the ground worried about practicalities. Long before the American-made disasters in Britain and Ireland in 1867, Mazzini was heavily criticised for dragging activists in Rome and Milan into useless sacrifices.[22] There was also the recurring phenomenon of the unwanted or unexpected expedition: the band of exile adventurers who landed by sea or sneaked over the mountains, expecting their compatriots to rise up to meet them, but finding only apathy, confusion or hostility. This was the fate of the Bulgarian Legion in 1867–8 and of many, many Italian efforts prior to the final triumph of Garibaldi's Thousand in Sicily and Naples.

Another way to become a professional revolutionary was through imprisonment: an experience IRB activists shared with the rest of Europe, along with prison memoirs as key texts.[23] Blanqui was the political prisoner *extraordinaire*, emerging only briefly when political winds shifted in his favour, but doomed to return once his latest revolutionary gambit had failed.

What Irish republicans did not generally share was the extraordinary internationalism of continental revolutionaries. Italian and French liberals fought in Spain in the 1820s and 1830s; Poles and Germans served under Mazzini and Garibaldi as well as on Parisian barricades; and foreign volunteers flocked to help Polish rebels in 1863, many of whose leaders had been trained in Genoa.[24] Buonarroti, Mazzini, Marx and Bakunin all thought in terms of a European revolution – hence Young Europe and the International – and these dreams were widely shared. Paris, Geneva and London were the great European centres of exile, debate and camaraderie, where thousands of revolutionaries intermingled.

Individual Irishmen took some part in all this. James Stephens and John

O'Mahony made some connections with French republicans after 1848.[25] There was at least one prominent Irish guerrilla leader in Poland in 1863 – the Tom Barry of his day?[26] And the Fenians did hire the veteran Garibaldini Gustave Cluseret to advise them on strategy and tactics. But there was nothing like the same scale of engagement as between groups on the continent. The only major Irish volunteer effort was actually mounted against Italian nationalists: the Papal Brigade of 1860.[27] And, tellingly, neither Buonarroti's nor Mazzini's international networks included Ireland.

Why this lack of interaction with the rest of the revolutionary world? Ireland was very much part of the Anglo-American world, and the weight of emigration across the Atlantic – and the political attractions of the American republic – brought exiles there, rather than to Europe. London was obviously out of bounds, so there could be no hobnobbing with Mazzini and Marx in the British Library. Geneva made little sense as a destination. Another factor was the virulent anti-clericalism of so many democrats in Catholic Spain, Italy and France. The French Revolution, the Roman Republic and the Paris Commune were not where good Catholics – like the majority of Fenians – were to be found.

III

How did the social structure of the IRB compare with those of secret societies elsewhere? First of all, they shared an overwhelmingly urban base. Just as the two Fenian uprisings were focused on Dublin, so French revolutions were primarily Parisian, Italian outbreaks took place in Milan, Venice, Rome or Naples and Polish efforts were centred on Cracow and Warsaw. When such rebels ventured into the countryside to liberate their idealised 'people', they usually encountered mystified indifference – if they were lucky. Thus, the experience of the Irish Confederates in 1848 was matched by that of Italian nationalists in Calabria and the Veneto, and of Russian populists in the 1870s.[28] At least they didn't face the rage of peasants in Galicia or outside Cracow in 1846, who massacred the Polish gentry who rose in rebellion that year.[29]

Liberal constitutionalists of the 1820s, 1830s and 1840s tended to come from the middle and upper classes everywhere although, in Ireland, gentry and aristocratic participation was greatly limited by the sectarian divide in politics and life. Still, Young Ireland looked a lot like its counterparts in Poland or the Romagna.[30] Radical democratic groups, on the other hand, tended to have a heavily artisanal rank-and-file, with a more *petit bourgeois* leadership, whether in Cork or the Rhineland.[31] The Fenians' move down-market was echoed elsewhere.

It also appears that underground movements usually spread through the same kind of pre-existing networks. One set were veterans of earlier groups: Confederates and '49ers in Ireland; Carbonari in France and Italy; and, in general, in the organisational goldmine of exile communities. Among the working classes, trade and mutual aid societies seem to have been important everywhere, as were workshops and factories, pubs, taverns and cafés – and their owners. Family connections were obviously important as well.[32] Risk put a premium on trust, even if it was often misplaced.

On the other hand, it does not seem as if Dublin and Cork contained identifiably insurrectionary neighbourhoods as could be found in Paris and elsewhere. Nor was there in Ireland the tradition of *communes* as existed in Russia and Poland: households of like-minded young people dedicated to the cause. Another key revolutionary space the Fenians lacked was the university campus. Just about every European conspiracy from the early 1830s onwards had a significant cohort of students involved: a ubiquitous presence in demonstrations and on barricades, as well as in café society.[33] Irish colleges were never hotbeds of radicalism (at least not until Queen's University and People's Democracy), nor did Ireland have a very large student population to begin with. This meant that Fenianism lacked a comparable intellectual cutting edge and a vital bridge to the intelligentsia and the middle class.

IV

The moment of truth for every conspiracy – what Mazzini called 'the triumphant fact' – was the pay-off: the insurrection. In terms of planning or imagining, this came in two basic forms: urban and rural. The original inspiration for Babeuf's urban rising were the *journées* of revolutionary Paris, just as later secret strategists planned to replicate the successor outbursts of 1830, 1848, 1851 and 1871. Outside France, we can add Brussels in 1830 and Venice, Milan, Vienna, Berlin and Prague in 1848. None of these were actually planned beforehand but secret society men were usually confident that they could count on the same crowds to rally to their side with the same fervour once they acted. That action would be sudden and swift: a pop-up revolution. Out of the blue, the unsuspecting government would be overwhelmed as a secret army appeared on the streets to seize arms, barracks and public buildings, all in one co-ordinated, simultaneous operation. On its heels would appear a provisional government, often a new flag and constitution as well, all in the name of the people. Surprise and timing were the keys to success. Like an intricate bank heist, if the authorities became suspicious, if someone was careless, if almost anything went wrong – everything would be ruined. Blanqui was the great apostle of this methodology, and even wrote a manual on the subject: his 1839 rising was his one properly realised attempt at putting his ideas into practice.[34]

Where French revolutionaries faced a highly centralised government based in a hegemonic capital city, Italians and Poles – like the Irish – had a much more fractured and less urbanised geography to deal with, as well as governments based outside their own countries, in Vienna and St Petersburg. For this and other reasons, they gravitated towards the idea of a guerrilla war, with a cadre of activists leading bands of peasants against the armies of their oppressors. There was much debate on the best way to achieve this victory – complete with duelling manifestoes – and numerous attempts to put them into practice. The most notable and sophisticated effort came in Poland in 1863, with the onset of the world's first self-described 'people's war'.[35]

Irish revolutionaries contributed nothing to this literature and do not seem to have absorbed it either. It is not clear that anyone knew what exactly was supposed to happen in 1867 or 1916, especially outside Dublin. As a result, the Easter Rising is a possibly unique example of insurrectionary abstract art. The surprise, the proclamation, the tricolour, the seized buildings and barricades were all there, but the targets seem almost purely symbolic or even arbitrary: instead of the arsenal, city hall or barracks, they occupied a post office, a bakery, a public park. There was probably some military rationale involved – it is hard to tell since no record of the plan has survived – but there was certainly no intention of seizing power. Absurd or otherwise, it was most definitely theatre.

Another interesting Irish exception to the European revolutionary repertoire was the absence of barricades. These were the paramount symbol of rebellion (even more than the revolutionary beard, a convention the Fenians did adhere to) and they appeared everywhere in 1848.[36] Yet they were never part of the Irish tradition – except, of course, in Belfast, where they connoted sectarian division rather than popular unity. Again, it would seem that people, ideas and techniques circulated fairly freely in western and central Europe, but they did not make it to Ireland.

V

Questions of strategy and tactics raise the inevitable question: why didn't they ever work? Why is the history of revolutionary conspiracy one of almost unremitting failure, from Babeuf to Pearse?

The first problem was security, and the great likelihood of discovery and betrayal. Most plots were uncovered and quashed before they ever really got started. Informers played a role in this, but so did sheer amateurism and silliness. More than one mastermind left membership lists lying in plain sight – such was the fate of the great Bulgarian conspirator, Vasil Levski, who was captured in 1872.[37] It is somewhat ironic that systems designed to protect an organisation's leaders were most often subverted by those same people, at the expense of those below them. Whatever about codes and circles, few people were serious enough about what Lenin referred to as *konspiratsiia* – the art of not getting caught.[38] The rules of compartmentalisation were *always* broken and, in any case, recruits were usually drawn from the same interwoven networks and political and social milieus, and therefore knew each other anyway.

The second major problem with conspiracies was their inability to mobilise popular support. Of course, this was difficult to do using normal political means in those countries where such activity or expression was illegal – hence the perceived need for secrecy and revolution in the first place. Not necessarily impossible, however, as the Polish National Government and underground socialist parties in Germany and Russia proved.[39] And even the most secretive organisations typically sought some outlet for their propaganda. The Conspiracy of Equals used posters but later generations depended on the classic underground newspaper – indeed, the secret printing press carried almost as much symbolic value as the barricade. Sometimes this effort, however circumscribed, had greater long-term impact than any feeble uprising. Such was probably the case with Mazzini's *Young Italy*, and perhaps also with the *Irish People*.[40]

Still, however successful the underground might be in raising consciousness, there was no substitute for an actual political party – and publicity carried the inherent risk of discovery. And, however much secrecy and cellular organisation made sense, it was always going to work at cross purposes with the wider aim of convincing people to support the cause. Once the fighting started, it was too late to explain why. In this sense, secret societies were a self-defeating mechanism, and their tendency to introversion and solipsism encouraged the fantasy that 'the people' were with them, while their secrecy prevented them from realising that dream.

A more localised problem was that of location. Uprisings might force a change in government – at least temporarily – but they could usually only produce a real victory if they took place in a capital city, like Paris or Petrograd. Provincial cities like Milan, Cracow or Dublin might fall and it would not matter because the state and armed forces were elsewhere. Such a loss might represent a setback – and enough of them might come close to bringing down a Hapsburg-style regime – but cities can just be re-taken once the necessary forces are marshalled, as happened again and again in 1848–9, and as would be repeated at Easter 1916.

Finally, just about any rebellion was doomed no matter how well it was organised or concealed. Without access to real military resources, or without some catastrophic collapse of the opposing state and army, it was just a matter of the greater force prevailing. One thing a survey of revolutionary failure tells us is that we should think again about the special pleading that seems to surround Irish risings. If only the informer had been discovered; if only so-and-so hadn't been caught; if only it had been launched earlier, when everything was ready; if only they had waited until the time was right; if only the guns had arrived and the mobilisation order hadn't been countermanded; my dog ate it; the traffic was bad. Versions of these excuses exist throughout revolutionary history and they all seem like a dead-end for serious argument.

VI

There is failure to prevail and then there is failure to achieve anything at all – as in Ireland in 1803, 1848 and 1867. Mazzini's record was almost as bad and he worried about it. When he referred to the 'triumphant fact', what he meant was not outright victory but rather a spectacular event capable of inspiring others even in defeat, as opposed to an embarrassing, pathetic rout. He believed in the necessity of action as a principle, as did some Polish and Chinese radicals and even Blanqui, in a way. Patrick Pearse and other proponents of a 'blood sacrifice' were not alone.

Every national tradition had its share of failure but one striking difference between Irish and European rebellions was the scale of their violence. The Phoenix Park assassinations, the occasional killing of an informer, and the dynamite attacks in Britain can compare to Russian Populist efforts in 1878–81, but there is no Irish equivalent to the defence of the Roman Republic in 1848–9, the Polish slaughters in 1830–1 or 1846 or 1863, or to France in 1848 or 1851, let alone the Paris Commune. In contrast to their reputation, it was hard for Irish revolutionaries to summon up real bloodshed after 1798. This could be seen as either a curse or a blessing but the question remains: why not?

Neither the Fenians nor their nineteenth-century predecessors could produce a mass mobilisation, nor did they ever gain control of a national guard or a militia or any other serious armed force. So before 1916 there were never any real battles. It also mattered very much that there was no class conflict involved in these episodes: no 'reds versus whites', middle classes turning on the dangerous masses, or peasants exterminating their landlords. Finally, on the continent (and in Ireland in 1798), the worst revolutionary violence often came when the rebels were still in control, but facing defeat.[41] Atrocities at this stage were magnified by counter-revolutionary propaganda and rumour, prompting savage reprisals. Nothing like that took place in nineteenth- and twentieth-century Ireland.

Also deficient by continental standards was British state or 'white' terror. Papal, Hapsburg and Tsarist cruelties were sometimes exaggerated, but these governments were far more violent than Britain's.[42] The Manchester Martyrs may have struck a powerful chord with Irish nationalists but their deaths were drops in the bucket compared to the overflowing martyrologies of French republicanism or the Polish national struggle. Victorian liberalism played its part, as perhaps did reform-minded public opinion. Restraint on one side also undoubtedly helped encourage restraint on the other: a 'green' terror might well have unleashed an 'orange' response.

VII

This chapter started with the question of origins and will conclude with the question of how revolutionary secret societies end. For if the IRB's late arrival sets it apart, so does its survival long, long after its original contemporaries had disappeared. Young Italy did not make it past two decades, nor did the Polish Democratic Society, and most conspiracies – like that of Czech radicals in Prague in 1849[43] – were the work of mere moments by comparison. From 1858 to 1922 the IRB carried on for sixty-four years: easily the longest-lived such organisation ever.

Part of the explanation might lie in the simple fact that the IRB did not attempt a second insurrection until 1916, when it had the Irish Volunteers as a vehicle. If it had acted on its own again after 1867, it might well have sealed its fate. Instead, it displayed a most unusual adaptability. Uniquely in the annals of revolutionary secret societies, it fundamentally changed its strategy from insurrection to Buonarroti-style entryism, and was as successful at the latter as it was dismal at the former. Fenians joined and influenced the Home Rule movement, the Land League, the Gaelic Athletic Association, and ultimately the Irish Volunteers and Sinn Féin. That the IRB was able to use the Volunteers in 1916 and then completely take them over afterwards was a remarkable achievement. The role it played in the Irish revolution of 1916–23 – operating within a wider movement – is only matched by the power exercised by the South African Communist Party within the ANC and MK.[44]

Thus, Fenians contributed much to the advance of Irish nationalist endeavours, even if they did so as members of other organisations. This track record suggests a further reason for the continued operation of the brotherhood: it still performed a useful function as a kind of recruiting and training ground for political leaders, from Michael Davitt to Michael Collins.

So why didn't it continue past 1922? French conspiracies stopped after the advent of the Third Republic; Italians after final unification in 1870; Poles after 1918. Likewise, the IRB folded because most of its leadership felt it had achieved its great goal of independence. In any case, the organisation had been completely subsumed by the Irish Republican Army (IRA). When the anti-Treaty Volunteers broke away and set up their own executive and general staff, they felt no need to establish a rival IRB supreme council as well. In a weird reversal, the IRA in effect became the new IRB, and would prove to be even longer-lived than its ancestor.

NOTES

1. James Joyce, *Ulysses* (London: Bodley Head, 1960), p. 163.
2. For a foundational text, see Kurt Wolff (ed.), *The Sociology of George Simmel* (New York: Free Press, 1950), pp. 307–76.
3. See Jean Chesneaux, 'Secret societies in China's historical evolution', in J. Chesneaux (ed.), *Popular Movements and Secret Societies in China 1840–1950* (Stanford, CA: Stanford University Press, 1972), pp. 1–22.
4. See Tom Garvin, *The Evolution of Irish Nationalist Politics* (Dublin: Gill & Macmillan, 1981), pp. 14–52.
5. See Jill Harsin, *Barricades: The War of the Streets in Revolutionary Paris, 1830–1848* (London: Palgrave Macmillan, 2002), pp. 106–23.
6. A new translation can be found in Lars T. Lih, *Lenin Rediscovered: What Is To Be Done? In Context* (Chicago: Haymarket Books, 2005). On the role of the newspaper, see pp. 813–36; see also the discussion on pp. 433–88.
7. See Ian Birchall, *The Spectre of Babeuf* (New York: St Martin's Press, 1997).
8. Elizabeth Eisenstein, *The First Professional Revolutionist: Philippo Michele Buonarroti* (Cambridge, MA: Harvard University Press, 1959).
9. For this period, and these organisations, as a whole, see James Billington's extraordinary *Fire in the Minds of Men: Origins of the Revolutionary Faith* (New York: Basic Books, 1980), pp. 128–45, and Martyn Lyons, *Post-Revolutionary Europe, 1815–1856* (London: Palgrave Macmillan, 2006), pp. 56–97. On the Carbonari, see John Rath, 'The Carbonari: their origins, initiation rites and aims', *American Historical Review*, 69/353 (1963), pp. 353–70.
10. E. E. Y. Hales, *Mazzini and the Secret Societies: The Making of a Myth* (London: Eyre and Spottiswoode, 1956); Roland Sarti, *Mazzini: A Life for the Religion of Politics* (Westport, CT: Praeger, 1997).
11. Eugene Kisluk, *Brothers from the North: The Polish Democratic Society and the European Revolutions of 1848–1849* (Boulder, CO: East European Monographs, 2005), pp. 1–16.
12. Patrick Hutton, *The Cult of the Revolutionary Tradition: The Blanquists in Politics, 1864–1893* (Berkeley: University of California Press, 1981), pp. 1–99.
13. See Raymond Crew, *A Sterner Plan for Italian Unity: The Italian National Society in the Risorgimento* (Princeton: Princeton University Press, 1963).
14. W. Rudzka, 'Studies on the Polish insurrectionary government in 1863–4', *Antemurale*, 7–8 (1967), pp. 397–481.
15. Douglas Wheeler, 'The Portuguese revolution of 1910', *Journal of Modern History*, 44/2 (1972), pp. 172–94.
16. M. Þükrü Hanioðlu, *Preparation for a Revolution: The Young Turks, 1902–1908* (Oxford: Oxford University Press), pp. 143–81.
17. On Sun Yat-sen, the Revolutionary Alliance, and the Blanquiesque March 1911 insurrection, see T'ang Leang-Li, *The Inner History of the Chinese Revolution* (Westport, CT: Hyperion Press, 1977, 1st edn 1930), pp. 49–53, 71–80; Marie-Claire Bergère, *Sun Yat-sen*, trans. Janet Lloyd (Stanford, CA: Stanford University Press, 1998), pp. 173–97.
18. Thomas Pearcey, 'Panama's generation of '53: Patriots, Praetorians, and a decade of discord', *Hispanic American Historical Review*, 76/4 (1996), pp. 692–719; Luis Aguilar, *Cuba 1933: Prologue to Revolution* (Ithaca, NY: Cornell University Press, 1972), pp. 118–19.
19. See M. R. Beames, 'The Ribbon societies: lower-class nationalism in pre-famine Ireland' and Tom Garvin, 'Defenders, Ribbonmen and others: underground political networks in pre-famine Ireland', in C. H. E. Philpin (ed.), *Nationalism and Popular Protest in Ireland* (Cambridge: Cambridge University Press, 1987).
20. On this point, see Maura Cronin, *Country, Class or Craft? The Politicisation of the Skilled Artisan in Nineteenth-Century Cork* (Cork: Cork University Press, 1994).
21. See Sabine Freitag (ed.), *Exiles from European Revolutions: Refugees in Mid-Victorian England* (New York: Berghahn Books, 2003). A study of Chinese émigré nationalism – with many parallels with the Irish case – can be found in L. Eve Armentrout Ma, *Revolutionaries, Monarchists, and Chinatowns* (Honolulu: University of Hawaii Press, 1995). For a fascinating regional study of a later period, see Charles Ameringer, *The Democratic Left in Exile: The Antidictatorial Struggle in the Caribbean, 1945–1959* (Coral Gables: University of Miami Press, 1974).
22. Sarti, *Mazzini*, pp. 158–62.
23. See, for example, Maria Smith, 'The Spielberg remembered: nine prison narratives of the Italian Risorgimento' (Ph.D. thesis, University of North Carolina at Chapel Hill, 2001).

24. See Emanuel Halicz, *Polish National Liberation Struggles and the Genesis of the Modern Nation*, trans. Roger Clarke (Odense: Odense University Press, 1982), pp. 151–61. For a slightly later example of this internationalist impulse, see Gilles Pécout, 'Philhellenism in Italy: political friendship and the Italian volunteers in the Mediterranean in the nineteenth century', *Journal of Modern Italian Studies*, 9/3 (2004), pp. 405–27.
25. Marta Ramón, *A Provisional Dictator: James Stephens and the Fenian Movement* (Dublin: UCD Press, 2007), pp. 57–62.
26. His name is reported as O'Brien de Lacey: Norman Davies, *God's Playground: A History of Poland*, 2 vols (New York: Columbia University Press, 2005), vol. ii, p. 263.
27. R. Dudley Edwards, 'The Risorgimento and Ireland 1848–70', in R. D. Edwards (ed.), *Ireland and the Italian Risorgimento* (Dublin: Italian Institute, 1960), pp. 31–55.
28. See Paul Ginsborg, 'Peasants and revolutionaries in Venice and the Veneto, 1848', *Historical Journal*, 17/3 (1974), pp. 503–50.
29. Piotr Wandycz, *The Lands of Partitioned Poland, 1795–1918* (Seattle: University of Washington Press, 1974), pp. 134–5.
30. For Roman revolutionaries, see Leopold Glueckert, *Between Two Amnesties: Former Political Prisoners and Exiles in the Roman Revolution of 1848* (New York: Garland, 1991).
31. For the latter, see Jonathan Sperber's superb *Rhineland Radicals: The Democratic Movement and the Revolution of 1848–9* (Princeton: Princeton University Press, 1991), pp. 185–221.
32. For a study of Italian networks, see Clara Lovett, *The Democratic Movement in Italy 1830–1876* (Cambridge, MA: Harvard University Press, 1982), pp. 76–116.
33. For student radicalism in Germany and Austria, see Priscilla Robertson, 'Students on the barricades: Germany and Austria, 1848', *Political Science Quarterly*, 84/2 (1969), pp. 367–79; Rolland Ray Lutz, 'The German Revolutionary Student Movement, 1819–1833', *Central European History*, 4/3 (1971), pp. 215–41. For Russia, see Daniel Brower, *Training the Nihilists: Education and Radicalism in Tsarist Russia* (Ithaca, NY: Cornell University Press, 1975) and 'Student political attitudes and social origins: the Technological Institute of Saint Petersburg', *Journal of Social History*, 6/2 (1972–3), pp. 202–13, which reports some unique survey data.
34. See Harsin, *Barricades*, pp. 124–46.
35. Emanual Halicz, *Partisan Warfare in 19th Century Poland: The Development of a Concept*, trans. Jane Fraser (Odense: Odense University Press, 1975).
36. Mark Traugott, 'Barricades as repertoire: continuities and discontinuities in the history of French contention', *Social Science History*, 17/2 (1993), pp. 309–23.
37. R. J. Crampton, *Bulgaria* (Oxford: Oxford University Press, 2007), pp. 89–90.
38. See Lih, *Lenin Rediscovered*, pp. 459–69.
39. See Vernon Lidtke, *The Outlawed Party: Social Democracy in Germany, 1878–1890* (Princeton: Princeton University Press, 1966) and Ralph Carter Elwood, *Russian Social Democracy in the Underground: A Study of the RSDRP in the Ukraine, 1907–1914* (Assen: Van Gorcum, 1974).
40. Ramón suggests this was the case: *Provisional Dictator*, pp. 150–9.
41. See Glueckert, *Between Two Amnesties* and Steven Hughes, *Crime, Disorder and the Risorgimento: The Politics of Policing in Bologna* (Cambridge: Cambridge University Press, 2002), pp. 169–232.
42. For a reappraisal of Metternich's security policies, see Alan Sked, *Metternich and Austria: An Evaluation* (London: Palgrave Macmillan, 2008), pp. 123–243.
43. Stanley Pech, *The Czech Radicals of 1848* (Chapel Hill: University of North Carolina Press, 1969), pp. 237–62.
44. Stephen Ellis and Tsepo Sechaba, *Comrades Against Apartheid: The ANC and the South African Communist Party in Exile* (Bloomington: Indiana University Press, 1992).

Index

The Gaelic Athletic Association, 1884–2009

Mike Cronin, Paul Rouse & William Murphy (Eds)

This book brings together some of the leading writers in the area of Irish history to assess the importance of the GAA in Irish society since its founding in 1884 and is the first key academic book to centre on the GAA and Irish history. While there has been much written about the GAA, the bulk of work has concentrated on the sporting aspects of the Association – the great games and famous players – rather than the role that the GAA has played in wider Irish history. The chapters cover a large chronological span dating back to the origins of hurling, through the foundation of the GAA, its role in the political life of the nation and ending with an assessment of some of the main issues facing the GAA into the twenty-first century. Importantly the book also offers original and insightful work on areas including the class make up of the GAA, the centrality of Amateurism in the Association, the role of the Irish language and the ways in which films have featured Gaelic games.

April 2009   304 pages illus
978 0 7165 3028 2 cloth   €60.00/£45.00/$69.95

Series: The Irish Abroad

Irish Republicanism in Scotland
1858–1916

Fenians in Exile

Máirtín Seán Ó Catháin

The first historical narrative of Irish nationalism in Scotland, dealing with the exiled Irish
nationalist movement in Scotland as a whole
and not just focusing on the physical-force tradition within that movement. The book begins
with a discussion of the Irish in Scotland, and
follows the organisational birth and growth of
the Irish Republican Brotherhood and other
Irish nationalist groupings up to 1916. The
nature of Irish expatriate political organisation and activity is
discussed and Fenianism in Scotland is measured against its
counterparts in England and Wales, North America, Australasia
and South Africa. The immigrants' political development is
examined and the prevailing view of the Fenian tradition is challenged, placing the beginning and development of the movement
much more in the Irish diaspora than in Ireland itself.

2007   296 pages
978 0 7165 2857 9 cloth   €65.00/£45.00/$75.00
978 0 7165 2858 6 paper   €24.95/£19.95/$29.50